From Script to Stage in Early Modern England

Redefining British Theatre History

General Editor: **Professor Peter Holland**

Redefining British Theatre History is a five-volume series under the general editorship of Professor Peter Holland. The series brings together major practitioners in theatre history in order to establish ways in which previous assumptions need fundamental questioning and to initiate new directions for the field. The series aims to establish a new future for theatre history, not least by making theatre historians aware of their own history, current practice and future.

Titles include:

Peter Holland and Stephen Orgel (*editors*)
FROM SCRIPT TO STAGE IN EARLY MODERN ENGLAND

W. B. Worthen and Peter Holland (*editors*)
THEORIZING PRACTICE
Redefining Theatre History

Redefining British Theatre History
Series Standing Order ISBN 0–333–98219–3 (Hardback) 0–333–98220–7 (Paperback)
(*outside North America only*)

You can receive future titles in this series as they are published by placing a standing order. Please contact your bookseller or, in case of difficulty, write to us at the address below with your name and address, the title of the series and the ISBN quoted above.

Customer Services Department, Macmillan Distribution Ltd, Houndmills, Basingstoke, Hampshire RG21 6XS, England

From Script to Stage in Early Modern England

Edited by

Peter Holland

and

Stephen Orgel

Redefining British Theatre History Series
General Editor: Peter Holland
In Association with the Huntington Library

palgrave
macmillan

First published 2004 by
PALGRAVE MACMILLAN
Houndmills, Basingstoke, Hampshire RG21 6XS and
175 Fifth Avenue, New York, N.Y. 10010
Companies and representatives throughout the world

PALGRAVE MACMILLAN is the global academic imprint of the Palgrave Macmillan division of St. Martin's Press, LLC and of Palgrave Macmillan Ltd. Macmillan® is a registered trademark in the United States, United Kingdom and other countries. Palgrave is a registered trademark in the European Union and other countries.

ISBN 1–4039–3342–1 hardback
ISBN 1–4039–3343–X paperback

This book is printed on paper suitable for recycling and made from fully managed and sustained forest sources.

A catalogue record for this book is available from the British Library.

Library of Congress Cataloging-in-Publication Data

From script to stage in early Modern England / edited by Peter Holland and Stephen Orgel.
    p.   cm. – (Redefining British theatre history)
    Includes bibliographical references and index.
    ISBN 1–4039–3342–1 – ISBN 1–4039–3343–X (pbk.)
    1. Theater – Great Britain – History – 16th century. 2. Theater – Great Britain – History – 17th century. I. Holland, Peter, 1951– II. Orgel, Stephen. III. Series.
PN2589.F76 2004
792′.0941′09031 – dc22
                                                        2004049566

10 9 8 7 6 5 4 3 2 1
13 12 11 10 09 08 07 06 05 04

Printed and bound in Great Britain by
Antony Rowe Ltd, Chippenham and Eastbourne

Contents

IV.   Women's Work

List of Illustrations

Notes on Contributors

Richard Beadle is a Reader in English Literature in the Faculty of English at the University of Cambridge, and a Fellow of St John's College, Cambridge. He has written on many aspects of later medieval and early modern drama, and is the general editor of *The Cambridge Companion to Medieval English Theatre* (Cambridge University Press, 1994). A revision of his standard edition of *The York Plays* (1982) will shortly be published by the Early English Text Society, with a new second volume containing a history of the cycle and commentary on the text.

Anthony B. Dawson, Professor of English at University of British Columbia, has published several books, including a stage history of *Hamlet* for the 'Shakespeare in Performance' series (1995) and *The Culture of Playgoing in Shakespeare's England: a Collaborative Debate* (2001, written with Paul Yachnin). His edition of Shakespeare's *Troilus and Cressida* has just appeared in the Cambridge series (2003), and he is currently at work on an edition of *Timon of Athens* for the Arden, 3rd series.

R. A. Foakes, Professor Emeritus, University of California, Los Angeles, has a long-standing interest in Shakespeare and the theatres of his age. He is the author of *Illustrations of the English Stage, 1580–1642* (Scolar Press, 1985) and has recently published a revised version of his edition of *Henslowe's Diary* (Cambridge University Press, 2002), the account-book of the original owner of the Rose theatre. His recent publications include the Arden, 3rd series, edition of *King Lear* (1997) and *Shakespeare and Violence* (Cambridge University Press, 2002).

Andrew Gurr, Professor Emeritus at the University of Reading, has published several books and many articles about the Shakespearean period, and has edited six plays by Shakespeare and his contemporaries. His most noted books are *The Shakespearean Stage 1574–1642*, now in its third edition (Cambridge University Press, 1992), *Playgoing in Shakespeare's London*, now also in a third edition (Cambridge University Press, 2004), *The Shakespearian Playing Companies* (Oxford University Press, 1996), and most recently, *The Shakespeare Company, 1594–1642* (Cambridge University Press, 2004).

Peter Holland is the McMeel Family Professor in Shakespeare Studies at the University of Notre Dame. Among his books are *The Ornament of Action* (Cambridge University Press, 1979) and *English Shakespeares: Shakespeare on the English Stage in the 1990s* (Cambridge University Press, 1997). He is editor of *Shakespeare Survey* and general editor (with Stanley Wells) of *Oxford Shakespeare Topics* for Oxford University Press.

Natasha Korda   is Associate Professor of English at Wesleyan University. She is author of *Shakespeare's Domestic Economies: Gender and Property in Early Modern England* (University of Pennsylvania Press, 2002) and co-editor with Jonathan Gil Harris of *Staged Properties in Early Modern English Drama* (Cambridge University Press, 2002).

Scott McMillin   is Professor of English at Cornell University. He has written *The Elizabethan Theatre and the Book of Sir Thomas More* (Cornell, 1987), *Shakespeare in Performance: 1 Henry IV* (Manchester, 1991), and, with Sally-Beth MacLean, *The Queen's Men and their Plays* (Cambridge, 2001). He has also edited the *First Quarto of Othello* for the Cambridge Shakespeare, and the *Norton Critical Edition of Restoration and Eighteenth-Century Comedy* (2nd edn, Norton, 1996). He is currently writing a book on Shakespeare and his acting companies.

Stephen Orgel   is the Jackson Eli Reynolds Professor in the Humanities at Stanford. His most recent books are *Imagining Shakespeare* (Palgrave, 2003), *The Authentic Shakespeare* (Routledge, 2002) and *Impersonations: the Performance of Gender in Shakespeare's England* (Cambridge, 1996). His many editions include *The Tempest* and *The Winter's Tale* in the Oxford Shakespeare, and *Macbeth, King Lear, Pericles, The Taming of the Shrew* and *The Sonnets* in the New Pelican Shakespeare, of which he and A. R. Braunmuller are general editors.

Carolyn Sale   recently completed her dissertation, 'Contested Acts: Legal Performances and Literary Authority in Early Modern England' at Stanford University. Her essay on Thomasine White is part of a book project on the relationship of women, writing and the law in the English Renaissance.

Bruce R. Smith   is Professor of English at the University of Southern California. Among his books are two with particular relevance to theatre history: *Ancient Scripts and Modern Experience on the English Stage 1500–1700* (Princeton University Press, 1988) and *The Acoustic World of Early Modern England* (University of Chicago Press, 1999). His current work centres on passionate perception before Descartes.

Claire Sponsler   specializes in medieval drama and teaches at the English Department at the University of Iowa. Her books include *Drama and Resistance*

(Minnesota University Press, 1997), *East of West* (Palgrave 2000), and *Ritual Imports* (Cornell University Press, 2004).

Tiffany Stern   is Senior Lecturer in English at Oxford Brookes University. She is author of *Rehearsal from Shakespeare to Sheridan*, *Making Shakespeare*, and, with Simon Palfrey, *Shakespeare in Parts* (forthcoming), and has edited the anonymous *King Leir* and Sheridan's *The Rivals*. She has written articles on 16th–18th-century theatre history, Shakespeare, and book history, and is currently working on a book titled *The Fragmented Playtext in Shakespearean England*.

Series Introduction: Redefining British Theatre History

Peter Holland

On the surface, it doesn't look like much of a problem: conjoining the two words 'theatre' and 'history' to define a particular practice of scholarship has a long and illustrious history. Nor does it appear to over-complicate matters to add the word 'British', for all that the word is so furiously questioned at different moments of history (and especially at the moment). Yet what kind of history theatre history is and what kind of theatre theatre history investigates, let alone what the Britishness is of its theatre history, is endlessly problematic. For all the availability of shelves full of the outcomes of its practices, theatre history is in need of a substantial reassessment. This series is an attempt to place some markers in that vital project.

It is hardly as if theatre history is a new area of scholarly enquiry and academic publication. Within a general, varyingly academic mode of publication, one could point, in the UK, to the longevity of *Theatre Notebook*, a journal founded in 1945 by the Society for Theatre Research; its subtitle *A Journal of the History and Technique of the British Theatre* neatly sets out its scope and the assumed scope of theatre history. A number of US journals have had similar concerns, including *Theatre Survey* (from the American Society for Theatre Research) and more narrowly defined examples like *Restoration and Eighteenth-Century Theatre Research* or *Nineteenth-Century Theatre Research*. Lying behind such work is the complex institutional history of the formation of university drama and theatre departments on both sides of the Atlantic and their vexed and often still unformulated connection both to theatre training (the university as feed to a profession) and to departments of English Literature.

For the early modern period theatre historians might chart the subject's early twentieth-century history as being encapsulated by the work of E. K. Chambers (especially *The Elizabethan Stage*, 4 vols [Oxford: Clarendon Press, 1923]) or G. E. Bentley in his continuation (*The Jacobean and Caroline Stage*, 7 vols [Oxford: Clarendon Press, 1941–68]), phenomenal individual achievements of documenting theatrical events, theatre performers and theatrical contexts.

Their work might be matched for a later period by, say, E. L. Avery et al., eds, *The London Stage 1660–1800*, 11 vols (Carbondale, Ill: Southern Illinois University Press, 1960–8) or Philip Highfill, Kalman Burnim and Edward Langhans, eds, *A Biographical Dictionary of Actors, Actresses, Musicians, Dancers, Managers and Other Stage Personnel in London, 1660–1800*, 16 vols (Carbondale, Ill: Southern Illinois University Press, 1973–93). Further back still comes the fundamental work of such people as Boaden (*Memoirs of Mrs Siddons*, 2 vols [London, 1827]) and Genest (*Some Account of the English Stage from the Restoration in 1660 to 1830*, 10 vols [Bath, 1832]), who saw themselves neither as scholars nor as academics and yet whose work implicitly defined the accumulative function of data collection as a primary purpose of theatre history. Behind them comes the achievement of the greatest of eighteenth-century editors of Shakespeare, Edmond Malone.

Yet, seeing that there is a practice of theatre history is not the same as understanding or theorizing such a project. While many academics are engaged in the practice of something they would unhesitatingly term 'Theatre History' and while they would differentiate it carefully from a variety of other contiguous fields (e.g. performance theory or history of drama), there has been remarkably little investigation of the methodological bases on which the shelves of accumulated scholarship have been based or the theoretical bases on which Theatre History has been or might be constructed. Even within organizations as aware of the need for theoretical sophistication as IFTR/FIRT (Fédération Internationale pour la recherche théâtrale) the emphasis has been placed more squarely on performance theory than on the historiographical problems of theatre. In part that can undoubtedly be traced to the disciplines or institutional structures out of which the work has evolved: one would need to examine its early and still troubled connection to literary studies, to the analysis of drama and, most visibly, to the study of the history of Shakespeare in performance or, on another tack, to consider the ways in which theatre departments have structured their courses in the US and UK.

By comparison with the traditionally positivist accumulation of data that marks, say, *Theatre Notebook*, one could, however, see signs of the emergence of a new concern with the processes of historiography as it affects the specific study of a massive cultural institution like theatre in, to take just one significant example, the collection of essays edited by Thomas Postlewait and Bruce McConachie, *Interpreting the Theatrical Past: Essays in the Historiography of Performance* (Iowa City: University of Iowa Press, 1989). But, while individual theatre historians are demonstrating an expanding awareness of the specific areas of historiography relevant to their work (e.g. economic history) and while theorizing of performance including its historical traces has grown immensely over the past fifteen years, there is little enough to set out on a large scale the parameters of something that might hope by now to see itself as a discipline.

The shelves of libraries and bookshops and the reading lists of courses do not show major resources for understanding what theatre history is, while an unending stream of books offering to help students understand the history of theatre pours from presses. In part this may be connected to the absence of departments of theatre history and the further substantial absence, within theatre departments, of courses concerned to do more than teach theatre history as an assumed and shared methodology based on an acceptance of what constitutes evidence and of how that evidence generates the potential for meaning.

Redefining British Theatre History sets out, extremely ambitiously, to make a major statement by bringing together, in the course of its series of five volumes, some fifty major practitioners in theatre history in order to establish ways in which previous assumptions need fundamental questioning and in which a future for the field can be enunciated in modes as yet undervalued. It aims to be a significant review of where we are and what we think we are doing.

The project began from an unusual collaboration between research library and publisher. My gratitude goes first and foremost to Dr Roy Ritchie of the Huntington Library and Josie Dixon of Palgrave Macmillan for contacting me to see whether I would develop a proposal that would create a series of conferences and subsequent volumes based on a single theme. Their support, not least financial, has been crucial in bringing the project to a reality both in the pleasures of the conference and the creation of this book. If we succeed, *Redefining British Theatre History* should chart the beginnings of a new future for theatre history, not least by making theatre historians newly and self-consciously aware of their own history, their practice and their future.

Introduction: a View from the Stage

Stephen Orgel

The ideal of theatre history is to see with the eyes of the past, but it is an elusive, and in some ways illusory, ideal. Theatre history is no different from any other kind of history, and the past it reveals changes as both what we conceive to be evidence and what we want from the past changes. Over the last half century, our view of the Early Modern stage has changed radically. In particular, it has come to look increasingly unlike a theatre seen from the playwright's perspective – the playwright, needless to say, has almost invariably been Shakespeare. That central fantasy of traditional bibliographical studies, the possibility of reconstructing the author's original manuscript from the evidence of published texts, is largely irrelevant to the issues discussed in these pages, which focus on plays not as poetry and narrative, still less as chapters in the development of the Renaissance artist's mind, but as performances and events. The perspective is that of audiences, actors, theatre companies, patrons, architects and designers. Early Modern theatre in this view is more than a collection of (largely missing) scripts: it is a complex and often bewildering visual, acoustical, material and financial world, in which seasons, occasions, venues and competing companies figure more significantly than playwrights, and the central creative imagination is concerned less with the creation of play texts than with their transformation into successful performances.

If such considerations lead us away from poetry and drama, they nevertheless lead us directly to theatre. The essays in this volume are deeply concerned with questions of evidence, for the most part archival and archaeological; but almost all begin with puzzles or lacunae, things that seem wrong, or that traditional explanations no longer seem to explain; things that are now clearly apparent, but have been ignored or overlooked, or that the generalizations of theatre history have taken no account of and seem to have no place for. Claire Sponsler, writing about English pre-Reformation drama, puts the question most directly: given that the most important scholarly undertaking of modern theatre history has been a return to the archives, how do we even know a medieval play when we see one? The question arises precisely because we now know so much more than we did half a century ago: the documentation codified in the *REED* project has provided us with a huge amount of new information about the preparation, sponsorship, and performance of medieval drama, but has uncovered no new texts of plays. Is this, Sponsler asks, really the case? Would we know the text of a medieval play if we found one? What are the scribal signals that distinguish the manuscript of a play from that of, say, a literary dialogue, a narrative, or an allegory? Have we, in fact, had a number of medieval plays in front of us all along, and have we simply been ignorant of the relevant signs? In this case, recovering what Early Modern audiences saw requires a significant sophistication of our own reading skills.

Richard Beadle's argument about the nature of medieval drama extends Sponsler's question, and moves from the evidence of manuscripts to the evidence of performance. Beadle observes that despite its largely religious subject matter, medieval theatre was essentially secular. Material elements such as masks and costumes were central to it, and it depended heavily not merely on spectacle, but on spectacular stage effects. The subtext of such an argument is that to understand theatre as a cultural, social, and thereby historical phenomenon we must focus on its audience. The questions Beadle asks are not new – his starting point is Allardyce Nicoll's *Masks, Mimes, and Miracles* of three-quarters of a century ago – but they have, he observes, been forgotten. We need to ask, as 'essential questions: what did the audience *see*, and how did they *feel* about what they saw?' These are, needless to say, not simple questions, and even to suggest answers requires not only the fullest attention to archival and archaeological evidence, but a willingness to entertain a broad variety of speculative and tentative hypotheses.

For the practice of theatre history, 'What did audiences see?' is a far more productive question than 'What did playwrights create?'; in the investigations chronicled in this collection, the playwright's place, when it appears at all, is distinctly subsidiary, and the playwright has only a very small role in the creation of the theatrical event – to say nothing of the maintainence of a successful theatre company. Authors become visible, in fact, primarily when audiences are claimed to have seen something they should not have seen, something subversive, libellous, seditious, or heretical, for which a responsible agent must be produced, as in the extraordinary case of street theatre discussed by Carolyn Sale. Only when liability became an issue was there any real pressure for plays to be supplied with authors; even in the professional, institutional, and highly regulated contexts of the Globe, the Rose, the Fortune, drama was generally anonymous, and was always a collaborative enterprise, much more of a process than a product. These essays bring home to us how much is occluded when we focus on the texts of plays rather than the institution of theatre.

Tiffany Stern shows us how fluid and fragmentary even the texts can be, and how little our modern editions preserve of what would have been paramount for either the Early Modern audience or even the Early Modern reader. She cites the title page of the first quarto of *Richard III* (1597), which may well also have been the text of the playbill:

> *The Tragedie of King Richard the third. Conteining, His treacherous Plots against his brother Clarence: the pitiful murther of his innocent Nephewes: his tyrannicall usurpation: with the whole course of his detested life, and most deserved death.*

As she observes, this is not a summary of the play that modern editions would consider either adequate or marketable, and most of them either delete it or relegate it to a note. 'Yet this may well have been what early modern Londoners who were literate read: it may have drawn them to the theatre, and, later, made them buy the printed quarto' – it was, in short, for at least some of them, what the play was 'about'. The plays in print, moreover, are freqently what she calls 'patchworks', composed of elements put together from different manuscripts performed at different times, whose relation to each other is only indifferently understood by the printer. Songs, prologues, and epilogues tend to be especially vagrant. Stern graphically queries the notion of the play text, even within the playhouse, as an integral whole. It may, she says,

> have been made up of a loosely tied bundle of papers, consisting of a book of dialogue (or several . . .), some separate sheets containing songs and letters, other separate papers containing prologues and epilogues . . . and finally, perhaps, a separate bill / title page providing the lure that attracted the audience. That is not to say that all plays existed like this. After all, some kind of 'complete' text was submitted to the Master of the Revels – though what kind and at what stage is queried by this argument. Nevertheless, substantial bits of the play seem to have existed as separate but definable fragments, each raising the possibility of different authorship, and each capable of having other existences in other books, other places, and other contexts, being as much poems, jests, and advertisements as they were sections of the play. Even as bits of play text they may have differed in their level of permanence. Most permanent was, perhaps, the dialogue of the play, least permanent, perhaps, the prologue and epilogue. So plays could also have, internally, different levels of fixity.

How far we are from being able to relate playwrights and scripts to actors and performances in any historically valid manner is tellingly measured by Andrew Gurr:

Out of the total of 167 extant plays performed by the Chamberlain's/King's Men in the forty-eight years that they played, the 'allowed book' or licensed play book, the version from which performances were drawn . . . survives in only two nearly complete play manuscripts. Neither of them is by Shakespeare. That is less than 2 per cent of the total existing repertory of the leading company of the time. So the current shift of editorial target from the author's copy untouched by theatre hacks to the script as it was first staged, which is the announced aim of the collected Oxford edition of 1986 and of almost all subsequent editions and series of editions, must be acknowledged to be unattainable. If the Oxford target has any value as an ideal, which it must, we need to study the context for the other 98 per cent of lost texts to identify the practices of the companies who owned the play books.

The study of context means, for Gurr, 'giving precedence to the study of the playing companies and their combined repertories, and their intertextuality, over the study of authors and their versions of the texts in print' (and modern critical editions involve, almost without exception, significant rewritings of the surviving texts designed to enable us to treat them as objects of literary study). Gurr is appropriately cautious about the extent to which such a project may be realized, but if it is theatre we are concerned with, rather than bibliography, these are the issues we must address. They require us, at the outset, to revise our notions of what constitutes evidence and what we want out of history.

Renaissance plays themselves dramatize such issues. Anthony Dawson shows how *Othello* focuses precisely on the slipperiness of facts and the contingencies of interpretation; moreover, the uses to which Othello and Iago put the narratives they construe as evidence strikingly parallels the evidentiary uses to which modern commentators, whether critical or political, put *Othello* and the authority of Shakespeare. Dawson turns then to the equivocations, both textual and contextual, of *Troilus and Cressida*, to ask what kind of evidence they might constitute, and for what – the 1609 quarto first claimed that the play had been performed by the King's Men at the Globe, and then, in a cancelling title page and a new preface, asserted that it had never been performed at all or, at least, not in the presence of 'the vulgar'. Can these revisions, along with the play's uncharacteristically satiric tone, be used, as they have been, to argue that the play was specifically designed for the Inns of Court? As Dawson observes,

A key problem with the mode of argumentation in this kind of analysis is that assumptions about textual provenance are used rather too loosely to support assumptions about theatrical provenance and vice versa. Mutually supportive they can and must be, but there is also a danger of circular logic.

'All evidence,' Dawson concludes, 'is in some way staged; i.e., it only becomes evidence when it is made part of an argument or interpretation, usually one that is embedded in some kind of narrative. Hence it is in a strong sense always rhetorical' – or, we might add, theatrical.

This is intended as a cautionary argument, but it also acknowledges how carefully our evidentiary narratives need to be constructed in order to persuade; and how powerfully persuasive they are when the narrative is a good one. R. A. Foakes's case for a radical revision of our idea of the public theatres of Shakespeare's era is made through adducing the hardest of hard evidence, the archaeology of the Rose theatre. The case is persuasive precisely because it starts from the issue of what constitutes evidence, opposing the 'documentary evidence' of the Swan drawing, a copy of a lost original that did not pretend to accuracy to begin with, against the surviving physical structure of an actual playhouse, which, when examined, is found to contradict the Swan drawing in a number of significant respects. Nevertheless, the most influential modern reconstructions of the original Globe have been based largely on the Swan drawing. There is now doubtless far too much invested in its very dubious evidence for theatre history to have any revisionary effect on either the structure or the popularity of what is, preposterously, called Shakespeare's Globe; certainly no twenty-first-century Sam Wanamaker is likely to raise money for the construction of a historically plausible alternative, least of all one based on Henslowe's competing playhouse. But we really do now know a great deal more about the Rose than about the Globe, and this is a rare case where putting a text in its context really is possible. The Rose was the playhouse where *Tamburlaine* was performed, and Foakes's discussion of the staging of *Tamburlaine*, despite its honourable hesitations, qualifications, and uncertainties, is uniquely persuasive because it is able to begin with the actual space of performance.

Bruce Smith asks how we can recover what went on in that space. Early accounts of stage performances regularly stress the visual and kinetic elements, describing the Shakespearean stage as a world of action and significant gesture; whereas criticism has overwhelmingly concerned itself instead with the language of drama. But 'personation', the standard Early Modern term for what actors do, is not merely rhetoric and elocution; it is a function of the whole physical presence of the performer – theatrical performance is an act of embodiment. Smith's evidence comes for the most part from the texts of plays, that is, from language, but the language is designed to articulate and accompany the movement that together with it comprises the *action* of a drama. Such an argument requires us to consider the syntax of dramatic language with a new kind of attention. In expressing action, Smith observes, 'nouns have only limited usefulness. The most they can do is assert that something is *there* . . . Verbs turn nouns into entities that can act and objects that such entities can act upon. But the essence of movement is neither in the agents nor the objects but in the *upon'* – in prepositions. Smith focuses especially on the way prepositions in stage directions and dialogue locate performers and direct their, and the audience's, attention; a number of Shakespearean passages read quite differently if we see them, or more properly listen to them, in the context of the action they imply.

If Early Modern theatre is not to be treated as literature, but as a professional, cultural, financial institution, who did the work in it? We know a good deal about the performers, but the most striking aspect of that particular segment of the workforce was the absence of women within it, a significant gap that was filled by young men, who became, in effect, the apprentices of the company. This arrangement elicited little critical interest until fairly recently, although it was unique in Early Modern Europe: no other Western public theatre limited its personnel to males. The practice was, however, clearly considered both natural and entirely decorous by the English, whose attitude towards the contemporary continental tradition of actresses ranges from surprise to prurience. Scott McMillin interrogates the theatrical apprentice system in very specific ways: how were female roles designed so that the most inexperienced members of the group could perform them convincingly? How did the boys learn their roles? Since they were apprentices, how did the masters train them? These are not at all general questions, or ones that are assumed to be unanswerable; McMillin shows how the text of *Othello* enables us to reconstruct the process of rehearsal:

> More than half of Desdemona's cue lines are given her by one character, Othello. More than half of the cue lines she gives are answered by one character, Othello. More than half of her speeches can be rehearsed with one actor, the actor playing Othello, and probably that is how they were rehearsed. The master-actor probably rehearsed the boy actor one-on-one, teaching the boy how to respond, teaching him enunciation, gesture, movement.

The repertory is also an essential part of McMillin's subject – this comprised the work the actors did. We know that the King's Men played *The Alchemist* and *Othello* on succeeding nights at Oxford in 1610. 'One wonders which role in *The Alchemist* was assigned to the Desdemona boy. Did the Venetian wife who cannot bring herself to say 'whore' spend the previous evening playing Dol Common?' McMillin proceeds to unpack the relation of the repertory to the workforce in a uniquely enlightening way, noting the termination dates of indentures and the indenturing of new apprentices, and combining these with performance data – a boy-actor's life-expectancy as a woman, assuming that he joined the company at the age of eleven or twelve, would have been only six or seven years. The Desdemona King James saw at Whitehall in 1604 would not have been the Desdemona Henry Jackson praised at Oxford in 1610; but Burbage, as Othello, would have trained both.

If women were absent from the professional stage, they were not at all absent from the theatre. They constituted a large and visible presence among the spectators, and in fact, theatre represented an area of unusual freedom for women in Early Modern England: they could attend without their husbands, openly, often in groups, and without masks to conceal their identities. European visitors were often as shocked by this spectacle as English travellers were by the sight of women on the continental stage – how society constructs theatre depends heavily on what place women are conceived to have in it. In English theatre, their place was certainly as consumers – a large proportion of the audience consisted of women as paying customers, which means that the success of the enterprise was significantly determined by their receptiveness to what was presented. English drama, and English theatre, appear to us misogynistic in a number of respects, but there was something about the enterprise, and particularly about the all-male stage, that women liked.

Actors are not, however, the only workers in the industry of theatre. Natasha Korda uncovers the large system supplying the company, and finds it significantly maintained by women. Women were active in the needle trades and second-hand clothing business; they furnished costumes, fitted them, altered them, kept them in good repair. The costumes, it should be remembered, constituted the largest part of the company's investment, the most precious part of its inventory. The women who supplied and maintained them were indispensable. Women also performed for the company all the work that women traditionally perform throughout society – providing food, running the household, keeping domestic order – and since the boy-actors who took the roles of women were apprentices and lived in their masters' homes, the masters' wives, daughters, serving maids, were engaged in training the youths, not only as surrogate sons and incipient men, but as adult women too.

Finally, Peter Holland leads us back to the most basic problem in pursuing theatre history as a discipline, the amount of information that is missing and unrecoverable. Reading through the volumes of *REED* is maddenly frustrating. The *Records of Early English Drama* include a vast amount of information relating to theatrical production: notes of performances, theatrical preparations, payments for theatrical properties of all sorts, the issuing of licences to perform, as well as complaints, judicial hearings, litigation, fines; but they almost never record the titles of the plays involved. Travellers from the continent, similarly, often note in their journals a visit to the theatre, which may be described in some detail (as is the meal afterwards); but the name of the play is rarely mentioned. In sharp contrast to the standard history of English drama, which has been overwhelmingly text-based, the historical records reveal almost no interest in the texts of plays, even less in their titles, and absolutely none in the names of playwrights. We now know how rich and active a theatrical life cities like Bristol and York supported, but about what plays their citizens saw, we know next to nothing.

What, then, is theatre history a history of, if not plays? These essays show us how much there is to know about the richest and most complex of cultural institutions in Early Modern England, and how much of it we ignore when we think of drama merely as a collection of texts.

Part I
Questions of Evidence

1

Henslowe's Rose/Shakespeare's Globe

R. A. Foakes

Recently I was trying to organize a seminar of scholars from around the world, and found, to my dismay, that a number of them did not use computers or have email. Their resistance to using new methods of communication that would have eased my burden struck me as boneheaded at the time. But on reflection I realized that an inability to accept innovations and new thinking on the part of people who ought to know better is a common human trait. In the sixteenth century, for instance, a technological revolution in warfare took place with the development of guns, harquebuses, muskets or calivers and pistols, all brought into use by 1570. By 1590 the Dutch army had two men armed with guns for every one with a pike. Yet in this year Sir John Smythe in a tract called *Certain Discourses Military* lamented the use of guns and called for a return to the obsolete longbow, starting a debate that went on for some years. There was great nostalgia for old ways, heavy armour, lances and bows and arrows. Marlowe, ever inventive, must have startled the audience at the Rose before 1590 when Tamburlaine first cried out, 'Shoot him all at once', and a volley of calivers presumably echoed in the theatre as the Governor of Babylon, hung above the stage, was 'killed' with 'many bullets'. This must have been quite a *coup de théâtre*.

There is a well-known letter written by Philip Gawdy to his father in 1587 describing an incident in which the Admiral's Men borrowed calivers or light muskets having 'a device in their play to tie one of their fellows to a post and so to shoot him to death'. The hands of one of the players 'swerved' and missed, killing a child and a woman 'great with child'.[1] This anecdote may report hearsay and greatly exaggerate, for no other account of the incident is known, but if it refers to Marlowe's *Tamburlaine, Part 2*, which was certainly in the repertory of the Rose in 1594–5,[2] it may tell us something about how the company staged the shooting, not necessarily by hanging the Governor in chains, as Tamburlaine commands,

> Go, draw him up,
> Hang him in chains upon the city walls
> And let my soldiers shoot the slave to death.
> *(Part 2*, 5.1.107–9)

Theridamas shoots first, then all Tamburlaine's soldiers on the command, 'Shoot at him all at once', leaving him with 'many bullets in his flesh'. So guns were presumably used, and though they would not have been loaded with real bullets, firearms might misfire and cause such an accident as Gawdy describes.[3] Did the players contrive to tie the Governor to, or hang him up on, one of the posts supporting the frame as representing the 'city walls'? Where would the Governor have been hung or tied?[4] Let's consider this matter in relation to the remains of the Rose. In Phase 1 (1587) (Fig. 1) the sides of the trapezoid stage abutted on to the inner frame of the theatre not, as might seem logical, at one of the main posts, but more or less halfway across bays. There is no sign in the foundations of any steps from the arena on to the stage, and the remains show the theatre may have had one main entry to the south, opposite the stage area. When the playhouse was enlarged in Phase 2 (1592) (Fig. 2), the whole stage area was reconstructed, and pillars for a canopy were added, but it is notable that the basic design of the stage was retained, with the sides again abutting halfway between the main posts of the bays.[5]

What was the purpose of this design feature? The players must have had a way of getting up to and down from the upper levels above the stage. If the line of the side walls was carried through to the rear of the building by a partition, the spaces adjacent to the stage could have been used as stairwells for actors using the balcony. It is conceivable that they could have been open to the incoming audience for admission and exit before and after a performance, and closed off by a curtain or folding partition during it. No turrets for side entrances have been found, and this design would have relieved pressure on the main entrance. The Governor of Babylon (or his effigy) could then easily have been hung on or tied to the main post adjacent to these stairs. This incident is one of many that contribute to the spectacular staging of the play. *Tamburlaine, Part 2*, has at least eight different geographical locations, and fifteen of its eighteen scenes call for one or more processions of kings or leaders; nine times the stage directions require such characters to enter 'with a train' of followers in addition to the named characters, a term used here more than in any other play.

It is not easy to imagine how this play was presented at the Rose in 1594. Take, for example, the sequence of scenes running from 2.2. to 3.3: in 2.2 Orcanus, Gazellus, Uribassa and their 'train' are marching from Orminus (entry stage right?) to Natolia, and encounter Sigismond of Hungary with his Christian army (entry stage left?). A battle ensues (offstage?), and Sigismond comes

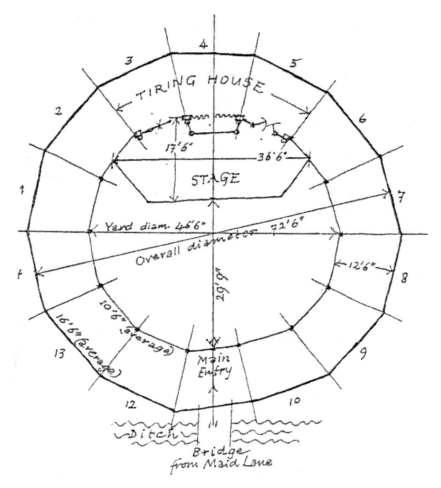

Figure 1. Schematic ground-plan of the Rose, Phase 1.

out wounded as the Christians are defeated. Orcanes and his army enter again, and the body of Sigismond is carried off. In the next scene, set in Larissa, Zenocrate is revealed (center stage?) in tableau behind an arras in her 'bed of state', attended by three physicians, three sons, three followers, and Tamburlaine, and I assume all ten players plus Zenocrate in bed emerged on to the stage. Tamburlaine announces he intends to burn the town of Larissa. In 3.1 (Turkey; stage right?), seven named kings enter plus other lords in procession with swords, sceptres, etc., and Calapine is crowned Emperor of Turkey. Then in 3.2 (Larissa, center stage?), Tamburlaine with his three sons and Usumcasane,

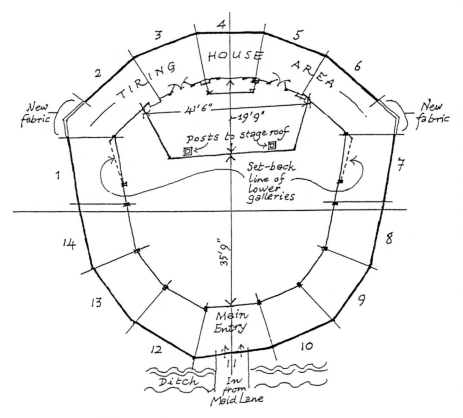

Figure 2.   Ground-plan of the Rose, Phase 2.

drums sounding a march, and Zenocrate's hearse carried by four soldiers, enter with 'the town burning' (as painted on a curtain?). This scene is followed by a processional entry in 3.3 (stage left?) for Techelles, Theridamas, and 'train' in a new location, Balsera; they 'Summon the battle' against the Captain and his wife and son, who appear aloft. These scenes require in sequence a minimum of six, eleven, ten, nine, and eight players on stage, not allowing for soldiers, followers, and other mutes. The scenes take place in Orminus, in Larissa, in Turkey, in Larissa again, and in Balsera. The complications of staging these scenes, perhaps with indications of different geographical locations, suggest that all three bays may have offered wide spaces for discoveries, for processional entries, and for scenes such as 4.1, where Calyphas and others play cards in the opening of a tent, readily contrived in a bay with an arras part drawn. The centre bay, flanked by two bays at an angle, could have provided a dominating position for the entries of Tamburlaine, who might have emerged from it in all his state entries, as with the hearse of Zenocrate, and his three entries in a chariot drawn by captive kings. The trapezoid shape of the stage would have been suited to processional entries and marching round the perimeter, and it is notable how Marlowe crowds what was a relatively small area.

The 'plot' survives for a revival, in the late 1590s or possibly 1600, of George Peele's play *The Battle of Alcazar* with Edward Alleyn playing Muly Mahamet. The plot interestingly shows that the staging was often more elaborate than the Quarto of 1594 suggests. For instance, in the 'plot', but not in the Quarto, pages are required to accompany courtiers or ambassadors on stage in three entries; and in Act 3 the 'plot' calls for an elaborate dumb-show involving Nemesis, three devils, three ghosts, and three Furies with scales, who kill three of the characters in the play and have vials of 'blood' to show for it. Here, as frequently, the plot spells out how many persons are needed on stage, and what properties are required, whereas the printed text merely has a stage direction that reads 'Enter the Presenter and speakes'. The plot here, and frequently else-where, provides a fuller and more detailed sense of how the play was staged than the printed text, and this may have been the case with *Tamburlaine* as well. The 'plot' also contains the names of twenty-five actors, eleven sharers, seven hired men and seven boys, and shows the Admiral's Men performing with extravagant casting, such as two mute pages to accompany a chariot, and with lavish spectacle. *Tamburlaine*, which may have been the first, and was cer-tainly the most famous, of what I call the Rose spectaculars, also required a large cast, and may have been, like *The Battle of Alcazar*, even more breathtak-ing than the printed text suggests. Have we taken enough account of the use of 'plots' in the Elizabethan playhouse in considering the staging of plays, and the possible inadequacies of stage directions in printed plays?[6]

I began by pointing to examples of the difficulty many of us have in accept-ing innovations; we tend to cling to old beliefs, old ways of thinking. Does this apply to theatre history as much as to computers or weapons? I think it may do. Some of the main features of the Rose theatre proved to be startlingly dif-ferent from accepted ideas about Elizabethan theatres. The Rose had fourteen sides, thus invalidating the assumption of scholars that all arena theatres would have been symmetrical, and would have four sides like the square Fortune, or a multiple of four sides, usually sixteen, twenty or twenty-four. Speculation about the public theatres had generally assumed that they had large square or rectangular stages. So it was a major surprise to discover that at the Rose the stage was proportionately smaller, and trapezoid in shape. The inner wall of this theatre served as the rear of the stage, and appears to have provided three capacious entrances and exits, each about 10 feet 6 inches wide. I have also commented on the spectacular staging requirements of *Tamburlaine*, and the large casts used in such plays, as well as the use of 'plots' to give directions. All this evidence has been available, in plain view, as it were, yet it was pretty much ignored when the Globe reconstruction was planned, in great measure because of the difficulty in moving beyond the well-known De Witt drawing of the Swan. This drawing, which shows only two doors for entry on to the stage fostered the assumption that the Globe too may have had only two doors, with perhaps some kind of recess between them. The two stage doors at the reconstructed Globe are double wooden doors fitting into a round arch and 'boarded, as shown by de Witt'[7] (Fig. 3). The shape of the stage and the flat *frons scenae* in the new Globe are also based on this sketch, as can be seen in the photograph taken at a performance of *Twelfth Night* (Fig. 4). This shows a moment in 1.5, with characters spread across the stage, from left to right: Olivia, Curio, Sir Toby Belch, a Priest (added in this production), Feste and Maria. It seems that directors feel they have to use the corners of the stage, even if, as here, doing so sets actors far apart. Maria has come to announce the arrival of Curio, and does so from a distance, so that the players look scattered in what is a domestic scene. It is worth asking why designers relied on the de Witt drawing rather than the evidence of the Rose remains.

The drawing has been frequently reproduced, and, as the only known illustration of the interior of an Elizabethan theatre, made about 1596, it has greatly influenced received ideas of the nature of other playhouses in the period. It is in fact a copy made by Aernout van Buchell of a drawing sent to him by his friend Johannes De Witt, whose original drawing has never been found. It has perpetuated the idea of Elizabethan theatres as having a bare stage and minimal facilities. It shows a flat stage façade with two doors, imitated at the new Globe as noted earlier, though a third central stage opening has been added there, since some plays require the display of large properties or the use of three entrances. When De Witt visited the Swan it struck him, according to van Buchell, as the largest and most splendid of the four theatres he saw, but its history is chequered, to say the least. It was located in the manor of Paris Garden, well to the west of the other Bankside playhouses, and Francis Langley, who had it built, may have hoped to attract a different audience from the other theatres to be ferried across the Thames to Paris Garden stairs. In 1597 Pembroke's Men played there, but offence given by the lost play *The Isle of Dogs* brought about the restraint on playing imposed in July 1597.[8] Only two companies, at the Rose and the Theatre, were allowed in the order of 1598 permitting playing to be resumed, and little is heard of the Swan until 1611. Only one play, Middleton's *A Chaste Maid at Cheapside* (printed 1630), has a title page directly linking it with the Swan. There are more references to other forms of entertainment at the Swan, to fencing, extemporaneous versifying, and feats of activity, than to performances of plays.

As to van Buchell's sketch, Johan Gerritsen has shown that De Witt probably, as was his habit, sent a copy, reduced in size, of his original sketch to van

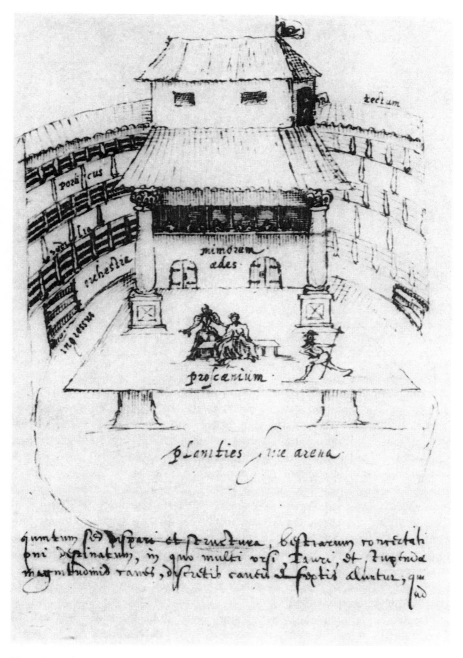

Figure 3. Johannes De Witt's drawing of the Swan theatre, ?1596, as copied by Aernout van Buchell.

Figure 4. The stage at the reconstructed Globe theatre in London, showing the flat *frons scenae*, round-arched doors, large rectangular stage, and columns supporting a cover over the stage, in Act 1, Scene 5 from *Twelfth Night* (2002).

Buchell, who then scaled it up to the larger sketch that survives; in other words, van Buchell's drawing is a copy of a copy.[9] Moreover, Gerritsen studied the drawings of De Witt and van Buchell that are known, and showed that van Buchell had a very different style of drawing from De Witt, and was much less accomplished, so that a coherent interpretation of buildings he drew is often impossible.[10] The details of the Swan drawing are indeed hard to interpret. It shows a huge hut above the stage standing high above the roofline, though the early seventeenth-century view of London that has the best claim to authenticity shows huts at the Rose and Globe, but none at the Swan. If it had one, it must have been removed by 1600, because none is shown in John Norden's panorama made in that year.[11] The drawing also contains an ambiguous representation of what have been interpreted variously as the bases under the stage of two implausibly fat columns supporting a flimsy canopy, or trestles carrying the stage boards, or openings in curtains hung round the stage to conceal the area underneath.

Van Buchell added a commentary, headed, in Latin, 'from the observations of London by Johannes De Witt', which is commonly reprinted as De Witt's 'letter to his friend',[12] explaining his drawing. It may be van Buchell's own reworking of whatever De Witt drew and wrote. Towards the end he notes 'Cuius quidem forma quod Romani operis umbram videatur exprimere supra adpinxi', or 'I have drawn above what traces of Roman work it seems to express in its form.' E. H. Gombrich has shown how an artist drawing a building begins 'not with his visual impression but with his idea or concept', as Matthias Merian did some years later in his engraving of the cathedral of Notre Dame in Paris, made about 1635, in which he depicts the windows as having round or Roman arches, when in fact they had pointed Gothic arches.[13] This same process can be seen in the drawing of the Rose by C. Walter Hodges considered above (Figs. 1 and 2) in which he gives the centre bay at the rear of the stage a balcony, for which the archaeological remains provide no evidence. De Witt or van Buchell also began with an idea, the concept of a Roman theatre, and set out to sketch the Swan as if it were a Roman theatre.[14] The commentary on the drawing headed 'from the observations of London by Johannes De Witt', whether it copies De Witt's words or includes interventions by van Buchell, shows they perceived the Swan as a kind of Roman amphitheatre[15] in terms of pictorial conventions most probably derived from the treatise *De Amphiteatro* (1584) written by their former instructor at the University of Leiden, Justus Lipsius. We do not know how far van Buchell reworked De Witt's observations and drawing, but he goes on to describe what else De Witt saw in Britain, beginning 'Narrabat idem se vidisse' – 'he also reported seeing' – referring to De Witt in the third person.

There are other reasons why this sketch should not be trusted. Gerritsen found drawings by De Witt and van Buchell of a wall plaque on the outside of a church in Antwerp commemorating Cornelis de Vriendt, architect of the Antwerp Town Hall, and a comparison of them reveals something of van Buchell's relative incompetence as a draughtsman, though the monument no longer exists. De Witt (Fig. 5a) shows a plaque mounted on a wall with a separate figure to one side, apparently female, with huge wings and holding a long horn or wind instrument into which she is blowing. This was interpreted by Gerritsen as a figure representing Fame. Van Buchell also noted in a comment below his drawing (Fig. 5b) that the monument was on the outer wall of a Franciscan church, but drew it, perhaps basing his sketch on descriptive notes he had made, as if it were free-standing and depicted a diminished winged figure of uncertain gender standing on top of the plaque and blowing into two smaller bugles. De Witt shows the plaque as rectangular, with scrolls above supporting a small figure on a plinth. Van Buchell gives the plaque shoulders with two small figures reclining on them, and attaches it to an elaborate base supporting the winged figure. Possibly De Witt was interested in recording the appearance of the monument, while van Buchell was more concerned with the inscription on it. Van Buchell's sketch, with its much fussier and complicated detailing, has little in common with De Witt's.[16]

More directly relevant to the Swan drawing is van Buchell's sketch of another building, the façade of St Mary's church in Utrecht (Fig. 6). The church had

Figure 5. (*a*) Memorial to Cornelis de Vriendt on the outer wall of a church in Antwerp, as drawn by Johannes De Witt, 1610–11. Courtesy of the University Library, Utrecht.

Figure 5. (*b*) Memorial to Cornelis de Vriendt on the outer wall of a church in Antwerp, as drawn by Aernout van Buchell (1565–1641). Courtesy of the University Library, Utrecht.

been damaged in a siege in 1576 when the north-west tower, missing in the sketch, was ruined by artillery. The lowest storey shows fat Roman columns, a wide doorway with a Roman arch in the centre, and four lancet windows flanked by more wide blocked Roman arches. Well above these van Buchell depicts a blind arcade of somewhat squashed Roman arches with fat columns. The south-east tower is truncated because van Buchell lacked space on the page of his *Diarium* to show it fully. This tower is shown as aligned with the façade

Figure 6.   Drawing of the west façade of St Mary's Church, Utrecht, by Aernout van Buchell (1565–1641).

of the church, and what looks like a free-floating thick slab projecting from it is impossible to interpret. Pieter Saenredam, an artist noted for his skill in perspective, drew this same façade later, in 1636 (Fig. 7), in a sketch that shows how van Buchell widened the central arch enormously without recording the window immediately above the door, how he misrepresented two large windows in making all four on the ground floor into lancets, how he made all the columns much fatter, moved the blind arcade well above its correct position, and got everything out of scale.[17] In Saenredam's drawing the tower is set back from the façade and a small sloping roof covers the gap between the wall of the façade and the wall of the tower. Because he misrepresents the tower as rising from the façade this roof appears in van Buchell's sketch as an incomprehensible slab. The carpenter's sheds erected as lean-tos on either side of the building had been removed by 1662, when Saenredam made a painting of the church, revealing that the blocked ornamental arches they concealed were Gothic, not Roman as van Buchell drew them. Van Buchell had an enthusiasm

Figure 7. Drawing of the west façade of St Mary's Church, Utrecht, by Pieter Saenredam (1636).

for Romanesque architecture, which is what led to his interest in the Maria-kerk in Utrecht, of which he said, 'It truly is a very beautiful building, presenting not the barbarian [i.e., Gothic] but the ancient Roman style'.[18] He transferred this enthusiasm to his drawing of the Swan.

I think the sketch of the theatre is in many ways untrustworthy, besides being hard to interpret, but we can get help in understanding the Swan from another source. When Henslowe and Alleyn decided to abandon the Rose and build the Fortune, they advised their builder, Peter Street, to copy some features of the new Globe. We do not know how innovatory the first Globe was, that's to say, in what ways it was an improvement on the Theatre or the Curtain, but evidently Henslowe wanted his new playhouse to have the latest features, and he did not seek to model it on the Rose. In 1600 he chose to incorporate improvements made in the 1599 Globe. This seems to make excellent sense. Why then does the contract for the Hope theatre, built in 1613 as a 'game place or playhouse' fit 'both for players to play in and for the game of bears and bulls to be baited in the same', call for it to be 'of such large compass, form, wideness and height as the playhouse called the Swan', and to be 'made in all things and in such form or fashion as the said playhouse called the Swan'?[19] The obvious answer is that the Hope was modelled on a twenty-year-old playhouse that offered a design for a multi-purpose space for plays and other activities. Some improvements were required: for instance, a canopy cantilevered over the stage with no supports, and a roof tiled rather than thatched. The contract says nothing about stage doors, or how acrobats or animals were to be brought into the arena. The most likely reason for copying an old theatre in building the Hope is that it was like the Swan, so it makes sense to think of the Swan as like the Hope.

According to the contract, the Hope was to have 'a stage to be carried or taken away, and to stand upon trestles, good, substantial and sufficient for the carrying and bearing such a stage'. It is therefore probable that the supports for the stage in the Swan drawing are also trestles. The columns shown in the Swan drawing I assume are wildly out of scale. The foundations of the Rose reveal the bases of columns added to support a canopy when the theatre was enlarged in 1592, columns that extended up through the stage boards.[20] If the pillars at the Swan were similar to those at the Rose they would have remained in place when the stage was taken away. The pillars may have been something of a nuisance, interfering with sight lines, when the Swan was used for feats of activity, as by the acrobat Peter Bromville in 1600, which would explain why a cantilevered canopy was required at the Hope. It is hard to imagine how such a theatre would have looked when used for bear-baiting or for activities of various kinds, but some idea may be suggested by an engraving of the Fechthaus, or fencing-house as it was known, opened in Nuremberg in 1628, a square building analogous to the Fortune, which, like the Hope, was designed as a multi-purpose theatre (Fig. 8). Soon after it opened a company of English players gave eight performances there, and town records show that receipts were substantial. The players took slightly less than half as their share, the rest going to the city or to charity, hence the detailed records, which show that 2665 people attended the first performance, and more than 12000 came to see the eight plays.[21] An engraving of 1651 displays the interior of this theatre set

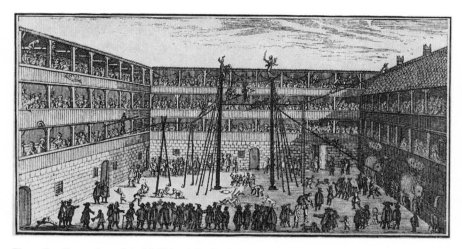

Figure 8.   Engraving, dated 1651, of the Fechthaus at Nuremberg, built in 1628, showing acrobats and other entertainers putting on a show in the arena.

up for acrobatics, rope dancing, tumbling, and other feats of activity.[22] The doors and small window grills in the three visible walls around the square arena may indicate holding stalls for animals, and the engraving provides no clues as to how the area might have been converted for staging plays. If this engraving is puzzling because it is hard to imagine how the arena looked with a stage set up, the Swan drawing is puzzling because it is hard to imagine how the arena might have looked without a stage.

The Swan drawing has been reproduced over and over again as something of a key to imagining an arena theatre because it is the only known interior view of a London playhouse. Its unreliability is sometimes acknowledged by theatre historians, but then ignored when they go on to take it as a model for understanding Elizabethan stages, and its influence has been enormous, as, for instance in relation to the stage at the reconstructed Globe. The measurements of the stage at the new Globe are derived from the contract for the Fortune, 43 feet wide, 'and in breadth to extend to the middle of the yard'.[23] The shape, however, is derived from the Swan drawing. What the Fortune contract specifies is only that the stage shall 'extend' to the middle of the yard; it says nothing about the shape, but adds that the 'Stage shall be placed & set As also the staircases of the said frame in such sort as is prefigured in a Plot thereof drawn'. The contract had earlier called for 'such like stairs Conveyances & divisions without & within as are made & contrived' at the Globe, referring to external staircase turrets (which the Rose did not have), and internal staircases presumably to enable the audience to circulate. The staircases within the frame I think would have been similar to those contrived at each side of the stage at the Rose, to provide access to the balconies or various levels used by the players; staircases of this kind were in fact incorporated into the plans for the reconstructed Globe. The 'plot' or plan that 'prefigured' these stairs and the shape of the stage is lost, but it would also perhaps have shown whether there was a flat *frons scenae* as depicted in the Swan drawing, for this is not mentioned in the contract. Was a plan of the stage also needed because the measurements stated did not relate to its shape? Was it, like the stage at the Rose, trapezoid? Should the designers of the new Globe at least have allowed for this possibility, and designed their stage with removable corners so that we could have learned which shape works better?

Most of the leading dramatists, including Shakespeare, launched their careers at the Rose, so what went on there should be of the greatest interest, yet the evidence about it is treated differently from that relating to the Globe. In the case of the Globe, scholars rely heavily on the printed texts of Shakespeare's plays, asking what were the minimum requirements in terms of actors, staging and properties for performance, and they read back from his dramas to determine the working features of the playhouse accordingly. He bestrides the Elizabethan stage like a colossus, since his plays predominate in what is known of the repertory of the Chamberlain's Men; but in fact only eleven plays other than those by Shakespeare have been identified as in the repertory of the Chamberlain's Men before 1600, and no text survives for three of them. By contrast, Henslowe lists well over 200 titles of plays performed at the Rose. In the absence of information about the rest of the repertory, Shakespeare's plays, all known only from printed texts, have been searched minutely for evidence of staging.[24] The constant turnover of plays at the Rose included a lot of hackwork, and we like to read forward from Henslowe's Diary as listing the work of less prominent playwrights in a theatre generally seen as inferior to the Globe. So the Rose plays that survive tend to be given far less attention.

I commented earlier on the plot of *The Battle of Alcazar*, which shows that for this play much more action took place on the stage at the Rose than the printed text reveals. Printed texts and extant manuscripts show that authors varied greatly in their treatment of stage directions, which are often sparse and inconsistent. Readers after all could get by with comparatively little in the way of directions, and few authors took such trouble as, for example, Ben Jonson did to help his readers understand what he was about. The company staging a play, however, needed a clear guide to the action, and, as the seven plots that survive from the Rose indicate, they hung up for the actors a chart outlining the dramatic action and noting what might be needed in the way of properties and stage aids. There is evidence that companies continued at various theatres to use similar working documents for stage production: so, for example, the Duke in Middleton's *Women Beware Women* (1620s?), 5.1.129, seeing that the courtiers are not following the outline of the masque, consults the paper he holds, and says 'Why sure, this plot's drawn false; here's no such thing'. Also in John Ford's *Lover's Melancholy* (1628) there is an entry for 'Corax with a paper plot'.[25] Only a few plots remain, rough and often incomplete manuscripts, and only for the Rose, but their existence is enough to show that the author's directions may have been expanded, changed or ignored in the staging of plays. So how much weight should we give to the directions found in printed plays? There is yet another layer in the staging of plays, represented, alas, by only one example, the actor's part for Edward Alleyn's performance as Orlando Furioso. He was a leading actor and sharer, and could perhaps put his own mark on a role in a way not possible for all; but no doubt others, like Richard Burbage, were able to do likewise. Alleyn's script abbreviates or omits many directions found in the Quarto of the play, and adds some not in this printed version, directions that indicate stage business and actions specific to his part, such as 'he walketh up & downe' and 'he whistles for him'.

It may be that working practices changed over the years, and that we should not lump together Elizabethan and Jacobean stage directions. However, at the Rose there were three documents involved in the production of a play: the play script as read over by the company, the stage plot, and the actor's parts. Should we take these factors into account in assessing the significance of stage directions in, for example, the Globe plays of Shakespeare, some of whose early plays were staged at the Rose? If so, then editors and critics might feel less concerned to treat stage directions in these plays as gospel, and more willing to suggest ways of expanding or modifying them where the action indicates that the plot or an actor might have introduced stage business.

If a long-standing attachment to the Swan drawing and to grand conceptions of the Globe as the premier theatre of the age continue to affect interpretation of the evidence, another factor is the association of the Rose with Henslowe and the Globe with Shakespeare. Henslowe was long regarded, in the words of Sir Walter Greg, as an 'illiterate moneyed man . . . who regarded art as a subject for exploitation',[26] and this taint has faded only gradually, never completely. He was clearly not illiterate, however odd his spellings in his *Diary* may sometimes be, and he was certainly a businessman who needed to make a profit out of his theatres; but he still tends to carry the stigma of someone who regarded *art* as there for exploitation. The implicit contrast has always been with the Shakespeare and the Globe as representative of high art. In his widely used survey of *The Shakespearean Stage*, 3rd edition, 1992, Andrew Gurr presented an image of Henslowe as an 'unscrupulous mismanager' who employed a bunch of 'hack-writers' to patch up plays or scribble new ones in collaboration, and who imposed an 'autocratic rule' on the players.[27] The sweet and gentle Shakespeare could be thought of as belonging to a better class of people, and the Chamberlain's Men as democrats, at least from 1599 when a group of sharers gained part ownership of the Globe, in contrast to the authoritarian sway of Henslowe over the Rose and Fortune. In other words, Shakespeare could be thought of as belonging to a morally superior company that escaped the stigma of profit-making.

The contrast is marked by the way in which the Rose has come to be thought of as Henslowe's property, run as a business, while the Globe, now revived on Bankside, is advertised as 'Shakespeare's Globe', the house of great drama. It is important to bear in mind the chronology of these theatres: the Rose flourished in the 1590s, while the Globe belongs to the 1600s, and we have to allow for changes and new fashions. At the Rose plays were devoured: 'the most extraordinary feature of the repertory was its huge appetite'.[28] In the 1590s there was no accumulation of good old plays that could be revived, and many of the dramas staged there had a very short life, so that the Admiral's Men were constantly contracting for new plays. There is no reason to suppose practices were different for the Chamberlain's Men during this period. Probably things were calmer during the 1600s, and the demand for new plays at the Globe and Fortune less strenuous. Even so, there is no reason to suppose that the basic pattern of playing changed radically, or that the theatres operated differently. The owners and sharers in the company were all looking to make profits and a good living.

In this essay I have been considering what seem to me important issues in theatre history as these affect our understanding of the Elizabethan and Jacobean stage. The very language we commonly use may carry built-in assumptions, as in the naming of the reconstructed Globe as 'Shakespeare's Globe'.[29] This implies superiority over other theatres of the period, as well as a very questionable sense of authenticity. The long history of speculation about the nature of the Globe carried much more weight in the design than the evidence provided by the discovery of the remains of the Rose, which was associated with profit-making and lesser dramatists. Ideas of the stage area at the Globe, about which no direct evidence survives, have continued to be strongly influenced by van Buchell's dubious drawing of the Swan, while the evidence of his incompetence as a draughtsman has been set aside, and the solid evidence provided by the remains of the Rose undervalued. In relation to our understanding of the working practices of the players, the stage 'plots' and an actor's part in the Dulwich archive have also been neglected. The Rose, after all, was the theatre at which almost all the leading dramatists (including Shakespeare) learned their trade, yet we are seduced by the stature of Shakespeare into understanding the theatre practices from his Globe plays rather than from the business deals, contracts and records to be found in Henslowe's *Diary*. This is not a problem unique to the early modern period, as Jane Moody has shown in her demonstration of the importance of illegitimate theatre, especially in relation to Shakespeare's plays, in the Romantic period. There too literary historians of the period have privileged the mental theatre of the great Romantic poets, and neglected what was actually happening on London stages.[30] Like other kinds of history, theatre history is an ongoing narrative, constantly subject to modification as new findings emerge, but also often trapped in inherited assumptions and myths. The reconstituted Globe on Bankside has been enormously successful as a popular tourist attraction, and has publicized itself as Shakespeare's Globe. Yet for all the input of experts, it is not the kind of experimental theatre some of us hoped for, but instead has a stage area based on the Swan drawing and on a dubious interpretation of the Fortune contract. This establishes for thousands of visitors a fixed idea of an Elizabethan stage that may well be erroneous in many respects.[31] My concern has been to draw attention to the way long-held assumptions can exert control over theatre history, and to illustrate the difficulty of accepting new evidence when it conflicts with traditional beliefs. At the very least I would suggest we need to be constantly vigilant, to be prepared to revise cherished opinions, and to be aware of the prejudices that may be fostered by the terms we use, as in calling the Rose Henslowe's playhouse and the Globe Shakespeare's theatre.

Notes

1. E. K. Chambers, *The Elizabethan Stage* 4 vols (Oxford: Clarendon Press, 1923), II.135; Glynne Wickham, Herbert Berry and William Ingram, *English Professional Theatre, 1530–1660* (Cambridge: Cambridge University Press, 2000), 277.
2. *Henslowe's Diary*, ed. R. A. Foakes (2nd edn, Cambridge: Cambridge University Press, 2002), 26–7.
3. See Charles Edelman, '"Shoot at him all at once": Gunfire at the Playhouse', *Theatre Notebook*, 57 (2003), 78–81.
4. Edelman supposes that the Governor would have been tied to a stage post such as was lacking at the Rose in 1587, and that the performance to which Gawdy's comment relates took place at the Theatre; but the Governor is hung 'upon the city walls' (5.1.108), which suggests a location above the main stage.
5. Andrew Gurr, 'New Questions about the Rose', *Times Literary Supplement*, 18 April 2003, 14–15, points out that many questions about the Rose are as yet unanswered, and further analysis of the remains may require us to revise present interpretations. However, I don't think further analysis will change our concept of the main structural features as it existed in 1594.
6. For further commentary on this issue see my essay, 'Raw Flesh/Lion's Flesh: a Cautionary Note on Stage Directions', in *In Arden: Editing Shakespeare*, ed. Ann Thompson and Gordon Mcmullan (London: Thomson Learning, 2003), 25–37.
7. John Ronayne, 'Totus Mundus Agit Histrionem. The Interior Decorative Scheme of the Bankside Globe', in *Shakespeare's Globe Rebuilt*, ed. J. R. Mulryne and Margaret Shewring (Cambridge: Cambridge University Press, in association with Mulryne and Shewring, 1997), 121–43, citing 135. Gabriel Egan's essay on 'Reconstructions of the Globe: a Retrospective', *Shakespeare Survey*, 52 (1999), 1–16, brings out the influence of the De Witt drawing on schemes for reconstructing this playhouse.
8. *Henslowe's Diary*, 240.

9. Johan Gerritsen, 'De Witt, Van Buchell, the Swan and the Globe: Some Notes', in *Essays in Honour of Kristian Schmidt*, ed. Peter Bilton et al. (Oslo, 1986), 29–45. I am summarizing material from an essay on 'The Image of the Swan Theatre' which I contributed to *Spectacle and Image in Renaissance Europe*, ed. André Lascombes (Leiden, New York and Cologne: E. J. Brill, 1993), 337–59, a volume that has been largely overlooked in accounts of the Elizabethan stage, and is not mentioned in Andrew Gurr, *The Shakespearian Playing Companies* (Oxford: Oxford University Press, 1996) or in Wickham et al., *English Professional Theatre, 1530–1660*. See also Gerritsen's later note, 'The Swan Theatre Drawing: a Review', in *Folio*, 2 (1995), 33–8.

10. Gerritsen, 'De Witt, Van Buchell', 37–8; Foakes, 'The Image of the Swan Theatre', 346.

11. Norden was a cartographer and surveyor who drew from observation. The later decorative panoramas of London, by J. C. Visscher (1616) and Matthias Merian (1638) have no independent authority. There is no evidence that Visscher visited London, and his engraving is based on Norden's, while Merian's in turn is based on Visscher's. These two both give the Swan a hut, perhaps because the other Bankside theatres had them. See R. A. Foakes, *Illustrations of the English Stage 1580–1642* (Stanford: Stanford University Press, 1985), 10–13, 18–19, 27–8.

12. Most recently in *English Professional Theatre, 1530–1660*, 441, which misleads in heading a partial translation of what van Buchell wrote as 'Johannes de Witt describes the playhouses in a letter to his friend.'

13. See E. H. Gombrich, *Art and Illusion* (Princeton: Princeton University Press, third printing, 1969), Part 1, Section II, 'Truth and the Stereotype', 66–74. The quotation is from 73.

14. The anonymous translator (John Dover Wilson? – or perhaps Allardyce Nicoll?) altered 'forma' to 'formam' in a transcription in *Shakespeare Survey*, 1 (1948), 23–4 of van Buchell's sentence, 'Cuius quidem forma quod Romani operis umbram videatur exprimere supra adpinxi'. This 'correction' has been adopted by others, and is included, for example, in the 'original Latin' cited in *Shakespeare's Globe Rebuilt*, ed. J. R. Mulryne and Margaret Shewring, 189, and translated as 'I have drawn it above since it appears to imitate in its shape the form of a Roman structure.' What van Buchell wrote has a significantly different meaning, roughly, 'I have drawn above what traces of a Roman structure it seems to express in its form.' He did not draw the Swan because it was shaped like a Roman theatre, but set out to sketch it in the style of a Roman theatre.

15. John B. Gleason noticed the probable derivation of the term 'amphiteatra' from Justus Lipsius in 'The De Witt Drawing of the Swan Theatre', *Shakespeare Quarterly*, 32 (1981), 324–38, but he assumed the term was De Witt's, which it may have been, though all we can be sure about is that it is what van Buchell wrote. He also noted structural analogies with the vertical half-section of a Roman amphitheatre as represented in chapter 13 of *De Amphiteatro*, which shows gladiators fighting in the arena, with the solitary figure of a Roman emperor seated watching.

16. See Gerritsen, 'De Witt, van Buchell', 36–7, and 'The Swan Theatre Drawing: a Review', 36–7.

17. I am indebted to June Schlueter for drawing my attention to the images of the west façade of St Mary's church by van Buchell and Saenredam. For her important investigations into the origins of the Swan drawing and the life of De Witt, see 'Genus *Cygnus*: Thee Species of the Swan', in *Medieval and Renaissance Drama in England* 16 (2003), 192–217. My interpretation of the pictorial evidence bearing on the Swan is different from her more cautious reading.

18. Citing the passage as translated in *Pieter Saenredam: the Utrecht Work. Paintings and Drawings by the 17th-century Master of Perspective*, ed. Liesbeth M. Helmus (Utrecht: Central Museum, 2000), 18. The Mariakerk was in decay by the 1590s, after being damaged in a siege in 1576, when the north-west tower was destroyed.

19. The contract is reprinted in Wickham et al., *English Professional Theatre*, 598–600.

20. Citing Julian Bowsher, *The Rose Theatre: an Archaeological Discovery* (London: Museum of London, 1998), 50.

21. See Karl Trautman, 'Englische Komoedianten in Nürnberg zum Schlusse des Dreissigjahrigen Krieges (1593–1648)', *Archiv für Litteraturgeschichte*, 14 (Leipzig, 1886), 113–36; the Fechthaus opened in June 1628.

22. The print is reproduced in Gustav Könnecke, *Bilderatlas zur Geschichte der deutschen Nationalliteratur*, 2nd edn (Marburg, 1895), 172, with the caption 'Das Fechthaus zu Nurnberg', built 1628, from a print of 1651.

23. The contract is printed in *Henslowe's Diary*, 306–10.

24. Little is known of the repertory of the Chamberlain's Men, other than Shakespeare's plays, prior to their move to the Globe. Roslyn Knutson lists fourteen plays, including the three parts of *Henry VI*, in which Shakespeare had a hand, and four that were staged at the Rose; see *The Repertory of Shakespeare's Company 1594–1613* (Fayetteville: University of Arkansas Press, 1991). By contrast, *Henslowe's Diary* contains the titles of 280 plays, though some of these belong to the period 1600–3; see Neil Carson, *A Companion to Henslowe's Diary* (Cambridge: Cambridge University Press, 1988), 82–4.

25. See Martin Brückner and Kristen Poole, 'The Plot Thickens: Surveying Manuals, Drama, and the Materiality of Narrative Form in Early Modern England', *ELH*, 69 (2002), 617–48, especially 635–40. 'The plot of the Play, called England's Joy' was issued as a broadside announcing a date for a performance at the Swan on 6 November 1602; although this was a hoax, it suggests that audiences were familiar with the idea of a stage 'plot'.

26. *Henslowe's Diary*, ed. W. W. Greg, II (1908), 112, cited in *Henslowe's Diary*, ed. Foakes, xxix.

27. Cambridge University Press, 58–9. In his later book, *The Shakespearean Playing Companies* (Oxford: Clarendon Press, 1996), 93–104, Gurr presents a more sympathetic and much fuller account of Henslowe's activities.

28. Gurr, *The Shakespearian Playing Companies*, 101.

29. Commenting on John Orrell's *The Quest for Shakespeare's Globe* (Cambridge: Cambridge University Press, 1983), Susan Cerasano registered her scepticism about his claims for the accuracy of Hollar's drawing on which his arguments are based, and prophesied as long ago as 1986 that any reconstruction would become for the public 'The Globe Playhouse, Shakespeare's Own'. See *Medieval and Renaissance Drama in England*, 3, 265–95, especially 273.

30. Jane Moody, *Illegitimate Theatre in London, 1770–1840* (Cambridge University Press, 2000).

31. The reconstructed Globe may also be greatly oversized in relation to the original. John Gleason reports that radar surveys of the Theatre and the Globe show that both had a diameter of about 72 feet like the Rose. See 'New Questions about the Globe', *Times Literary Supplement*, 26 September 2003, 15. If valid, this evidence might explain why De Witt/van Buchell says that the Swan was the grandest and largest of the Bankside theatres, not the Theatre, the main timbers of which were used to frame the Globe.

2
Masks, Mimes and Miracles: Medieval English Theatricality and its Illusions

Richard Beadle

Masks, Mimes and Miracles was the title of a book published in 1931 by the British theatre historian Allardyce Nicoll, which sought to show that there was 'a regular line of "theatrical" continuity' from the Roman mimes, or low comedians, down to the medieval *joculatores*, popular entertainers, whose practical skills went on to provide some of the most distinctive features of the miracle, mystery, and morality plays; a continuity that finally came to reside in the late sixteenth-century Italian *commedia dell'arte*, where the stock characters and their masks bear an extraordinarily close resemblance to Classical images of performers in the Atellan farces.[1] Like most who wrote about early theatre history before the late 1960s, Nicoll's working assumptions were of an evolutionary type that have generally been discarded by the scholarly world, though they still inform many popular accounts of how medieval drama developed. But at the same time, Nicoll differed markedly from those of his time who taught that European drama was reborn in the Latin liturgy of the early Christian Church, was gradually vernacularized, moving at the same time out of the environs of the Church into the secular world of the marketplace and the streets. Nicoll's instinct was that theatrical continuity lay in the secular sphere all along, that it did not depend on a record of scripted play texts, but relied upon material phenomena like masks and masking, in the persistence of certain distinctive acting styles and 'turns', and in a natural human desire to see mysterious and bewitching devices and conjuring tricks – what we now call, in a different medium, 'special effects'.

As Meg Twycross and Sarah Carpenter point out in their recent valuable book *Masks and Masking in Medieval and Early Tudor England*, there is no way of either substantiating or disproving Nicoll's thesis, because the documentary record is too fragmentary, and such evidence as there is is too elusive of secure interpretation.[2] But if one is seeking to redefine late medieval and early modern theatrical history, it may be time, in the light of new information, to bring back into focus some of Nicoll's preoccupations in *Masks, Mimes and Miracles*.

Not only is his book still a valuable source of documentation and illustration, but it has the virtue of sustaining an audience-orientated point of view towards theatre history, instinctively implying essential questions: what did the audience *see*, and how did they *feel* about what they saw? These may sound like naive propositions, and maybe they would be in drier, theoretically oriented environments of thinking, but when applied to late medieval English theatre they assuredly are not. Writing recently about the current state of knowledge concerning the York Corpus Christi cycle, Peter Meredith observed as follows:

> In many ways, the York Play is the best documented of all the English Mystery cycles. There is the text, almost complete; there is a city which retains many of its medieval features and one in which the route of the Play is almost entirely preserved; there is voluminous civic documentation; and there are considerable, though more limited, craft records. Despite this, it is difficult to think of any 'fact' about the Play which is not open to question or at least to variant interpretation.[3]

Students of the York cycle have become accustomed to keen debates of a quite radical nature about their material, as, for example, about twenty-five years ago, when a dispute suddenly broke out over whether the long-held conventional belief that the York plays were performed on wagons, along a processional route through the streets of the city, was not in fact an antiquarian myth. The text, it was argued, was designed for a private indoor performance before a coterie audience drawn from the civic elite. So for a good many years there was scant agreement that a universal audience saw plays on pageant wagons in the street at all, let alone what they felt about them. A better edition of the records, and practical research in the form of restaged processional performances on university campuses, and eventually along parts of the original route through York itself in 1988 and 1992, have gradually restored the status quo, but that is where agreement about what the audience saw currently ends.[4] The unresolved debate at the moment arises out of the physical experience of trying to manoeuvre heavy, two-storey pageant wagons along Stonegate and Petergate in 1988 and 1992 – York streets that are in places little more than twenty feet wide to this day, taking into account some of the medieval jettied or overhanging upper storeys still in existence on some buildings. Prior to these productions, most people had rather vaguely assumed that the wagon-stages played side-on, across the street, like little proscenium stages, though there was still room for disagreement about whether they all faced the left-hand or the right-hand side of the street. Now there is growing conviction in some quarters that York pageant wagons did not play side-on at all. Rather, they played end-on, as transpicuous thrust stages coming down the street towards the audiences assembled at the stations. Consequently, we are in the midst of another far-reaching reconsideration about 'what the audience saw'. For generations we have been predisposed by more recent theatrical history to see plays in the wide lateral orientation of the proscenium stage, and we have perhaps rather idly assumed that our medieval ancestors configured their pageant wagons as miniature proscenium stages, playing across the street area. But there are increasing signs that this would not work. We have hardly begun thinking about how these plays might have looked if they had to be blocked for end-on wagon presentation, in a receding, and probably an ascending perspective, with the audience on three sides.[5]

A macro-theatrical matter such as the orientation of the York pageant wagons is plainly of importance, but the remainder of this study will be devoted to exploring certain less conspicuous features of medieval English theatricality, and their impact on the audience. Twycross and Carpenter on masks and masking in early theatre are a model of scholarly caution in the face of frag-mentary and chronologically sporadic evidence, and there are various things about which they rightly prefer not to commit themselves. However, in the light of their work, and as far as the English cycle plays are concerned, it now seems safe to hazard the existence of a convention, whereby all the actors who played the numerous supernatural figures who appear in these plays had their facial features concealed, either by a mask or visor, or by full face-painting. The facial concealments were colour coded, with gold for God, red for angels, and similarly for saints in heaven or good souls at the Last Judgement, and of course black masks or head-pieces for devils, demons, and the damned souls in Hell. Though it is likely to be surprising or unsettling to our habitual assumptions, it appears that this convention extended to God in his incarnate form as Jesus Christ, who appeared either with a golden mask or visor, or with his face gilded: there is a delightfully phrased payment in the records of the Chester cycle for 'gilding the face of the little God', relating to Christ's appearance as a boy to dispute with the learned doctors in the Temple at Jerusalem. But it seems we now have to start thinking of a golden-faced Christ in the extreme and bloody realism of the Crucifixion play.

If the supernatural masking convention is applied to the forty-six or so pageants that go to make up the York cycle as a whole, it appears that masked actors are on stage at some point in the great majority of them (some forty), more often than not mingling with the unmasked figures. There would also have been at least three pageants in which all the actors would have been masked, and no human faces would have been visible at all, which included the important plays at the beginning and the end, the *Creation and the Fall of Lucifer* at the beginning of time, and *Doomsday*, the Last Judgement that is yet to come. So one may presume that down to the last of the normally annual performances of the Corpus Christi play in 1569, whether the *Fall of Lucifer* or *Doomsday* was being played sideways across the street or whether the pageant-wagon was set up for end-on presentation, the audience would have been looking at a fully masked performance. This is perhaps an element in theatre history that needs defining *ab initio*, rather than redefining.

Twycross and Carpenter see masks in the mystery cycles as in some ways related to the widespread seasonal and festive masking prevalent in medieval culture, such as the donning of animal masks at certain times of the year, and the social custom of mumming. But, equally clearly, they see the cycle play masks as without specific precedent in formal kinds of theatre in the West during the post-Classical period.[6] Medieval theatrical masks are instead more likely to represent an independently developed semiotic system resembling or paralleling masked playing in non-European cultures, something that is closer to the use of masks in African or Indian or Japanese traditional theatrical forms. Modern scholarship's need for defamiliarization here poses some significant problems, since the dialogue in the mysteries is only rudimentarily stylized, as stanzaic verse, but otherwise uses the everyday common vocabulary and colloquial idioms of its audience, a language that often carries a strong, humanly emotive thrust in scenes of violence, pathos and demonstrative religious sentiment, of which there are a great many. But in contrast with this, the visual articulation of the plays – which is where masks figure – was markedly representational: all manner of spiritual things are given concrete form, of which masks are only one, and the actors who play divinities, demons, and other visitors from the spirit world are no more and no less than what their masks represent. In the medieval English theatre this factor would have brought with it significant advantages, since in the cycle plays the part of God the Son, for example, might be taken by many different actors in successive pageants (upwards of twenty at York), but the figure itself would have maintained a single gilded or visored countenance throughout to the audience. It is also worth pondering that the Latin word for mask, *larva*, at first meant 'spectre' or 'ghost' or 'evil spirit', and it went on doing so until well into the medieval period; likewise its Germanic counterpart, *masca*, 'evil spirit', from which our modern word 'mask' is derived. By the fourteenth century, what we might call the 'neutral' theatrical sense of *larva*, simply meaning a face-mask, has emerged, and so the English preacher John Bromyard can write about *Ludentes enim in ludo, qui vulgariter dicitur miraculos, larvis utuntur* ('Players in the kind of play that are called miracles in the vernacular make use of masks'), and the inventory of the York Creed play in the fifteenth century has a *larva aurata*, a golden mask, for Christ. Nonetheless, the etymological origins of *larva* and 'mask' in the supernatural, and specifically in the fear of the supernatural, are striking, and we should bear them in mind.

The dialogue and stage directions of the mystery cycles appear to disclose no self-consciousness or even awareness of masking. There are many plays where unmasked characters confront masked figures, such as the eighth pageant in the York cycle, where God as a divine artificer gives the landlubberly Noah an extended practical lesson in shipbuilding. But there is no indication that the actor playing Noah registers or reacts to the fact that the actor playing God is masked, or looks strange. If Noah is perturbed by God's sudden intervention in his life it is because he is 500 years old and God is telling him to go and build an ark. It is as if there is another convention, that it is the audience who see and respond to the masks, but that the ordinary human figures who appear in the plays do not. If such a convention did exist it would be close, but not quite identical in function, to the iconographical significance of many stage props which the religious drama shares with the visual arts of the period. There would be no surprise on the audience's part in seeing the Virgin Mary wearing the crown or diadem with which she was commonly pictured, as she searches anxiously through the streets of Jerusalem for the little God with the golden face whom she has lost; or Adam in the mysteries and Mankind in the morality always equipped with his spade. The diadem and the spade are as much iconographically prompted ideas in the minds of the audience as they are physical objects on the stage, and so it must have been with masks. But if the semiotic significance of masks in these plays is fairly clear, the nature of their living theatrical potency is more difficult to discern. This is no doubt partly because our late medieval and early modern ancestors had accumulated upwards of 200 years' experience of the practicalities of masked playing, whereas most of us, whether we are audiences, actors, directors, or theatre historians, have little or none.

A kind of theatre that extensively renounces facial expression as a communicative medium is sacrificing a lot, so there must also be a strong sense of any corresponding gains, and it is therefore impossible to continue analysing masked playing without thinking about such things as acting style and acoustics, areas where specific technical expertise is called for. Some considerations, however, are fairly plain. Masked actors, without the resources of facial expression, lose a significant proportion of their individuality, and have to learn how to move in unfamiliar ways. The audience for its part also has to recognize a different language of gesture, especially of head movements, because the head usually has to be moved more slowly behind a mask, and the actor's sightlines are restricted. Relatively small head movements by a masked actor make a much stronger impression than they do when performed by unmasked performers, as witness the remarkably detailed sets of instructions for head movements used by masked actors preparing to perform in the Japanese Noh theatre.[7] Without facial expression, other movements of the body take on greater significance: a masked actor's gestures tend often to be symbolic, and postures to be emblematic. Auditory values are also altered, and are apt to reinforce the otherworldly significance of the mask itself. The sounds made by masked actors tend to be slightly eerie, and they call for a different

level of audience attention, since without facial expression or an accompanying gesture one cannot necessarily tell when a masked actor is about to speak,
or indeed, where there is more than one, which of them is speaking.

Let me consider the other large and seemingly naive question posed at the
outset: what did the audience feel about what they saw under these conditions?
John Bromyard, the fourteenth-century Dominican preacher mentioned above,
writing again about masks, also remarked that in his time only two sorts of
people regularly wore them: actors and thieves. Though actors seldom wear
masks nowadays, thieves and others who are up to no good often still do, not
just to conceal their identity, but also because they know that a balaclava or a
stocking over the face goes a good way towards frightening most of us, even
without resorting to more direct means of doing so. As we have seen, whether
one invokes the Latin or the Germanic word for mask, the name of the object
shadows its etymological roots in a fear of the supernatural. If the late medieval
theatre had extensive recourse to masks, one major reason was surely in order
to connect itself with that region of the audience's emotional spectrum where
fear and awe reside, to create potent illusions of the presence of the numinous
in everyday life, and of the imminence of apocalyptic destruction, which
engaged directly with their beliefs, as they were usually expressed and objecti-
fied in Christian dogma. Ultimately, the effect of masking in the mystery plays
was unerringly implicative, as were so many features of medieval dramaturgy.
By the end of the York Corpus Christi cycle, for example, the audience were
effectively being drawn within the illusion of the *Doomsday* play, being given
a choice as to whether they will be wearing the radiant masks of the saved or
the tormented masks of the damned as they rise out of their graves at the sound
of the last trumpet.

The approach suggested here seeks to take the fact of the masking of the
supernatural figures in the mysteries as one of the central and governing facts
of late medieval theatricality, rather than one of its curious and marginal
epiphenomena. It is perhaps worth beginning to think about how other visual
aspects of early theatrical experience – the mimes and the miracles, the acting
styles and the special effects – look from the perspective of the special sense of
illusion created by the presence of masked actors. First of all, the disputed topic
of the acting style in medieval theatre: 'Was the acting highly stylised, or
moderately naturalistic?' asks Meg Twycross in her classic account of 'The
Theatricality of Medieval English Plays', and she goes on:

> We shall never really know. The use of masks for supernatural characters,
> the gilding of God's face, haloes, and the way some characters carry attrib-
> utes, suggests a certain measure of stylisation; as does the rhetorical struc-
> ture of the dialogue. But it is possible for both to co-exist in the same
> performances: they are not opposites, but a matter of degree.[8]

This is an eminently sensible approach, but it might yet call for qualification in as much as one could argue that it is the minimally naturalistic fact of extensive masking that defines the nature of the illusion, rather than masked performers functioning as an adjunct to a predominantly naturalistic style of playing.

As observed above, the texts of the plays appear to show no sign that the more naturalistically depicted figures were expected to 'play off' the slower, gestural acting style that the masked performers are likely to have used. To be sure, the colloquialism of much of the dialogue encourages us to feel that a directly mimetic or everyday acting mode would be appropriate where, say, Noah's wife, or the Shepherds travelling to the manger, or King Herod were concerned, the kind of total actor/role identification that we expect to see in TV soap operas and most movies. Maybe this was the case, but one can on the other hand point to some marked counter-indications which might lead us to wonder whether even the roles of the ordinary human beings depicted in the plays were in fact acted rather less than wholly naturalistically.

One is the oft-remarked frequency of direct address to the audience in the mystery plays. This hardly calls for illustration, but it is worth remarking that theatrically its affiliations lie with informal traditions of acting that survive in vaudeville, revue sketches, English seasonal pantomime and the like – much closer to Brecht than to Stanislavski. Another non-naturalistic feature is much more subtle, and can be located in a submerged but pervasive feature of the diction of the mystery play scripts, which becomes very noticeable in the word-frequency ranking lists in the recently published concordances to the texts of the cycles. This is something that calls for more detailed documentation than can be provided in the present context, but as I have recently tried to show elsewhere, the language of the plays strongly foregrounds certain performative and deictic lexical sets, the most important of which are composed of numerous synonyms for the concepts of working and doing, coming and going, giving and taking, looking and seeing. This means that what is *said* in the dialogue is strongly integrated with what the actor is seen by the audience to *do*. It is a lexically restricted style in which diction is specifically and consistently designed to draw attention to action, often implying as it does so a movement or a physical gesture on the actor's part.[9] In essence this is a type of oblique variant of the more obvious kind of direct address to the audience mentioned a moment ago: lines like 'Behold, I pluck this apple', 'Now go we up to Jerusalem', 'See how I strike this nail through bones and sinews' are not spoken for the benefit of the other characters in the story, but to cue demonstrative movements and gestures. Ultimately, one can argue that the scripted element in these plays is managed in such a way as to support an acting style which is much more gestural than would be called for under purely naturalistic condi-

tions, and that it tends to assimilate in the direction of the kind of stage movement envisaged above for the masked performers. Meg Twycross is undoubtedly right to emphasize that very different acting styles could coexist within
the same play in this kind of theatre, though it is not something we can easily
grasp. But one might need to add that the tone, as it were, would be set by the
stage presence of the more mysterious, but at the same time more manifestly
artificial actors in masks. Even when we are looking at texts that seem designed
for the ordinary mimetic acting style we are chiefly familiar with, we may be
forced to recognize counter-currents within that style – these overt and covert
types of direct address to the audience just described – because it implies a kind
of theatricality which prefers to advertise itself as illusion, rather than try to
disguise the fact.

A theatrical style that simultaneously installs and undercuts its naturalistic
effects can afford to worry less about the audience's willing suspension of
disbelief, and it creates a lot more room for the accommodation of those
performing skills and turns which emerge from the para-theatrical world of
popular entertainment: silent mime, sleight of hand, conjuring tricks, ven-
triloquism, acrobatics, juggling, pyrotechnics, and the more elaborate technical devices that we nowadays associate with the work of professional illusionists, shadowy figures whom Chaucer and others in the fourteenth and fifteenth
centuries knew as *tregetours* – 'thise subtile tregetours' of the *Franklin's Tale* and
the *House of Fame* – the special effects people.[10] Such things are everywhere in
the mysteries and are no less likely to feature in the moralities and other theatrical genres of the time. It might be said that they are stage miracles, which
can make the audience see something that isn't really there, or cause them to
experience something that cannot happen in the everyday world outside the
theatrical illusion. So in the York plays, Moses can lay down his rod before
Pharaoh and make it turn into a serpent, and then back into a rod again. Or
in the Wakefield First Shepherds' play, the shepherds can sit down to what one
expects is going to be a snack of bread and cheese, but somehow conjure
up at great speed from their bags a twenty-one-course banquet of hot
and cold dishes, many of them from the haute cuisine of the time. Or in
the Chester play of the Purification of the Virgin, the ancient priest Simeon
can display a page of his manuscript bible to the audience, where the ink in
which the words 'Ecce virgo concipiet' are written turns from black to red
and then to gold before their very eyes. Popular superstition associated
numerous conjuring tricks like these with witchcraft, and interesting explanations of how they were done can be read in Reginald Scot's *Discovery of
Witchcraft* (1584), a book familiar to early modernists of various kinds, but
not perhaps as well known as it might be to theatre historians. It contains,
for example, detailed instructions, with diagrams, for how to manage

a mock-beheading on stage, which might yet be brought to bear on the famous episode in the fourteenth-century English romance *Sir Gawain and the Green Knight*, where King Arthur tries to pass off the Green Knight's walking and talking after his head has been chopped off as an illusionist's trick: 'Wel becomes such crafte upon Cristemasse', he says; this is the sort of thing these subtle tregetours get up for 'laykyng [*playing*] of enterludez' in the festive season.[11]

Stage miracles, if one can call them that, and a whole range of ingenious devices and contrivances of a mechanical type, are commonplace in late medieval theatre, and one suspects that their theatrical appeal would be rather greater than the enactment of real miracles, like making the blind see, or the raising of Lazarus. Often, but not always, the conjuring tricks and ingenious devices do in fact enact supernatural interventions in the ordinary course of nature, which can give them a degree of ambivalence – we know they are the devices of actors and stage technicians, but in the divine scheme of things on which the cycle is based they present the illusion of miracles which are as real as those that the plays derive from Scripture. This effect finds its most extreme manifestation not in the mysteries but in the only English miracle play proper, the Croxton *Play of the Sacrament*, where a group of Jews are depicted as acquiring a consecrated host, and subjecting it to a series of tests to see whether it really is the body and blood of Christ.[12] The conjuring tricks and special effects the actors have to use become progressively more elaborate. First, in a mock crucifixion, they try to nail it to a post, but as they do so the hand of the actor who is holding it steady comes apart from his arm, and the wafer sticks firmly to the detached hand – a fairly straightforward device. Then they lay it on a table and stab at it with dagger, whereupon it starts to spurt blood at them: a cleverer effect, of which we have a description in an early sixteenth-century French analogue of the Croxton play:

> Then by a device which has been made, let a large quantity of blood spring up high from the said Host, as if it was a pissing infant, and let the Jew be covered and bloodied by it, and make his person very wet.

Next, they try to seethe the wafer in a cauldron of oil, but the oil boils over and turns to blood, a contrivance which is mentioned later in another post-medieval rationalist exposé of witchcraft, Thomas Ady's *A Candle in the Dark* (1656). Finally, as the *pièce de résistance*, the bread is incinerated in an oven, but then the oven bursts asunder, blood gushes out at the seams, and an image of Christ himself appears, which later is made to turn back into bread before the audience's eyes. Something similar was done in the contemporary French *Miracle de la Sainte Hostie*, where the sacred host is described as 'rising on a cloud and becoming a small infant, this being done by engines and devices' (*engines et secrets*).[13] The Croxton play seems to offer us the total coalescence of conjuring tricks and illusionists' devices with the 'real' miracles attributed to the sacred host in sermon exempla and theological discourse: transubstantiation as both essential theatricality and doctrinal concept.

It may be objected that the foregoing account, which should be regarded as no more than cursory and preliminary, has held the scripts of late medieval English plays at arm's length, whilst speculating about their visual effects, but this seems to me, for the time being, a secondary concern where their essential theatricality is at issue. We encounter here a kind of theatre which was especially comfortable with its illusions, if one can put it like that, the work of eclectic playwights who were not afraid to assimilate the widest possible variety of theatre arts, and actively to display them as what they are: illusions. One suspects that if we choose to come at the redefinition of this kind of theatre from the direction of its masks, its mimes, and its miracles, then the scripts will look after themselves.

Notes

1. Allardyce Nicoll, *Masks, Mimes and Miracles* (London: Harrap, 1931). The influence of Hermann Reich's monumental *Der Mimus*, 2 vols (Berlin: Weidmann, 1903) is powerfully felt throughout Nicoll's work.
2. Meg Twycross and Sarah Carpenter, *Masks and Masking in Medieval and Early Tudor England* (Aldershot: Ashgate, 2002), 189.
3. Peter Meredith, 'The City of York and its "Play of Pageants"', *Early Theatre*, 3 (2000), special volume, *The York Cycle Then and Now*, 23–47 (39).
4. Much of the controversy of the late 1970s and early 1980s revolved around Alan H. Nelson's reinterpretation of the York evidence for processional performance in *The Medieval English Stage: Corpus Christi Pageants and Plays* (Chicago and London: Chicago University Press, 1974). For photographs showing the recent street productions on pageant-wagons in York see John Marshall, 'Modern Productions of Medieval English Plays', in *The Cambridge Companion to Medieval English Theatre*, ed. Richard Beadle (Cambridge: Cambridge University Press, 1994), 290–311 (298–9).
5. For an up-to-date and balanced summary of the issues in question here see John McKinnell, 'The Medieval Pageant Wagons at York: their Orientation and Height', *Early Theatre*, 3 (2000), special volume, *The York Cycle Then and Now*, 79–104.
6. Twycross and Carpenter, *Masks and Masking*, 193, 200, 336–41.
7. Kunio Komparu, *The Noh Theatre: Principles and Perspectives* (New York, Tokyo and Kyoto: Wetherhill/Tankosha, 1983), 229–39.
8. In *The Cambridge Companion to Medieval English Theatre*, 37–84 (43).
9. Richard Beadle, 'Verbal Texture and Wordplay in the York Cycle', *Early Theatre*, 3 (2000), special volume, *The York Cycle Then and Now*, 167–84 (173–4).
10. Laura Hibbard Loomis, 'Secular Dramatics in the Royal Palace, Paris, 1378, 1389, and Chaucer's "Tregetours"', *Speculum*, 33 (1958), 242–55. See also Louis B. Wright, 'Juggling Tricks and Conjury on the English Stage before 1642', *Modern Philology*, 24 (1927), 269–84.

11. *Sir Gawain and the Green Knight*, ed. J. R. R. Tolkien and E. V. Gordon, revised by Norman Davis (Oxford: Oxford University Press, 1967), lines 417–72.
12. Edited by Norman Davis in *Non-Cycle Plays and Fragments*, Early English Text Society, Special Series, 1 (Oxford: Oxford University Press, 1970), 58–89.
13. Cited by Darryll Grantley, 'Producing Miracles', in *Aspects of Early English Drama*, ed. Paula Neuss (Cambridge: D. S. Brewer, 1983), 78–91 (83, 85).

3
Theatre Without Drama: Reading *REED*

Peter Holland

The name of the play

Imagine a scrap of conversation. 'Hi, what are you doing tonight?' 'I'm going to the theatre.' Now fill in the next line of dialogue. Of course, what is said next depends on the circumstances but it is a reasonable assumption that, in most contexts, the next line will be something like 'What's the play?' It won't be if, say, the second speaker is the local fire officer whose job is to see whether fire precautions are being properly observed, nor if s/he is going to his or her place of work as artistic director or usher or actor or dresser. But in the modern culture of theatre the only reasonable exception among playgoers would probably be from someone heading to, say, London's half-price ticket-booth in Leicester Square since the determination to see a play, any play, will only be resolved into a particular choice when what is available cheap is known.

For an early modern playgoer the systems of advertising might well result in rather less advance knowledge, but turn my exchange into the past tense ('What did you do last night?' 'I went to the theatre' 'What was the play?') and even the early modern spectator might have some means of answering, even if s/he could not identify the title, let alone the playwright – and not only the knowledge with which to do it but, one might expect, the wish to do so, even if the answer were along the lines of 'Oh, something about a prince of Denmark and his mother'.

Look now at the thick red line of volumes that continues inexorably to stretch across the shelves of the well-stocked university library, the sixteen collections in twenty-two volumes that have so far appeared from the Centre for Research in Early English Drama in the ongoing magnificent achievement of *Records of Early English Drama* (*REED*), the most recent, the three volumes and 1900 pages for *Kent: The Diocese of Canterbury*, appearing on the last day of 2002, the whole series covering to date twelve counties, six towns and one diocese.[1] Indeed, my choice of imperative, 'look', was deliberate, for most scholars of early modern drama have looked at the thickness of the volumes, the extent of the shelf-space, and turned away. *REED* can say more about drama and theatre outside London than had ever been imagined earlier, in, for instance, London-centred works like Chambers' *Elizabethan Stage* or Bentley's continuation, or the tiny extent (by comparison) of attention to performance beyond London in the substantial achievement (for its time) of the two volumes of Murray's *English Dramatic Companies*.[2] Yet *REED* remains largely unread – or at least, given its effective unreadability, unconsulted.

But search the thousands of pages, the tens of thousands of records of dramatic performance, ignoring the even higher incidence of records of payments for music, and try to find the name of a play. Read diligently enough and you will strike lucky. Like the compilers of the *REED* volumes themselves, as they trawled through civic, household, parish, and legal records in local records offices and other major depositories in England and elsewhere, the perseverance of the searcher will eventually be rewarded. In Bristol, for instance, the compiler of the mayor's audits in the period from July 1576 to October 1578 took prescient pity on the thirst for knowledge of future drama historians:

> Item, paid to my Lord Chamberlayns players at thend of their play called the red Knight before master mayer and thaldermen in the yeld hall the sume of xx s.[3]

And there are similar items for payments of 22 shillings to 'my Lord of Leycesters Players' when 'the play was called Myngo', of 13 shillings and 4 pence to 'my Lord Sheffildes players' when 'the play was called the court of comfort' and three occasions where the audit gives something that may or may not be the play's title, for when 'my Lord Berckleys Players' were paid, 'the matter was what mischeif workith in the mynd of man', for the performance by 'my Lord Charles hawardes players' (i.e. the Admiral's Men) 'their matter was of the Queen of Ethiopia', while for 'the Erle of Bathes players' 'the mattier was quid pro quo'.[4] Drama historians have tended to assume that the last three are the titles also but perhaps the form of wording here means what it says, describing subject-matter and not an act of naming.

Such riches have to be offset against three frustrations for this run of good luck: firstly, there is no comparable information about title or subject for the four other performances by professional companies within the same period (or the dozens of others across the decade) for which records of payments appear in the Bristol mayor's audits; secondly, nor is there any for the two payments to 'mr Dunne Scholemaster' for the 'charges of his last playes' in this same tranche of time;[5] thirdly, and of course none of the six plays identified by name or 'matter' seems to have survived, unless their 'matter' lurks behind other plays printed or manuscript.

In the absence of the plays themselves and in the absence of, for instance, details about the takings, what can be done with the information so far, short of hypotheses about the subject-matter of lost plays? The conventional response was 'very little'. As John Astington remarked in 1978 at the outset of *REED*, 'Texts have been and remain the center of theatrical studies, partly because of the literary tradition in the humanities, and partly through the autonomous life of dramatic texts themselves.'[6]

Patrons and touring

Yet *REED* has been part of and provoked changes in what we can do with such material. As early modern theatre history has developed in the last quarter-century, so there have been responses of increasing complexity to the accumulating materials, the heaps of fragments, the contents of those large red volumes, responses that have reached out towards adjacent fields. One route, the one that has generated some of the most outstanding work using the *REED* materials, has been to work on patronage of theatre companies and the patterns of company touring. That work has now begun to intersect with the sustained investigations of patronage structures for the writing and dissemination of non-dramatic texts in the early modern period, work given its current importance and impetus through the conference-derived volume on *Patronage in the Renaissance*, edited by Guy Lytle and Stephen Orgel in 1981.[7] Studies of patronage in early modern theatre necessarily concern themselves in part with theatre beyond London, even as such studies are starting at last to define the distinctive qualities of theatrical patronage, especially in the remarkable recent collection edited by Paul Whitfield White and Suzanne Westfall.[8] Patronage is fundamental to many of the structures of production and consumption of both drama texts and theatrical performance in the period, both in London, in aristocratic entertainment, and in civic performance beyond the capital.[9] Yet, as I shall be arguing much later, the concern with and concentration on patron-defined companies has narrowed the perspectives on early modern performance.

There has been a tendency to assume that studies of touring, which necessarily connect with patronage studies, will remain unclear until they can be based on the fullest picture that *REED* will eventually provide. But Sally-Beth MacLean has published a series of brilliant investigations of touring systems,[10] most strikingly in her study, with Scott McMillin, of *The Queen's Men and Their Plays*,[11] by far the most exciting study of a single early modern theatre company yet to appear. Siobhan Keenan's recent book-length study of touring, an adequate bringing together of what has been known and can be understood from the researches of *REED*, past and as yet unpublished, similarly shows how touring becomes a means of constructing a totalizing history, an overview of dramatic activity.[12]

MacLean and Alan Somerset have been developing a website on patrons which, when it moves beyond the pilot stage next year, will enable searching by patron, place of performance or company as well as providing for patrons details of offices held and properties owned, the kind of information that the appendices on patrons and travelling companies have provided in individual *REED* volumes.[13] Such research treats the individual fragment of the historical record – 'Item paid to my Lord Clyntons players at the end of their play before master mayer & his brethren xiij s. iiij d.'[14] – and reassembles it into a network that embraces Clinton's company and their practice of playing: where, when and how much they were paid. The first prototype site, following Robert Dudley, patron D532a, lists his titles, offices, spouses, and properties, and then assembles the extant records of performances by players, bearwards, and musicians, listing by date, place, auspices, payment and whatever else may be known – though not the name of the plays performed, of course.

But the site's sample questions about performance, their understanding of what might be asked of this database, also necessarily indicate the narrowness of the materials with which they are working: again, they cannot ask what was played, only questions of the who, where, when, how much varieties, allowing, for instance, comparisons, so that it would enable one to know that, in my Bristol sample, the payment range went from 10 shillings (for Lord Berkeley's and Lord Howard's players) through 13 shillings and 4 pence (for Essex's, Lord Clinton's, Lord Sheffield's and the Earl of Bath's players) to 1 pound (for Sussex's Men and a different visit by the Earl of Bath's players) and finally 22 shillings (for Leicester's). It is intriguing to find Leicester's actors playing a church in Plymouth in 1559 and another in Dartmouth in 1570 as well as in guild halls, to find their payments ranging from 6 shillings to 30, and to trace their playing under the jurisdiction of ecclesiastical and university authorities as well as civic. But it is also most intriguing when the bare records suddenly flower into a fragment more knowledge: that there was, for instance, a payment at Bristol in October 1573 'for taking down the table in the mayers courte and setting yt vp agayne after the said players werre gonne'.[15] The usual cannot command attention in the way the exceptional does.

At its best, in, for example, Andrew Gurr's study of the London theatre companies,[16] metropolitan and provincial playing are integrated into an account of the interaction in company history between playing at their London home and travelling, making extensive use of *REED* materials to document the travels. But, as theatre historians, considering the kinds of material *REED* or, earlier, the Malone Society collections of records for particular locations made available,[17] realized, records for touring began to diminish unnervingly in the seventeenth century and the implication, for such positivist historians, coupled with the increasing prominence of payments by civic authorities made to prevent companies from playing, was that there must have been a distinct decline in touring, that the metropolitan companies became, so goes one explanation, increasingly reluctant to spend time unprofitably on tour, if their contact with civic authorities only prevented them from playing. Keenan's account,[18] in line with conventional thinking, seems not to have taken into account the superbly revisionary version offered by Andrew Gurr in 1994.[19] For Gurr, refusing to read the absence of evidence as necessarily equivalent to the absence of playing, argues that the change in the quantity of record is a consequence of a change in the structures of authority controlling playing, that, precisely because of the increased power vested in or claimed by successive Masters of the Revels to authorize playing throughout the country by the issue of travelling licences, there was no need for any contact with the local authorities and hence no need for a record. Gurr's reprinting of a lengthy decision in the matter in Hythe in Kent in 1615, demonstrating what Gurr calls 'a valiant attempt to impose order on the chaos that procedures had evidently fallen into', shows one way to reimpose the previous system rather than accept the overriding control that the structures supporting the king's sovereignty sought to impose over previously local rights.[20]

I shall return to the implications of such work later, but it is crucial to recognize that, for a project whose output is so fiercely determined by local placing, the work of assemblage of the fragments has been to create a yearning – not necessarily of *REED*'s editors' making, though many are complicit in this – for a master narrative of company and patron, to see the dominance of the unit of actors as something marked by its mobility, to move from local record towards a grand history defined by a larger geography, a displacing of locale into a sequence that combines time and distance, requiring, for instance, in MacLean's studies of touring circuits, an understanding of the major road systems of early modern England, with their Roman, medieval, and renaissance layerings of systematizing travel, precisely, that is, a sense of the modes of communication that make the dissemination of information practicable.[21] Ever since I realized years ago that Shakespeare wrote *Hamlet* while working alongside more than one actor who had played at Elsinore, it has seemed to me that companies' touring might have provided significant sources of information to playwrights, and one extension from the mapping of touring to the processes of creation of the surviving plays that would be worth investigating would be to chart how many places in which action is explicitly set had been on that company's touring circuit.

Yet it is also striking that MacLean's work, like Gurr's, has been dominated by those companies that were London-based, a continuance of the tradition of London-dominated, metropolitan histories; the parameters of Gurr's study of the 'Shakespearian' playing companies, for instance, are the London playing companies, while MacLean's road-maps trace the routes of equivalent companies. Murray's two volumes of often inaccurate and now much mocked records were divided between London companies and provincial ones and, though the divisions blur (he, for example, defines as provincial Lord Berkeley's players, a troupe which, because they played in London, also figure in Gurr's study[22]), his accounts cover a significant number of companies and patterns of localized touring beyond anything that MacLean and Gurr have yet focused on. The Bristol *REED* volume lists, from the expert work of Arleanne Ralph, by my count fifty-three patrons of players (pp. 300–19), many of whom were, of course, lending their names to companies that figure in the records of London playing but many of whom do not, including, by my count, two of the eight in those two years of Bristol records I have been using as a sample (the Earl of Bath's and Lord Sheffield's), one of which might reasonably be seen as a local company but the other having a patron whose seat was in Yorkshire.

Even the analysis of touring, then, has been based on a London-centrism that, through its dominance, falsifies the general perception of the quantity, range, and distribution of such activity. If such a transforming of the records' articulations is marked for civic sources like Bristol they are even more marked for household records, especially when London is a long way off. The remarkable information from the household accounts of the Walmesleys during their ownership of Dunkenhalgh Manor and the Shuttleworths at Smithills and Gawthorpe Hall, all three estates in Lancashire, and the equally intriguing evidence from the Kent records for Sir Edward Dering at Surrenden all militate strongly against the acceptance of the structures of touring which concentration on, as it were, national companies creates.

Shakespearians have spent long enough recently wondering about the William Shakshafte referred to in the will of Alexander Hoghton in 1581 but we have, I think, ignored the significance that Hoghton was encouraging his brother Thomas to take advantage of Alexander's stock of 'playe Clothes yf he be mynded to keppe & doe keppe playeres. And yf he wyll not keppe & manteyne playeres. Then yt ys my mynde & wyll that Sir Thomas Heskethe knyghte shall haue the same Instrumentes & playe clothes'.[23] Hesketh was certainly keeping players in 1587 when his troupe was recorded as leaving Knowsley, the house of the Stanleys of Derby near Prescot. The Stanleys often had players at Knowsley including Leicester's company and repeated visits from the Queen's Men. Hesketh's players were, then, in distinguished company but the tiny quantity of information about them suggests that they kept their performances to local houses. If they toured in any significant way their circuit would appear to have been a Lancashire one.

The Knowsley records are unsurprising but those of Dunkenhalgh show more strongly the mixture of local and national players. The thirty years of accounts from 1613 to *REED*'s terminal date of 1642 show visits by the King's Men, Lady

Elizabeth's Men and Derby's, for instance, but also such local companies as those of Lord Monteagle, Lord Stafford, Lord Eure, Sir Cuthbert Halsall and Sir Edward Warren, the last of whom even the researches of David George have not managed to identify, though he is likely, in my view, to have been a relative of the John Warren of Woodplumpton and Poynton whose players also appeared at Dunkenhalgh.[24]

But there were more besides. There are regular payments at Dunkenhalgh and at Gawthorpe to 'Distley' (or 'Dishley') and his company from 1609 onwards. As a payment of 30 shillings on 7 October 1612 makes clear, Distley was a member or leader of Dudley's company, 'giuen to distley and his companie my Lord dudley his plaeres',[25] but the frequent visits to Dunkenhalgh in the 1620s make no mention of the patron, simply and repeatedly to 'disley the Plaier'.[26] Bentley argued that that company is never referred to as Dudley's after the 1612 reference and that Distley's troupe 'was not improbably a local organization, since four of its six appearances are recorded at Gawthorpe Hall, and it is never recorded farther afield than Leicester'.[27] But Distley was in 1618 identified as leading a short-lived company under the patronage of Lord Shrewsbury, playing at Londesborough; by 1619 he was leading a group explicitly recognized by the Earl of Cumberland's steward as 'my Lod: Dudley his players', thereby disproving Bentley's assumption.[28] What is striking is that the company is in the Dunkenhalgh records identified by the name of leading actor, not patron; it suggests, in ways that need to be taken account of, the weakening of the patron's presence and the increase in the importance of the lead actor, as if the King's Men became known on tour as 'Burbage and his company', something which, so far as I know, did not occur.

Also regularly to be seen at Dunkenhalgh was the company of Richard Bradshaw (probably not the same man who was in the Dudley company in 1595 but possibly the one who was at Reading in 1630 and Banbury in 1633), playing there seven times.[29] And then there was William Perry, known for twenty-five years as the leader of a provincial company which worked under various names from 1617 including Queen Anne's, the Children of the Revels to the late Queen Anne, the King's players, the Red Bull company and 'His Majesty's servants for the city of York' but at Dunkenhalgh always 'pirrie & his companie'.[30] Ellis Guest, who falsely represented his company as 'the lady Elizabethes players', was also there, though on one occasion paid for not playing.[31] Such companies, whatever their patronage status were known by actor's name, a change in the attitude towards the company that is significant.

But there was yet one further kind of acting company paid for their visits to Dunkenhalgh. Players identified by their town of origin played there, often at Christmas, including actors from Downham, Ribchester, Clitheroe, Whalley, and Burnley, local amateur groups, perhaps like the ones who were given 4 shillings by the Earl of Cumberland in December 1606, 'the yong men of the towne being my lo: Tenantes & servants to holp them to furnishe themselues for going this x[th]imas tyme a playing vnder my lo: name'.[32] Of such local groups *REED* volumes have much to say but we seem not to have noticed, since the focus of attention has been so substantially on charting the major companies' work, mapping their routes across the country. At Dunkenhalgh provincial and amateur troupes were equally as likely to be performing as the major London-based companies.

There is a further kind of provincial performance which the surviving records relating to Sir Edward Dering demonstrate, one which leads even more substantially away from the touring routes. In the 1620s, Dering frequently saw plays on his trips to London and in Maidstone. He often paid for fiddlers who performed at his home at Surrenden in Kent. But there are no records for visits by theatre companies to Surrenden. Instead, Dering seems regularly to have produced plays, using his family and members of his household as cast. In order to mount the plays he bought playbooks in London. In a period from the death of his first wife Elizabeth in June 1622 until his remarriage in 1625 he bought 156 playbooks, including two copies of the Shakespeare First Folio and a copy of Ben Jonson's *Works*, all three of which were paid for on 5 December 1623, the earliest known purchases of the Shakespeare Folio.[33] Usually the accounts are predictably silent over the names of the plays he bought: what were the titles of the fifty-six playbooks he bought in four batches on a single day, 28 November 1623? But the six playbooks he bought on 4 December 1623 were all copies of 'Band, Ruff and Cuff',[34] presumably one of the two editions of the little dialogue performed at Cambridge and both published in 1615 when Dering was a student at Magdalene College.[35] On 16 March 1624 he bought '3 playebookes of ye woman Hater', Beaumont's play, presumably copies of the 1607 edition.[36] In both cases it is a reasonable assumption that he intended to perform them at Surrenden, though why he would need as many as six copies of 'Band, Ruff and Cuff' which has a cast of only three is far from clear.

In February 1623 Dering paid 'mr Carington' – probably Samuel Carrington, the rector of a nearby parish – 'for writinge oute ye play of King Henry ye fourth att 1 d. ob. per sheete'.[37] This was Dering's well-known and very adroit adaptation of the two parts of Shakespeare's *Henry IV* into one play and it was probably for that production that he paid 17 shillings and 6 pence 'ffor heades of haire and beardes' on 18 February.[38] Dering wrote his longest addition to the play, eight lines for the first speech of the adaptation, on a scrap of paper, on the back of which were two cast-lists for characters in John Fletcher's *The Spanish Curate*, presumably also intended for performance at Surrenden, whether or not it actually took place.[39] The proposed actors included Sir Edward and four other members of his family, Sir Thomas Wootton and Francesco Manucci who worked for Sir Thomas, and various unidentified individuals, possibly some local gentry but certainly at least one servant in the household, 'lacke of ye buttery'. Dering was obviously interested in recently printed plays: the planned performance must have been between October 1622 (when the play was licensed) and summer 1624 (when Manucci left Wootton's employ).[40]

As well as putting on plays from his student days in Cambridge and adapting plays from the London theatres, Dering almost certainly tried his hand at least once at writing an original play. The surviving scenario for acts 1 to 3 of a play is, apparently, in Dering's hand and seems most likely to be a sketch for a play with author's notes about settings and customs.[41] Dering outlined a drama set in Thrace and Macedon, using Speed's *A Prospect of the Most Famous Parts of the World* (1627) as a research resource. Dull though the play promised to be, it defines another significant part of what was plainly a flourishing country-house theatre culture at Surrenden, generated not by visitors but by the thespian passions of its owner.

Gaps in the records

If the product of the *REED* volumes had been to complete an understanding of the local records then the move towards overarching narratives of touring might have been both possible and, within the boundaries of the evidence, legitimated. But *REED* volumes have been necessarily marked by two modes of incompleteness. The first is the inevitable consequence of the inadequacy of survival and the incompleteness of the research. Even in those cities whose records survive with a remarkable completeness, the evidence is still necessarily only a fragment of the information one might wish and *REED*'s editors, however assiduous, are always bound to have overlooked something, for they can only pragmatically look in likely places. Theresa Coletti, in the most substantial critique of *REED* so far mounted, weakened her case by falsely ascribing to the project a dream of wholeness, the mirage of assembling a body of evidence that would adequately represent the nature of early and early modern dramatic activity.[42] The dream of wholeness that *REED* incorporates is nothing more idealistic than finishing the project within the parameters it has established for itself, in other words covering the country with a sustainedly aware knowledge of the inadequacy of such coverage. It is striking that both critique and defence of *REED* have been substantially mounted by medievalists. The problem of *REED*'s structure as a consequence of periodization as well as the pre-web, limited technology model that eventuates in heavy and unsearchable volumes both deserve fuller consideration. No one now, I take it, would define such a project with print-based delivery.

But *REED*'s further problem is the displacement of the material from the context within which it has particular meanings. Let me return again to the material from Bristol for that period of slightly over two years. Apart from the ten performances by theatre companies, Mark Pilkinton, the editor for the

Bristol volume, records nine payments to the four members of the city's waits
– and such payments, almost always in the same wording and with the same
payment, occupy many hundreds of pages-worth of the *REED* volumes, the
repetition crying out for tabulation so that other materials could stand out in
stronger relief – and payments for 'my lord of leycestres Bereward for shewyng
pastyme with is Beares'[43] and the Queen's bearward for a similar show, for gunpowder for a salute of cannon accompanied by trumpet or drum as the mayor
passed by (three times), and similar processional events, including payments

- to five trumpeters from the ships from 'Cataya' (presumably Cathay, i.e.
  China)[44] as the mayor and the aldermen came back from the sermon at the
  college, preached, as it happens, by John Northbrooke, vehement opposer
  of drama and author of *A Treatise wherein Dicing, Dauncing, Vaine playes, or
  Enterluds . . . are reproued*, published the same year, 1577;[45]
- for a musician who married the daughter of a burgess as he was admitted
  to the liberties;
- and for repairs consequent on the play performances, for the visit of Leicester's company resulted in repairs to a board and the doors of the guildhall,[46]
  while that of the Lord Chamberlain's servants (that is, Sussex's Men) was so
  popular that 'the cramp of Iren which shuttyth the barre' at the guildhall
  doors had to be mended, 'which cramp was stretchid with the presse of
  people at the play'.[47]

REED's rules require the inclusion of anything to do with such civic
pageantry and ceremony, music and drama and it is a rich haul. But these five
pages of the *REED* volume are drawn from over 180 pages of the mayor's audit
book. As Patricia Badir eloquently demonstrated by taking a sample sequence
of payments from the common expenses of the Corporation of Beverley for
1565, while five records for *REED* would be excerpted from the thirty payments,
the selectivity occludes what she describes as 'the embeddedness of the record
of early English drama . . . amongst other information pertaining to the material ordering of urban space', continuing

> My point here is not to suggest that the archive document is in any sense
> ideologically neutral. However, when the payment to the player or bear ward
> is accompanied by provisions for cushions and gunpowder, the carting
> of a prostitute, the wages of the swineherd and the business expenses of
> urban oligarchs, the status of the document exceeds that of polemical
> demonstration.[48]

Indeed, one of the difficulties with which the *REED* editors, both individually
for the published collections and the thirty-three volumes under way and

collectively under the guidance of Alexandra Johnston, Sally-Beth MacLean, and the team in Toronto, have grappled is quite what constitutes an event that should be recorded. Anne Brannen, who is editing the Cambridgeshire volume, has wrestled with the question of whether to include an event recorded in the Ely visitation reports for 1592 when one Arche of Hinxton 'was cited for being "so drunken the same night that the wife of John Swan departed this life that he did conterfet himself a spirit having with him also diuerse other companions abusing themselves in the same order"'.[49] Clearly not a theatrical performance, these drunken ghosts constitute for Brannen a possible form of 'societal ritual drama', taking part in a form of ceremony to mark the passing of Mrs Swan (p. 19), but certainly an event in the category of 'dramatic activity', (p. 20) albeit while intoxicated, and, although obviously unsanctioned, a communal disguising. If they deserve an entry by virtue of their pretending to be that which they are not, then other events appear as civic ceremony, precisely for the reverse reason, for being very publicly that which they are (like the processing of mayor and aldermen). On those grounds, one might argue that even Badir is unduly limited about which of the Beverley records ought to appear, for the payment to Edward Thomason for the use of his horse and cart 'about this Towne with a whore'[50] is for a very public ceremony of the community's self-definition, something that is no more or less dramatic than, say, Mary Frith's self-display in London theatres. Other scholars have brought together the evidence for fascinating parish ceremonial events, whose records are scattered throughout *REED*, like church-ales, Robin Hood games and summer or king games (both of which may or may not have been plays but certainly included some elements of playing), and rushbearings, all local events which are distinctly theatrical but which fall well outside the conventional parameters of early modern drama.[51]

Read carefully and with a proper awareness of the strategies for exclusion, *REED* might well prove to be most exciting for its redefinitions and explicit and implicit questionings of what comes within the parameters of drama. If my title suggests that *REED* is about the record of performances without a named play then my emphasis in a moment will be on the possibilities of drama without theatre, for *REED* has offered the possibility of redefining what dramatic activity is in the early modern period. To go back yet again to those two years in Bristol, my second frustration about the records marked a kind of drama that theatre history has ignored: school drama, those plays put on at Christmas by Mr Dunne of the Bristol free school of St Bartholomew. If amateur drama, the most active area of modern Shakespeare production, is also the most completely ignored, then something is similar for the earlier period too, both in terms of school and university drama and of a much broader range of amateur performance. We have not, that is, theorized the position within the central strategies of theatre history of almost any form of event that is non-metropolitan and/or non-professional, precisely those areas of activity that *REED* most completely documents. Instead we have, as it were, abandoned the work to those working on the *REED* project itself, as if they have taken over our more general responsibility for investigating such materials.

Drama without theatre – satires and jigs

Some of the strongest arguments about *REED*'s limitations have been formulated in terms of the temptations of narrative, both within New and Old Historicism, the lure of the construction of history as *récit*, as if *REED*'s structural organization is predicated on formations of material that narrativize the archives in constricted ways defined by a previous, rather unselfconscious mode of historiography. The movement from lists of payments to something else seems to require either charting or narrativizing and I have been exploring limitations in the former. But *REED*'s work is also strikingly a container of forms of narrative, tightly localized, for all their occasional national vibrations. In the move that I want now to make from theatre without drama to drama without theatre, it is with a form of narrative that I want to indulge, noting as I do so that drama outside London necessarily took place outside the kinds of physical structures that defined theatre in London, for, with the four marked exceptions of the Wine Street Theatre in Bristol from 1604, Barker's Bristol playhouse from possibly 1614, the theatre at Prescot in Lancashire from about 1593 to possibly 1615 and the York playhouse of 1609, even the vast resources of *REED* have found no evidence of provincial playhouses.[52] Drama outside London was essentially performed without theatres and the narratives of their performance are necessarily interrelated with the places (inns and churches, town halls and great halls) in which they occurred.

I am aware that the narratives I am concerned with are ones known before the relevant *REED* volumes published – or in one case will publish – the materials. Indeed most of them depend on the work of C. J. Sisson in his study of *Lost Plays of Shakespeare's Age* in 1936 and an article on 'Shakespeare Quartos as Prompt Copies' in 1942.[53] Yet the force of Sisson's superb work has not been rethought and deserves reconsidering. Such narratives dramatize the range of local practices of drama across forms about which theatre history still needs to teach historians of early modern drama.

What should we make, for instance, of the survival of performances of the Preston Corpus Christi play as late as 1595? Peter Greenfield hypothesizes that the play might have been toured to great houses in its last few years.[54] Other tours by local players in other parts of the country might have included similar local biblical texts, perhaps again to great houses but also to other venues for performance. Perhaps most intriguing is the parish play put on by the parishioners of Methley in Yorkshire in 1614, a play performed on four successive days in a large barn next to the parsonage before 'a multitude of people', according to Richard Shann who noted at least part of its cast-list in his commonplace book.[55] The play was called *Canimore and Lionley* and, though John Wasson rather pushes the evidence in suggesting possible links to Shakespeare's romances (he is on firmer ground linking it to *Sir Clyomon and Sir Clamydes*),[56] this tale of Prince Canimore, the son of King Padamon, and Princess Lionley, the daughter of King Graniorn, their dukes and knights, a countryman, a ghost and, most belatedly, a vice figure, 'Invention the paracite', speaks of a kind of drama whose existence in the provinces this late has never been suspected and which transforms our historical mapping of the development of provincial drama. To find a vice figure so late reconstructs our narratives of the sequences of early modern drama.

Take, too, the sheer range of public drama that made up the extraordinary events of the Wells shows of 1607.[57] The intersection between traditional festivities, ones whose relation to Christianity had always been vexed, and the needs of the parish of St Cuthbert's to raise money to repair the church was the major matrix for the events, overlaid with the conflicts between the revellers and the wishes of Constable Hole – and it is worth emphasizing that Hole was no poor Dogberry but a clothier who had employed as many as 300 people in his workshops. Starting as a procession with drumming and dancing to bring in the May and set up the maypole in the High Street on 1 May, the shows moved towards the first drama, when the early-morning drumming on 3 May became street dancing led by George Greenstreet and Thomasine White as Lord and Lady of the May, probably involving two bowers at either end of the High Street and probably at two separate times that day, mid-afternoon and then a long and complex dance with up to forty couples, perhaps lasting from 5 until 10 p.m.. Dancing and music by this point have begun to include the drama of character, the taking on of roles to define a popular festivity, with two local people cast in it, a model of movement between performance and audience through dance that is as fundamental to the entertainment here as to the aristocratic forms of the interaction between performers and audience in the court masque.

A week later and the local annoyance with Hole and his possible mistress Mrs Yarde generated the pageant of the painted spotted calf, instigated by a gentleman, Edward Carye, in response to Mrs Yarde's description of the maypole as a painted calf. Paraded through the streets and shot at, the calf was also voiced by one of the company dressed in 'Satire Skynns' who would cry 'ba, like a Calf'.[58] The appearance in Somerset of a satyr is striking, a local transformation of a classical figure – is the status of Carye as gentleman significant here in originating this classical show? – but it is an English echo of those 'three carters, three shepherds, three neatherds, three swineherds that have made themselves all men of hair' and who 'call themselves saultiers' in *The Winter's*

Tale (4.4.322–5), that wonderful combination of satyrs and jumpers that might please Tom Stoppard. Over the succeeding days in May there were shows including morris-dancing, children of both genders dressed up as adult women, more performances by the lord and lady of the May and, on Trinity Sunday, 31 May, a Robin Hood play in the marketplace.

The June shows, five days of events each led by one of the town's verderies, the taxing districts named after the principal streets, included processions with the statues of giants and traditional drama of St George and his dragon-slaying accompanied by up to thirty of his knights and Irish footmen and including the King, Queen, and Princess of Egypt with their court, a show that was popular enough to be staged for the visit of Queen Anne in 1613. On 17 June there was a show of the Goddess Diana, played by a child dressed in white and carried on men's shoulders and/or in a coach, accompanied by up to six of the cathedral choristers in white linen, possibly their vestments, on horseback or walking, singing music that may have been hymns, anthems, or settings of the psalms, and probably also with Actaeon and his hounds, an extraordinary combination of pagan and Christian, classical show and appropriated religious music, an almost blasphemous integration of two cultures organized by the residents of Chamberlain Street and the Mercers. The show of 18 June modified its traditional style to libel Hole and his circle and included the characters of a haberdasher or hatter, a woman spinning, a usurer and a scrivener or notary, a pewterer, and a grocer and his assistant, as well as some kind of performance in which the characters 'did act some thinge in representacion of the trades men'.[59] The final show a week later included William Gamage with the holing-game, in superbly lewd mockery of Hole, a notary, and a figure with a cribbage board and playing cards.

In addition to all this, Gamage's prison ballad, 'william gamege his idle Braines', mentions appearances by Noah working on his ark, the pinner of Wakefield, Old Grandam Bunch making puddings from a filthy gut, two men in hairshirts carrying an egg on a cowlstaff and, preceding the shows, a naked feathered boy 'who In his hand a sword did beare / still making roome before them ther'.[60]

The Wells shows display a mixture of classical and Christian, traditional and occasional. Above all, their most distinctive work is visibly local and ephemeral, immediate and libellous. Local dramatic performance is often libellous and is connected with the complex phenomenon of ballad libels and similarly localized events which Adam Fox has explored.[61] *REED* records other examples that Fox did not cover, like the verses about John and Elizabeth Condytt of Dorchester which in 1608 they accused Matthew Chubbe and others of having written, copied, and distributed, and which they 'did also themselues read or cause the same to be read to diuers persons at seuerall tymes',[62] a public performance, though not a play. Part of the antagonism between the Condytts and the Chubbes was generated by Chubbe having allowed 'Certene stage players intituling themselues the servantes of the Lord Barteley' to perform on the Sabbath day, even though their licence from the town specifically refused such permission.[63]

But as the ballad-libel and other forms of verse-libel modulate into the dramatic they acquire connections with other dramatic forms. At Kendal in Westmorland, for instance, the Corpus Christi play had finally been suppressed in 1605 but in 1621, in reaction to James I's proclamation of 1620 urging land-lords to convert customary tenancies to leasehold, a play was performed at Kendal Castle whose primary purpose was to attack those who tried to elimi-nate tenants' rights. The play, partly, it appears, supported by some landlords who not only provided actors but also provided clothing and pressured the local authorities to allow performance, included 'a representacion of Hell and in the same did personate and acte manie Lordes of the Mannors of the said Countie which they did libellouslie and disgracefullie then and there represent to bee in hell to the greate abuse of the said Lordes'.[64] Though the actors denied – as one might expect – that any representation was individual but was merely a generalized depiction of rapacious landlords exploiting the poor, the defence does not convince, and the Kendal play of 1621 seems to have been another example of drama as local libel.

A less highly political example occurred in Claverly in Shropshire where a marriage-case, an argument about who would marry the daughter of the Reverend John Ridge in 1622, resulted in Humfrey Elliott, a gentleman, and Edward Hinkes, yeoman, spreading abroad 'by publishinge and devulginge generally false and slanderuse tales and Reproaches' against Elizabeth, taking the form of 'diuers scandalus and Infamus lybellus verses Rymes plaies and enterluds'.[65] Specifically, John Ridge, his daughter Elizabeth and his son-in-law William Pratt describe this libel 'in nature & forme of a plaie dyaloggwise wherin it was devysed that one of the actors should bee apparelled in womens apparell & bolstered & sett forth as though shee were great with Child & should apparsonatt the said Elizabeth vnder the name of Ienney' while another actor characterized Hinkes 'vnder the name of Iockey'.[66]

This verse play, which was included in the bill of complaint, was, the com-plainants claimed, performed on a Sunday,

the Saboth daie . . . in the presence of a great Number of your Maiesties subiectes so assembled purposly . . . to heere the same at Claverly . . . and did also malliciusly vnlawfully and scandalus<ly> saie repeate and acte the same both at Claverly & at dyverse and severall other tymes and places within the said County & elswhere . . . the s<a>id actors & Con-federats much reioysinge at the sainge actinge plainge & Repeatinge therof.[67]

What is more, there was another libel by the conspirators, 'in the nature [&] fforme of an Interlude or plaie in prose' which was also performed all over the place. In that one as well an actor, one John Bett, was 'Attyr<e>d in womens apparell' playing Elizabeth, or rather 'a most Impudente bould audaciuse strumpett' representing Elizabeth.[68] Incidentally and significantly, the bill of complaint indicates that, in Claverly at least, adult men played female roles, whatever may have happened on the professional stage.

The defendants of course denied that the play had anything to do with the Ridges and Pratts and that, what is more, John Ridge and his daughter and his son-in-law were present at performances in Claverly and Bobington, 'Ridge himselfe havinge ended Eveninge prayer that day very erly in the afternoone and soener then vsually of purpose that there might be tyme for the actinge of the same play for the recreacion of the spectators'.[69] The play, so far as the defendants argued, was one in a series of local performances about which

> Samuell Hill and ffrances Day . . . say that for these twelue yeares last past or more these defendants with others have for the lawfull merryment and recreacion of themselves and theire neighbors for the most parte yearly in sommer tyme acted some interlude or play . . . and that the said Samuell hill hath for the most parte acted the parte of the Clowne or foole.[70]

The play they describe was totally different, with a completely different list of characters, though there was a problem with an ad lib:

> at one of the tymes of actinge the same play one of there fellowe actors called danyell whose Sirname these defendants knowe not actinge the part of one called Bravado in that play when he should as his parte was have said Iustics mittimus daughter said in steade thereof Master Ridges daughter but for what cause or reason he soe said all these defendantes say they knowe nor doe thinke that the same was soe spoken with any intent to defame or scandalize the said Elizabeth . . .[71]

What is set out here is a tradition of local drama with new plays being written and locals regularly taking part. Whatever the truth of the complainants' case, the play that is included, named *ffooles fortune*, is a comic drama which might well – but need not – be a libel on Ridge and the Pratts but which, as a piece sung to popular tunes, Sisson identified as a jig.[72]

There is no form of Elizabethan drama more ignored or under-investigated than the jig. Baskervill's study of 1929, *The Elizabethan Jig and Related Song Drama* (Chicago: University of Chicago Press, 1929) seems to be the beginning and end of substantial work. Indeed, as far as I can tell, the jig seems never to be referred to throughout Cox and Kastan's *New History.*[73] As a popular form seen on the professional stage and clearly a devised and potentially libellous form for local drama its importance as a point of interconnection between urban and provincial theatre seems peculiarly important. It was obviously seen as amenable to local, topical drama, precisely that form which Sisson brilliantly traced in lost London plays like Chapman's *The Old Joiner of Aldgate.*[74]

Sisson's other regional example, which he called 'Michael and Frances', was written by Francis Mitchell, servant to one Edward Meynell, the Catholic squire of Hawnby, near Rievaulx in Yorkshire, after Meynell heard from a friend George Ward about a scandal concerning Michael Steel, Ward's neighbour, who had apparently thrown out his wife and was living with his servant and mistress Frances Thornton, a cousin of Mrs Steel. Meynell and Mitchell heard the story at Christmas 1601; by spring 1602 they had spread the text of the jig widely with copies in Bedale, Northallerton, and Topcliffe; by the summer a copy was sought by Sir William Bellasis, 'long desirous of a coppie of the . . . Jygge',[75] who sent his man for one; and, at some point, Mitchell and/or Meynell and/or Ward had 'geuen the same to stage players who by practice and procurement haue at the ending of their playes sunge the same as a Jygg to the great sclandall' of Michael Steel.[76] These performances appear to have been at Christmas 1602 at Osmotherly and Meynell deposed that, because the matter was already part of a legal action by Steel, he 'did cause them to leave off singing the said songe.'[77]

Jigs, whether libellous or not, were dangerous enough for an order for their suppression in all London playhouses to be issued in October 1612 after the 'tumultes and outrages' the arrival at the end of every play of 'divers cutt-purses and other lewde and ill disposed persons in great multitude' caused at the Fortune Theatre.[78] Whether in amateur drama like that at Claverly in Shropshire, as an afterpiece to professional performance in Osmotherly in Yorkshire, or on the London stage, jigs created a particular opportunity, both as drama and as theatre, both in relation to audiences and to acts of writing, that should alter our perception of the practice of early modern theatre. *REED* teaches us that they were often immediate, amateur, exhilarating, hugely popular, ephemeral, topical, and fun. As entertainment jigs created a stir that more conventional forms of drama rarely managed. In Yorkshire, at least, they were far more important as events, as occasions, than any more usual play. But of them conventional theatre history remains resolutely silent. Even given our fascination with carnival and popular forms, jigs, perhaps the most Bakhtinian and subversive form of the exuberant carnivalesque, have been suppressed from our discourse, even though theatre outside London, as Sisson showed nearly seventy years ago, can offer examples of texts where all London jigs are lost.

Touring in Yorkshire – drama and audiences

The Yorkshire volumes of *REED* have yet to appear. When they do, they will give us the full available documentation about the Osmotherly performers, for their activities are my final example of drama outside the confines of theatres.[79] It seems probable that the troupe performing the 'Michael and Frances' jig were the company led by Robert and Christopher Simpson, shoemakers in Egton, who were identified as players from 1595. Catholic recusants and often brought to court for it, the Simpsons led a company which included at least one boy, Thomas Pant, apprenticed in 1607 but clearly spending his time acting for them rather than learning his trade.

Sisson and Boddy have traced the pattern of their tours, principally but not solely in private houses – for they also 'played open in the town' in some places[80] – ranging from great houses of aristocrats to some yeomen's homes, many but again by no means all, the homes of Catholics. Sisson, who does not present the evidence, claimed he could 'make a list of some dozen or so great houses where they acted every year, with regular patrons, acting one or more plays'.[81] This is, in other words, a regular circuit by a company which, while primarily defined by their religion (which is what brought them regularly into court, often after being on the run, and hence into the records), were also offering a more general and less politicized, dangerous or subversive entertainment.

Perhaps influenced by local festive drama in Egton like the 'Plough Stots', perhaps by the local schoolmaster, Edward Nickson, a recusant, perhaps even coached by seminary priests trained in play performance at Douai, the Simpsons ran a company that was able by 1611 to tour under the protection of Sir Richard Cholmley of Whitby and Roxby whose letters served both as licence and as introduction, even though Cholmley denied their existence in court and claimed not to know that the Egton troupe were what the prosecutor called 'a sort of obstinate popish recusants . . . who had taken upon themselves to become common stage players'.[82] They were not the only company touring the area of Yorkshire at this time but they were significantly the largest. Their substantial troupe of up to fifteen (including Pant and another boy) intersected, in personnel and touring routes, with another, run by Richard Hudson of Hutton Buscel, a smaller group containing in 1615/16, when their tour of one-night stands can be precisely documented, two men, one youth and four boys.[83]

The Christmas tour of 1608/9 of the Simpson or Cholmley company covered Pickering, Helmsley, Thirsk, Ripon, Nidderdale, Richmond, and Northallerton, a wide swathe across Yorkshire, and they reached Gowthwaite in Nidderdale, home of Sir John Yorke, for performances at Candlemas (2 February) 1609. The disgruntled Thomas Pant is one of the main sources for accounts of the events thereafter which landed Yorke and his wife in prison, forced them to pay a heavy fine, and kept the Star Chamber occupied for some years. The result is a mass of records which allow for the tracing and questioning of the particular interrelationship between company and audience and play, a case-study in our understanding of the meaning of drama texts in relation to their audiences.

The company's repertory consisted of at least four plays: *Saint Christopher, The Travels of the Three English Brothers, King Lear,* and *Pericles.* The first was a saint's play about the conversion of Rephabus. Richard Simpson claimed that 'that booke by which he and other persons did act the said play . . . was a printed booke, And they onelie acted the same according to the contents therein printed, and not otherwise'.[84] But the play text does not seem to have survived. The company's members – and this was part of Sisson's interest in them – claimed, indeed, that all their play texts were printed books. As was stated by William Harrison, an actor who played the clown in the company's plays and who is the sole source for the fact that the company played *Lear* and *Pericles* (and which part did he play in *Pericles*? Which is the play's clown role?): 'these plaies which they so plaied were vsuall playes And such as were acted in Common and publicke places and Staiges . . . and such as were played publicly and printed in the bookes'.[85] There is no suggestion, even from those most interested in bringing down the Yorkes, that *Saint Christopher* was not printed, nor that, as Schrickx argued, it was printed at some dangerous place like the Catholic seminaries on the continent,[86] nor that the play, if performed as printed, was offensive, even though its concerns were clearly Catholic: the conversion of a saint, the Catholic and very much non-Protestant sacrament of penance, and the power of the crucifix.

The problem with *Saint Christopher* was an interlude added to the play at Gowthwaite

and at Mr. Bowes his house at Ellerby and at Mr. Conyers at Hatton Wisk and at Mrs. Katheryn Rattcliffe of Ugthorp and divers other gentlemens houses, and was left out when they played open in the town or at any of the places when the people were not popishly affected or when the master of the house was a protestant.[87]

One witness even claimed that the play had been performed at the house of Sir Stephen Proctor, the fiercely puritan justice who was the prime mover behind the prosecution. The spectacular addition showed a debate between a 'popish priest' and 'the English minister' in which the minister relied on the bible while the priest countered with the need for the cross, the iconic symbol of Catholicism. In the debate the priest 'convict[ed]' the Anglican upon which conviction the devells with thundering and lightning and with great noyse compassed the minister about and carried him away as it were to hell. Then the Angell, which part the aforesaid Pant played, came in and tooke the popish priest by the hand and led him away.[88]

Another witness reported that 'he that plaide the foole' (i.e. William Harrison) was also in the scene and 'did clap the Englishe minister on the shoulder and mocked and flowted him, and said, "Well, thou must away anon" '.[89] That the subject matter of the additions appealed to the audience at Gowthwaite is clear and the news of the performance was good recusant propaganda: one witness reported that those who had missed the performance were told 'if they had seen the play as it was plaid at Gowthwaite, they would never care for the newe lawe or for goinge to the church more'.[90] But I also want to emphasize its use of very traditional stage spectacle, complete with thunder and lightning, devils and an angel, like the earlier conjuring of Lucifer who entered 'with all his trayne and flaunt of fyre',[91] in a manner that is remarkably close to the staging needs for *Dr Faustus*.[92]

Saint Christopher may have been an old play – certainly the surviving English saints' plays were much earlier – and its playing may indicate the continuance in North Yorkshire of kinds of drama that would have been deemed ridiculously old-fashioned in London, like the Methley parish play with its vice 'Invention'. But no one actually suggested that it was an old play and the Simpsons' other three plays were strikingly new: *The Travels of the Three English Brothers*, by John Day, William Rowley and George Wilkins, was written, performed and printed in 1607; *King Lear* was printed in 1608; and *Pericles* (a play that may also have involved Wilkins) in 1609. The first and third of these we know to have been popular in London and the Simpsons were playing the great hits of recent metropolitan drama seasons, whatever else may have been their significance. *The Travels* includes a scene showing the pope remarkably sympathetically, hailed by Sir Anthony Sherley, who had converted to Catholicism by 1601, as 'the father of our Mother Church, / The stair of men's salvations and the key / That binds or looseth our transgression'[93] but, if the scene would have had particular resonances for a Catholic audience in Yorkshire, it was also played the same way in London. Reading *Lear* or *Pericles* as specifically Catholic plays is a complex matter beyond the scope of this chapter but, in any case, my argument is that we do not need to: the plays were popular in London and would have been so for any of the Simpsons' audiences and there is no suggestion that any of these three plays were reworked, with pointedly unstable texts, for different audiences.

Recontextualizing these plays in the circumstances of such performances is to see their potentials for taking on meanings variously according to those contexts. Reading *REED* is to see how such narratives redefine contexts in which early modern drama was read by its audiences, the meanings of its drama as well as its theatre. If realtors are prone to emphasize the importance of 'location, location, location', *REED* is a reminder of the ways the forms of drama, the making of theatre, and the reception of theatrical performance also depend on location. By reading *REED* and understanding the local, theatre historians will reread London plays, its theatres, and its audiences as no longer being general truths. *REED*'s awesome scale of specificity, the minutiae of the archival record, opens the possibility of reading beyond *REED* in similarly specific ways. But it can also remake our mapping of what drama is, what constitutes the theatricality of performance, how meaning is recoverable, and what makes some forms of early modern performance irrevocably other, irredeemably historicized, trapped in that immediacy of the topical and local, that unique moment and place of performance where theatre and drama must always meet.

Notes

1. For the sake of completeness, I list here the volumes that have appeared, all from the University of Toronto Press: *York*, ed. Alexandra F. Johnston and Margaret Rogerson (1979); *Chester*, ed. Lawrence M. Clopper (1979); *Coventry*, ed. R. W. Ingram (1981); *Newcastle upon Tyne*, ed. J. J. Anderson (1982); *Norwich 1540–1642*, ed. David Galloway (1984); *Cumberland/Westmorland/Gloucestershire*, ed. Audrey Douglas and Peter Greenfield (1986); *Devon*, ed. John Wasson (1986); *Cambridge*, ed. Alan H. Nelson (1989); *Herefordshire/Worcestershire*, ed. David N. Klausner (1990); *Lancashire*, ed. David George (1991); *Shropshire*, ed. J. Alan B. Somerset (1994); *Somerset, including Bath*, ed. James Stokes with Robert J Alexander (1996); *Bristol*, ed. Mark C. Pilkinton (1997); *Dorset/Cornwall*, ed. Rosalind Conklin Hays, C. E. McGee, Sally L. Joyce and Evelyn S. Newlyn (1999); *Sussex*, ed. Cameron Louis (2000); *Kent: Diocese of Canterbury*, ed. James M Gibson (2002).
2. E. K. Chambers, *The Elizabethan Stage*, 4 vols (Oxford: Clarendon Press, 1923); G. E. Bentley, *The Jacobean and Caroline Stage*, 7 vols (Oxford: Clarendon Press, 1941–68); John Tucker Murray, *English Dramatic Companies 1558–1642*, 2 vols (London: Constable, 1910).
3. *Bristol*, 112. In quoting from *REED* I have taken the liberty of ignoring their careful italicization of all expansions of scribal contractions.
4. Ibid., 115–17.
5. Ibid., 117 and 113.
6. John Astington, 'Comment' in JoAnna Dutka, ed., *Records of Early English Drama. Proceedings of the First Colloquium* (Toronto: Records of Early English Drama, 1979), 93–7 (p. 95).
7. Guy Fitch Lytle and Stephen Orgel, eds, *Patronage in the Renaissance* (Princeton: Princeton University Press, 1981).
8. See, in particular, Suzanne Westfall, ' "The useless dearness of the diamond": Theories of Patronage Theatre', in Paul Whitfield White and Suzanne R. Westfall, eds, *Shakespeare and Theatrical Patronage in Early Modern England* (Cambridge: Cambridge University Press, 2002), 13–42.
9. But see also Anthony B. Dawson and Paul Yachnin, *The Culture of Playgoing in Shakespeare's England: a Collaborative Debate* (Cambridge: Cambridge University Press, 2001).

10. See 'Records of Early English Drama and thre Travelling Player', *RORD* 26 (1983), 65–71; 'Players on Tour: New Evidence from Records of Early English Drama', in C. E. McGee, ed., *The Elizabethan Theatre X* (Port Credit, Ont.: Meany, 1988), 55–72; 'Tour Routes: "Provincial Wanderings" or Traditional Circuits?', *MaRDIE*, 6 (1993), 1–14; 'Touring Leciester's Men: the Patronage of a Performance Troupe', in White and Westfall, *Shakespeare and Theatrical Patronage*, 246–71; and 'A Family Tradition: Dramatic Patronage by the Earls of Derby', in Richard Dutton, Alison Gail Findlay and Richard Wilson, eds, *Region, Religion and Patronage: Lancastrian Shakespeare* (Manchester: Manchester University Press, 2003), 205–26.
11. Cambridge: Cambridge University Press, 1998.
12. Siobhan Keenan, *Travelling Players in Shakespeare's England* (Basingstoke: Palgrave Macmillan, 2002). See also the prominence allotted to Peter Greenfield's excellent summary of 'Touring' in John D. Cox and David Scott Kastan, eds, *A New History of Early English Drama* (New York: Columbia University Press, 1997), 251–68.
13. See http://www.utoronto.ca/patrons/Database-1.html for the first pilot, and http://eir.library.utoronto.ca/reed/index.cfm for the second version (covering Lancashire), both accessed 14 October 2003.
14. *Bristol*, 114
15. Ibid., 85.
16. *The Shakespearian Playing Companies* (Oxford: Clarendon Press, 1996).
17. The Malone Society series began with Chambers on 'Players at Ipswich' (*Collections*, ii.3 (1931)), 258–84 and included, for example, Giles E. Dawson's 'Records of Plays and Players in Kent, 1450–1642' (*Collections*, vii (1965)).
18. Keenan, *Travelling Players*, 165–85; see also, for example, Alan B. Somerset, ' "How chances it they travel?": Provincial Touring, Playing Places, and the King's Men', *Shakespeare Survey 47* (Cambridge: Cambridge University Press, 1994), 45–60; James Gibson, 'Stuart Players in Kent: Fact or Fiction?' *REED Newsletter* 20.2 (1995), 1–12. An early example is in John Wasson, 'Records of Early English Drama: Where They Are and What They Tell Us', in JoAnna Dutka, *Records of Early English Drama*, 128–44 (pp. 141–4).
19. Andrew Gurr, 'The Loss of Records for the Traveling Companies in Stuart Times', *REED Newsletter* 19.2 (1994), 2–19.
20. Ibid., 11.
21. See, in particular, the maps in MacLean, 'Tour Routes: "Provincial Wanderings" or Traditional Circuits?', 2–8.
22. See Murray, *English Dramatic Companies*, 2.26–8, Gurr, *The Shakespearian Playing Companies*, 168–9 and 177–8.
23. *Lancashire*, 156.
24. Ibid., 380.
25. Ibid., 173.
26. Ibid., 195, 197, and 199 for instance.
27. G. E. Bentley, *The Jacobean and Caroline Stage*, 7 vols (Oxford: Clarendon Press, 1941–68), 2.423.
28. See John Wasson, 'Elizabethan and Jacobean Touring Companies', *Theatre Notebook*, 42 (1988), 51–7 (p. 52) and Lawrence Stone, 'Companies of Players Entertained by the Earl of Cumberland and Lord Clifford, 1607–39', *Malone Society Collections*, 5 (1959), 17–28.
29. Bentley, *Jacobean and Caroline Stage*, 2.387–8.
30. Ibid., 2.529–31 and *Lancashire*, 193, etc.

31. *Lancashire*, 200, 204.
32. Wasson, 'Elizabethan and Jacobean Touring Companies', 56.
33. For Dering's book-buying, see *Kent: Diocese of Canterbury*, 913–26; T. N. S. Lennam, 'Sir Edward Dering's Collection of Playbooks, 1619–1624', *Shakespeare Quarterly*, 16 (1965), 145–53; and 'Books of Sir Edward Dering of Kent (1598–1644)', ed. Nati H. Krivatsy and Laetitia Yeandle in R. J. Fehrenbach and E. S. Leedham-Green, eds, *Private Libraries in Renaissance England: a Collection of Tudor and Early Stuart Book-Lists*, vol. 1 (Medieval and Renaissance Texts and Studies 87, Binghamton, New York, 1992), 137–264, esp. p. 141.
34. *Kent: Diocese of Canterbury*, 920.
35. See W. W. Greg, *A Bibliography of the English Printed Drama to the Restoration*, 4 vols (London: The Bibliographical Society), 1:466–7, 326 (a) and (b).
36. *Kent: Diocese of Canterbury*, 922.
37. Ibid., 917 and 1384.
38. Ibid., 917. For the adaptation see the facsimile edition, *The History of King Henry the Fourth as revised by Sir Edward Dering, Bart.*, ed. George Walton Williams and Gwynne Blakemore Evans (Charlottesville, Virginia: University Press of Virginia, 1974) and also Laetitia Yeandle, 'The Dating of Sir Edward Dering's Copy of "The History of King Henry the Fourth"', *Shakespeare Quarterly*, 37 (1986), 224–6.
39. *Kent: Diocese of Canterbury*, 916.
40. Ibid., 1383.
41. See J. Q. Adams, 'The Author-Plot of an Early Seventeenth Century Play', *The Library* 4th ser., 16 (1945–6), 17–27. Krivatsy and Yeandle ('Books of Sir Edward Dering', p. 141, see n. 33) write of it as being in Dering's hand, while, with typical caution, mentioning that 'he did copy out, if not compose' the scenario, and I defer to their knowledge of his hand, while tending to believe it unlikely that he was copying the plot, given the nature of its text.
42. See Theresa Coletti, '"Fragmentation and Redemption": Dramatic Records, History, and the Dream of Wholeness', *Envoi*, 3.i (1991), 1–13; her 'Reading REED: History and the Records of Early English Drama', in Lee Patterson, ed., *Literary Practice and Social Change in Britain, 1380–1530* (Berkeley: University of California Press, 1990), 248–84; and Peter H. Greenfield's thoughtful response, '"But Herefordshire for a Morris-daunce": Dramatic Records and the New Historicism', *Envoi*, 3.i (1991), 14–23, and his further consideration in 'Using Dramatic Records: History, Theory, Southampton's Musicians', *METh*, 17 (1995), 76–95. Coletti's arguments are also countered, in part, by Greg Walker, 'A Broken Reed?: Early Drama Records, Politics, and the Old Historicism', *METh*, 17 (1995), 42–51; see also Pamela M. King, 'Records of Early English Drama: Reflections of a Hardened User', *METh*, 17 (1995), 52–7, and her article with Meg Twycross adumbrating a project that would, by its use of 'multimedia computer technology' meet some of the problems, 'Beyond *REED*?: The York *Doomsday* Project', *METh*, 17 (1995), 132–50.
43. *Bristol*, 113.
44. Compare Sir Toby's calling Olivia 'a Cathayan' (Shakespeare *Twelfth Night*, 2.3.725; see also *Merry Wives*, 2.1.136).
45. See Pilkinton's note on p. 286 of *Bristol*.
46. This payment item (*Bristol*, 115) includes repairs to two pairs of stocks but it is not clear whether that work is in any way connected with the performances.
47. *Bristol*, 112.
48. Patricia Badir, 'Playing Space: History, the Body, and Records of Early English Drama', *Exemplaria*, 9 (1997), 255–79 (p. 259). ·

49. Anne Brannen, 'Creating a Dramatic Record: Reflections on Some Drunken Ghosts', *The Early Drama, Art, and Music Review*, 20 (1997), 16–24 (p. 17).

50. Badir, 'Playing Space', 258.

51. See, for example, David George, 'Rushbearing: a Forgotten British Custom' and Elizabeth Baldwin, 'Rushbearings and Maygames in the Diocese of Chester before 1642', both in Alexandra F. Johnston and Wim Hüsken, eds, *English Parish Drama* (Ludus: Medieval and Early Renaissance Theatre and Drama 1; Amsterdam and Atlanta: Rodopi, 1996), 17–30 and 31–40.

52. On these theatres, see Keenan, *Travelling Players*, 144–64 but on the Prescot playhouse, see also David George, 'The Playhouse at Prescot and the 1592–94 Plague', in Dutton *et al.*, eds, *Region, Religion and Patronage: Lancastrian Shakespeare*, 227–42.

53. C. J. Sisson, *Lost Plays of Shakespeare's Age* (Cambridge: Cambridge University Press, 1936) and 'Shakespeare Quartos as Prompt-Copies with Some Account of Cholmeley's Players and a New Shakespeare Allusion', *RES*, 48 (1942), 129–43.

54. See Peter Greenfield, 'Regional Performance in Shakespeare's Time' in Dutton *et al.*, eds, *Region, Religion and Patronage: Lancastrian Shakespeare*, 243–51 (p. 244). Greenfield notes too the survival of the Coventry cycle to 1579 (and see below on the Kendal play, suppressed in 1605). Many of the kinds of drama Greenfield documents are more extensively considered, by him and others, in his major recent source for the article, the fascinating collection of essays, many by *REED* editors, on *English Parish Drama*, ed. Alexandra F. Johnston and Wim Hüsken.

55. See John M. Wasson, 'A Parish Play in the West Riding of Yorkshire', in Johnston and Hüsken, *English Parish Drama*, 149–57 (p. 149).

56. Wasson, 'A Parish Play', 154.

57. See Sisson, *Lost Plays*, 162–77 and James Stokes' clarification of the sequence of events from the mass of the records in *REED*, 'Chronology of the Wells Shows of 1607', *Somerset*, 719–28, and Carolyn Sale's chapter in this volume.

58. *Somerset*, 722.

59. Ibid., 726.

60. Ibid., 715 (ignoring scribal corrections).

61. Adam Fox, 'Ballads, Libels and Popular Ridicule in Jacobean England', *Past and Present*, 145 (1994), 47–83.

62. *Dorset/Cornwall*, 174. The full materials cover pp. 173–98. Another argument over the public performance of a libel can be found for Melbury Osmond in 1622 (see *Dorset/Cornwall*, 225–30) and for Over Compton in 1617/18 (see *Dorset/Cornwall*, 231–8) as well as frequently elsewhere in *REED* volumes.

63. *Dorset/Cornwall*, 177.

64. *Cumberland/Westmorland/Gloucestershire*, 188; the case covers pp. 188–98 and the editors provide a characteristically clear summary of the events on pp. 235–6.

65. *Shropshire*, 24–5. The bill of complaint and answer are reprinted in pp. 23–39. See also Sisson, *Lost Plays*, 140–56.

66. *Shrophire*, 26.

67. Ibid., 32–3. Here and below I have added the obvious missing letters in the text's lacunae.

68. Ibid., 33.

69. Ibid., 39.

70. Ibid., 38.

71. Ibid., 39.

72. Sisson, *Lost Plays*, 147.

73. I cannot quite guarantee that it is never mentioned but it is not in any index, Baskervill's book is not in the bibliography, and there is no mention in any of the obvious essays.
74. Sisson, *Lost Plays*, 12–79.
75. Ibid., 133.
76. Ibid., 130.
77. G. W. Boddy, 'Players of Interludes in North Yorkshire in the Early Seventeenth Century', repaginated offprint from North Yorkshire County Record Office Publications, no. 7, Journal 3, April 1976, p. 11. Boddy's superb essay, still by far the best study available of the Simpson company, needs to be read alongside a few minor corrections by Christopher Dean, 'The Simpson Players Tour of North Yorkshire in 1616', *Notes and Queries*, 231 (Sept. 1986), 381.
78. Baskervill, *The Elizabethan Jig and Related Song Drama* (Chicago: University of Chicago Press, 1929), 116.
79. My account of the Simpson players and the performances at Gowthwaite is dependent on the following sources: Sisson, 'Shakespeare Quartos as Prompt-Copies'; Hugh Aveling, OSB, *Northern Catholics* (London: Geoffrey Chapman, 1966), 288–90; Boddy, 'Players of Interludes' (see n. 59); Willem Schrickx, '*Pericles* in a Book-list of 1619 from the English Jesuit Mission and Some of the Play's Special Problems', *Shakespeare Survey* 29 (Cambridge: Cambridge University Press, 1976), 21–32; John L. Murphy, *Darkness and Devils: Exorcism and 'King Lear'* (Athens, Ohio: Ohio University Press, 1984), 93–118; Masahiro Takenaka, '*King Lear* and History', *The Renaissance Bulletin*, 23 (1996), 27–31; Phebe Jensen, 'Recusancy, Festivity and Community: the Simpsons at Gowlthwaite [*sic*] Hall', *Reformation*, 6 (2002), 75–102, and reprinted in Dutton *et al.*, eds, *Region, Religion and Patronage: Lancastrian Shakespeare* – my thanks to Dr Jensen for allowing me to read her essay in typescript.
80. Murphy, *Darkness and Devils*, 109.
81. Sisson, 'Shakespeare Quartos as Prompt-Copies', 137.
82. On influences, see Boddy, 'Players of Interludes', 26–8; on Cholmley's connection, see Boddy, 'Players of Interludes', 18.
83. Ibid., 21.
84. Sisson, 'Shakespeare Quartos as Prompt-Copies', 138.
85. Ibid.
86. Schrickx, '*Pericles* in a Book-list of 1619', 23.
87. Murphy, *Darkness and Devils*, 109.
88. Ibid.
89. Boddy, 'Players of Interludes', 15.
90. Ibid., 16.
91. Murphy, *Darkness and Devils*, 109.
92. On the staging of thunder and lightning, see Leslie Thomson, 'The Meaning of Thunder and Lightning: Stage Directions and Audience Expectations', *Early Theatre*, 2 (1999), 11–24.
93. *The Travels*, in Anthony Parr, ed., *Three Renaissance Travel Plays* (Manchester: Manchester University Press, 1995), 5.38–40.

Part II
Interrogating Data

4

A New Theatre Historicism

Andrew Gurr

'No text without a context' is a New Historicist mantra, an apophthegm for cultural poetics. It is the mode of evocative images rather than facts and figures, anecdotes rather than dates. Yet anecdotalism is vivid precisely because it is so imprecise and statistic-free. I start from further back, with a few texts that I count as exemplary of the difficulties we have to overcome in rehistoricizing the early modern period and its drama. Our knowledge and our use of the texts and contexts of early modern drama are as imprecise as any anecdote. We have far too little information, poetically anecdotal or not, about the texts and their contexts that we seek to locate and use, especially when we invoke that current substitute for New Historicism in early modern theatre, performativity. We need to address both deficiencies, in text and in context.

First, the texts. I begin from a position first announced, with his typically iconoclastic authority, by Stephen Orgel in 1988. His paper 'Acting Scripts, Performing Texts', now reissued in the collection of essays that he ironically calls *The Authentic Shakespeare*, challenged the assumption that we have texts of the plays that can be assumed to offer reliable versions of what Shakespeare's company first put on stage. Orgel used that proposition to attack some standard editorial practices and assumptions. I would take his position some distance further, and with even more iconoclasm. I would say that almost no play texts survive from Shakespearian time in a form that represents with much precision what was actually staged. Out of the total of 167 extant plays performed by the Chamberlain's/King's Men in the forty-eight years that they played, the 'allowed book' or licensed play book, the version from which performances were drawn and from which performances deviated only in special cases, survives in only two nearly complete play manuscripts. Neither of them is by Shakespeare. That is less than 2 per cent of the total existing repertory of the leading company of the time. So the current shift of editorial target from the author's copy untouched by theatre hacks to the script as it was first staged, which is the announced aim of the collected Oxford edition of 1986 and of almost all subsequent editions and series of editions, must be acknowledged to be unattainable. If the Oxford target has any value as an ideal, which it must, we need to study the context for the other 98 per cent of lost texts to identify the practices of the companies who owned the play books. This approach must now assume the highest priority in studies of this period of theatre history.

That means in the first instance giving precedence to the study of the playing companies and their combined repertories, and their intertextuality, over the study of authors and their versions of the texts in print. The interaction between the plays within specific company repertories and the company's performative practices are the essential frame for any picture of plays as performed texts. Such an approach to theatre history is possible in a few exemplary cases, perhaps most notably, for reasons I shall come to, with Shakespeare's *Henry V* and *The Merry Wives of Windsor*. Secondly, such a revisionist view means that the play texts, still the most substantial relics of early performances, must be related to the distinctive repertoire of the company that performed them and the kinds of playhouse the company was using. Thirdly, the distinct types of staging used at particular playhouses must be related to the standardized forms in which the plays have come down to us. Evidence from the few surviving 'allowed books' provides a basis for rereading author-derived play texts as part of the necessary attempt to see what kind of staging they would have received. Above all, as an exemplar of the freedom the companies had to modify their written texts, we need to recognize the evidence that even the 'allowed books' were routinely cut in performance to fit the two hours' traffic of the stage that the prologue to *Romeo and Juliet* advertises. So first of all we must question the texts we use, and the targets we identify in sorting the variant versions and origins of the plays.

Should modern editorial ingenuity be directed to establishing the author's original intentions, or to the factory product that emerged on stage? How far should it aim at modernized versions for readers and the education market, and how far at a performative and perhaps a perfomed text? The case can still be argued for Shakespeare's plays that he, as a player in the company for which he was writing, knew exactly what he wanted to be put on stage, and that therefore his original version should prevail over the company's product after much rehearsal and modification. That suggests, though the case is not usually made that way, absolute primacy for the authorial text before the company got its hands on it and changed it. Such a view is not pronounced much today because it makes a revised version of the old New Bibliography idea, cleansing the text of its 'theatrical' interventions (and inventing new stage directions). In any case, aiming at the author's own version must be a target unique to Shakespeare's plays, since no other writer had the same inside role in his company or financial interest in its playhouses. Even his successors as resident writers for the King's company clearly lacked the peculiar expertise in staging that, for all his evident economy with stage directions, so many scholars and critics have worked to identify in Shakespeare. The surviving manuscripts of Massinger's plays written as resident writer for the King's Men show that he had little sense of what the company book-keeper wanted for his play script. In spite of all the evidence that the plays were written to be first published on stage, the range of variation between author and author, and between playing company and playing company are far too great for any one set of editorial principles to work satisfactorily for them all.

Then there is the too rarely asked question of whether the revisions the company made to each play text did manage to create a better, in any sense, text than the author's original concept. The company could and often did correct obvious errors that emerged in the process of preparing the play for the stage, and it could streamline a messy text to allow adequate doubling and trim away scenes that bulged uncomfortably outside the main line of the plot. But in that collaborative process they might introduce new features that did not fit the original conception. They might suppress or enlarge elements that a particular player took exception to or insisted on adding, however incongruous it might be to the general structure. A play that did not work well on its first staging could always expect to be modified, sometimes quite radically in later performances and in subsequent revivals. Which text from that long development process should an editor fix on? As Anthony Dawson has put it, following Jerome McGann, there was no play text, only textual events.[1]

I want here to test the usual answers to these questions by looking at some exemplary texts which put them to the test most strenuously. That means several plays by Shakespeare, all of which exist in at least two different versions, and one anonymous product, written for the Red Bull company in 1620. They all invite choices, between the author's versions and the company's, and decisions as to whether they are or should be written versions or stage scripts. Behind them all is the uncomfortable feeling that we still know far too little about early modern handling of play books and early staging than a new theatre history should have.

Following Orgel's line, and calling her work *Unediting the Renaissance*, Leah Marcus published in 1996 an examination of editions of Herbert, Herrick and Milton, plus (more usefully for our purposes) the two texts of *Faustus*, the quarto version of *The Merry Wives of Windsor*, the two versions of *The Shrew*, and Q1 *Hamlet*.[2] The book argues 'that the Shakespearean theater was far more predominantly "oral" than "literate" in its functioning, and that Shakespeare and his company only gradually came to conceptualize their plays in terms of readerly assumptions about how and where meaning is constituted' (37). This view she argues most fully in Chapter 5, on that much-contested patch of ground, Q1 *Hamlet*. Editions of early modern poetry and plays convert what was grasped orally into written texts that are often quite alien in form to their original function. For my purposes her most useful chapter is the one on *Merry Wives*, because in it she identifies two distinct versions of the play, each with its own character, the shorter of them appearing, like the first quarto of *Henry V*, to be the streamlined script that the company made out of the ample material their author sold them.

Marcus makes a good case for the quarto text of *Merry Wives* being distinct in its design and intended function from the Folio text. It is much shorter (she counts 1620 lines against the Folio's 2729), it is much less explicitly located in the area round Windsor, it has none of the Garter allusions and references to court matters, and it makes Anne Page's marriage to Fenton romantic rather than financial. She conjectures that it was cut to make a travelling version, a view I do not share, but her main inference is that the quarto text stands in its own right as a version that was very likely the normative version of the play staged by the Shakespeare company. That I think highly likely, insofar as any written text can represent the essence of a play on stage.

It seems a long time since editors of Shakespeare aimed at publishing the purely authorial text cleansed of any modifications making it ready for the stage. Harold Jenkins in the Arden 2 *Hamlet* twenty years ago was the last major editor of that play to base his text on the author's 'foul papers', the second quarto.[3] Three years later Philip Edwards in the New Cambridge edition used the Folio, with its evidence of use in the theatre. Two years after that George Hibbard used it even more baldly in the New Oxford single-play edition, deleting Hamlet's fourth soliloquy, 'How all occasions do inform against me', and citing it only in a footnote, where Jenkins had it in the main text, and Edwards kept it, but in square brackets. The editors of the collected Oxford edition of 1986 stated that their aim was to reproduce 'the more theatrical version of each play', whatever that might prove to be.[4] The difficulty of achieving that aim is that the theatre version, if there ever was a single one, got into print a lot less often than did the author's draft. The company which owned and staged the plays did what it pleased with what its writers supplied, and almost no versions survive in print or manuscript to tell us precisely what the company turned its 'raw material' (Peter Blayney's term) into. Apart from its assumption that Shakespeare's texts do not contain the right theatricality in what he wrote for staging at the Theatre or the Globe, the Oxford principle should make a better understanding of the company's routine practices into the highest priority. Yet what should we be doing? We have all seen author-centred studies that cannot cope with the fact that two-thirds of all the 600 Renaissance drama texts in English were written not by a single author but in collaboration. If you extend the collaborative process to players and company book-keeper, chaos is near to its second coming.

That rough beast is far less easy to corral than the Oxford principle assumes. We hope to value the play texts of Shakespeare and his successors because they are the only direct record of the original performances. Yet we do not even have the maximal authorized play scripts, the allowed books, let alone the more minimal versions that were staged. Almost none of the surviving repertory of 167 King's company plays in print or in manuscript do more than roughly approximate to the words the players spoke on stage, and they say almost nothing about their actions. In some distant future with more futuristic technology it might be possible to recreate something like the original company performances that the first Shakespearians created. In the lengthy meantime, though, the best we can do for now is assemble the main features of the company's habitual practices to make a platform on which we can reconceive the plays as they might have first (or later) been staged.

Ninety-eight per cent of the surviving texts from the Shakespeare company repertory went to the press from their writers, and reflect their concern to have their 'poems' read rather than remind readers of what they might have heard spoken on stage. The title page of Jonson's *Every Man Out of His Humour* in 1600 proclaimed that the text is 'As it was first composed by the Author B. I. Containing more than hath been publikely spoken or acted'. Barnabe Barnes' *Devil's Charter* in 1607 claimed to be 'more exactly revewed, corrected, and augmented since by the Author', and Webster's *Duchess of Malfi* of 1623 included 'diverse things Printed, that the length of the Play would not beare in the Presentment'. Modern readers and editors concerned not with the author's original but with the play as first staged must accept the reduced versions of the authors' own texts as no more than a rudiment, grossly inadequate written records of entities that were inherently fluid, even from one performance to another, as fixed as water, at least water at room temperature. Freezing those fast-moving events suspends them out of their natural flow.

Besides what we can infer with Leah Marcus from her comparison of the two versions of *Merry Wives*, one other of Shakespeare's plays, *Henry V*, survives in two notably distinct versions. The version we all know was printed in 1623 from the author's papers along with a lot of other play scripts the company had no use for. The other version was printed from a script assembled by the company for performance in 1599. The quarto text, printed in May 1600, less than a year after the play first appeared on stage, was typeset from a copy made by one of the players dictating it line by line to another (the compositor set all the lines, including the prose, as verse), from a script drastically cut and revised from the version seen in the First Folio. Every Chorus speech was eliminated; all the longer speeches had sections cut from the middle (not at the cue-ends); three scenes, including the churchmen's exchange with which Shakespeare opened his version, were deleted altogether; Act 3's Harfleur was reduced to three scenes, first Llewellyn beating the Eastcheap shirkers, then Henry threatening the Governor on the walls, and finally Katherine having her English lesson. Henry's 'Once more unto the breach' speech was left on the cutting-room floor along with the scaling ladders that a stage direction in the Folio text calls for straight after. Q1 *Henry V* is a perfectly coherent and stage-able play. The Folio's breach speech and the ladders do after all herald an attack that failed, since later the Governor appears up on the wall that the ladders were to have been laid on. Consequently, if we saw a version of what Shake-speare first wrote down in what became the Folio text, all the soldiers who did scale the walls, except for the Eastcheap crew who hung back till urged off-stage, not up the ladders, by Llewellyn, would evidently have died in an attack that failed. Shakespeare's Henry was a lot less inspiring at Harfleur than at Agin-court. That made a good reason to cut the ladders, and the opening speech of exhortation. The company streamlined Shakespeare's 3400 lines into half the length to make a two-hour show of English heroics. Oxford's principle required them to print not the author's foul papers but the quarto text.

Other Shakespeare plays may have been trimmed less thoroughly than *Henry V*. Sadly, though, the surviving printed versions give little direct evidence of what might have been cut. Every company's most crucial asset was its 'allowed book' of each play, signed by the Master of the Revels to license it for perfor-mance, the 'maximal' text from which the performances were made. Of the Shakespeare company's two surviving allowed books one is the manuscript the Master in 1611 called *This Second Maiden's Tragedy*, the other the defective manuscript of Massinger's *Believe As You List* of 1631, its locale revised from contemporary Portugal to ancient Carthage. Neither is as heavily cut as the quartos of *Henry V* and *Merry Wives*, though since we do not have any 'foul papers' for either play we cannot be sure what might have been done preced-ing the manuscript that has the Master's signature. The worked-over manu-scripts of *Sir Thomas More* with Tilney's markings on it and of *Barnavelt* with Buc's suggest that when the companies could afford them company scribes rewrote the messy foul papers. No certain copy survives of any 'allowed book' belonging to the Shakespeare company besides the one by Middleton or whoever and the one by Massinger. Nor are any likely to exist in print, since the last thing a company would do with its most precious asset, the allowed book with its enabling signature, was to hand it over to a printer.

Not that the 'allowed book' could tell us how any play was actually staged in any case. Its peculiar value was that it contained the maximum words that the company was licensed to perform anywhere in the country. The King's Men produced their allowed book of *A Game at Chess* to the Privy Council in their defence when quizzed about their performance of the 'Scandalous Comedie'.[5] Whether in London or on tour most performances would have been of shorter versions, since cutting was easy and added material would not be licensed. The company book-keeper held the allowed book, using it to check the properties he had to supply and to alert each player to be 'ready' on cue. Reduced ver-sions like the quarto *Henry V* would be made from it. Play books were heavily thumbed backstage, and Henry Herbert, the last Master of the Revels, had to reallow several old plays when the original manuscripts wore out.

It is just possible that some of the plays not printed until after the closure of 1642 had their source in allowed play books. One printed in 1657, *The Walks of Islington and Hogsdon*, actually prints Henry Herbert's licence on its final page: 'This Comedy, called, The Walks of Islington and Hogsdon, With the Humours of Woodstreet-Compter, may be Acted: This 2. August 1641. Henry Herbert.' Probably a Red Bull play,[6] it has some distinctive book-keeper notes of the sort we like to think were characteristic of prompt books. One note, for instance, says *'Splend stands within the Arras'* (B3v), the only known book-keeper annotation to use *'within'*.[7] It differs from authorial uses of stage directions like *'Trumpets within'* because the book-keepers were *'within'* themselves. Since their position was *'within'* the tiring-house, the term was normally employed from the audience perspective. The note in *Walks* indicates that the character was to be visible to the book-keeper from inside the back stage area. The use of such a preposition helps us to identify the manuscript from which the text was printed as what we rather too blandly and anachronistically call the prompt book. Such Beaumont and Fletcher or Middleton plays as were printed in the 1650s and 1660s do not offer much hope that more copies printed from the allowed/prompt books survive. Lacking the Master's note of authorization, no text can be said to represent with much accuracy the maximal version from which the staged texts were taken.

The allowed book had to be licensed some time before the first performance, though after copies of the individual parts had been transcribed. In a last word about Henry Herbert's work on Fletcher's sequel to *The Taming of the Shrew*, an old play book he was recensoring, he ordered that 'The players ought not to study their parts till I have allowed of the booke'. He insisted that his alterations must be transferred to the pre-existing players' scrolls of their individual 'parts'.[8]

Changes must have followed the first performance, but to the staging rather than to the now-fixed script. The easiest recourse when anything in the text proved awkward was always to cut. In the long process between first buying the author's draft and finally staging a familiar script the text was always in flux, however firmly the allowed book version might seem to have fixed it. Any written text produced from the long and fiddly process of preparation and rehearsal will be frozen into a quite unnatural form, and we read it as a fixity only because 400 years of respecting print and its fixity above the transience of the spoken word have habituated us to doing so. The texts we read today give us no more than an approximate access to the plays as they were staged during the company's life.

Another factor, one that confirms how completely the companies controlled their play texts, can be found in the recurrent notes in Herbert where he licensed additions to plays. At least twice he charged half of his usual £1 fee for an addition to a play. On 7 July 1624 he charged 10 shillings 'For the adding of a scene to The Virgin Martyr', and on 13 May 1629 the same amount 'For allowing a new act in an ould play'. On 12 May 1636 he charged the Fortune company a full £1 'for allowing the company to add scenes to an ould play, and to give it out for a new one'.[9] These notes signify the power of this last Master of the Revels over staged texts as much as the companies' readiness to tinker with their allowed books. More potently, though, it affirms their readiness to alter their play books from the experience of acting them even though they had to pay for their additions to be approved.

Cutting the maximal text in the allowed book was the standard practice, for whatever reason. The trouble with that is that we lack any indication of what might have been cut from the text as originally performed or from any subsequent version. We might well think that small incidents would be cut, like the sacrifice of Alarbus from the first scene in *Titus Andronicus*, for instance, since it appears neither in the German version of the play nor in the later ballad. But that is guesswork, like all except those identifiable in the *Henry V* and *Merry Wives* quartos. We could use the myriad prompt books from subsequent generations of stage productions to see what later directors found easiest to cut, but that would still leave us only with evidence located in the great what-if category.

That is my chief argument for the negative case. So to the context, and what positives we can find. Behind all this concern for the state of play texts is the question of what the original staging practices were, and what impact they had on the writing of the plays. In recent years we have had some experience of audience interaction in a Globe-type playhouse, and the energizing effect that an audience standing fully visible to the players has on their acting (and their speed of delivery), but such evidence is perilously close to the 'what-if'. What is there that can fairly tell us about the practices the leading companies of Shakespeare's time followed? I think we are slowly beginning to recognize a few of the features that devalue our own too-easy assumptions.

There is good reason to doubt the value of stage directions as reliable or even sufficient markers of how the plays were performed. On the evidence of texts by Webster and other authors, including *The Second Maiden's Tragedy*, Antony Hammond has argued with some cogent examples that action on the stage was more elaborate than the stage directions usually indicate.[10] Other possible contextual factors can be calculated with varying degrees of confidence. But we have to start by acknowledging all the individual features of body language, the gestural and dress practices that Mary Hazard calls 'silent language',[11] which are the most obvious features of early staging lost to us. There is nothing at all to say what visible emotions would have gone to register the intensity of moments like Romeo discovering Juliet dead, or what Coriolanus did when he faced his mother in Act 5.3, and as the stage direction orders, '*holds her by the hand, silent*'. We might hear a few whistles from the sidelines by John Bulwer, with his two books on a gestural language for the deaf, *Chirologia* and *Chironomia*, but they will not tell us much about how Burbage may have behaved when passioning Coriolanus or mad Hamlet.

The most notable concern needing fresh study is the consequences of three-dimensional staging. Thanks to our long-running tradition of picture-frame staging and its successor, the movie screen, we still think far too easily of staging in two dimensions. As a result we lose the force of stage blocking, and especially the difference between *locus* and *platea*, and its effects on stage choreography.[12] The central authority position, the *locus*, faces outwards, confronting the audience. The *platea* position, the street, is marginal, and puts its users next to the audience facing inwards to authority, with the audience often literally behind the players who stand there. That is basic to a play like *Richard III*, where for the first half of the play Richard prowls round the edge, confiding in the audience and fooling the occupiers of the authority positions, but in the last half of the play, once he has acquired the authority of the crown, he sits on his throne facing outwards, enacting a false control, in the opposite posture to that of his early antics. That is when we as audience lose the intimacy that he engineered for us while parading round the *platea*.

We have a long way to go before we can expect to have a good grip on how players moved on the Elizabethan stages. Some of that regrettable distance is self-imposed through our habituation with what I like to call two-dimensional staging, not just the old picture-frame facing the audience but the assumption that a spectator's proper position is facing the stage or the screen. That loses us much more than Weimann's distinction between *locus* and *platea*. Even modern theatre-in-the-round staging these days retains the us–them distinction of the picture-frame. The thrust stages Tyrone Guthrie developed still assume an audience grouped largely in front of the stage. The Olivier at London's National Theatre does not have any flanking seats for its audience, and even the Swan at Stratford, the best modern stage for Renaissance plays, has musicians not audience on its balcony. A few theatres are designed truly in the round – the Royal Exchange in Manchester, the Orange Tree in Richmond, London, the Arena in Washington, DC, for instance – but even they usually block the actor positions to face inward, actor to actor as in a movie, not outwards to the surrounding audience. The assumption that every stage has a front facing the audience and a back from which the actors enter is an entirely two-dimensional preconception. All the Elizabethan stages were three-dimensional. Consider the Inigo Jones design for his indoor theatre of 1616 (Fig. 9), the only reliable testimony we have to early theatre design for general audiences. We cannot be absolutely sure what the Jones plan and drawings were made for, though I am almost convinced by John Orrell's argument that

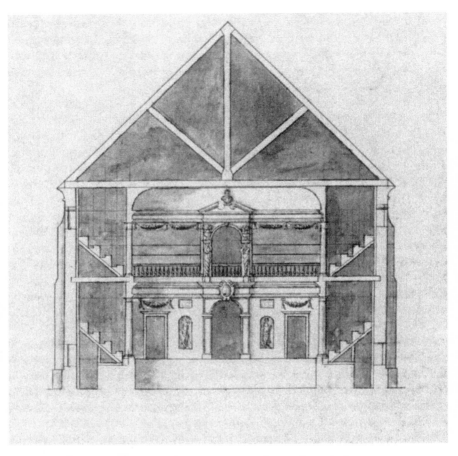

Figure 9. The stage end of Inigo Jones's drawing of an indoor playhouse.

he made them for the Christopher Beeston Cockpit in 1616, the first rival to the Shakespearean Blackfriars. They show the same configuration that Robert Fludd gave his *Orbis Terrarum*, some years later (Fig. 10), probably basing it on the Blackfriars with its flanking boxes and degrees on the stage balcony. This hypothetical stage makes ample provision not only for audience to sit in the boxes on each side of the stage but also to position themselves at what we consider to be 'behind', on the degrees that flank the stage balcony's central music room. A three-dimensional audience that literally surrounds the players was the Elizabethan norm. We have lost the arts and all the effects of such three-dimensional staging. An Elizabethan 'audience' was a crowd, listening in three dimensions. Modern 'spectators' are individuals, viewing and thinking in two.

Figure 10. Robert Fludd's *Theatrum Orbis* from his *Ars Memoriae*, 1623.

The early modern crowds in theatres were located in the auditorium according to their social and financial status, and in an age so status-conscious as the Elizabethan, the positioning of the highest-ranking audience members influenced how the players on stage could move. The *locus* or authority position gained in importance by the fact that the richest and most noble sat closest to it. A player addressing a stage monarch would thus doff his cap and bow to the highest among the audience at the same time as he kowtowed to the stage presence. Consider the implications of blocking for a centralized stage. It was concentric, the official speakers standing in the centre, while the commentators prowled around the flanks, and servants and messengers waited by the stage doors. The audience was closest to the commentators, and the commentators spoke their truths directly to them.

In *Richard III* Richard opens the play in soliloquy to the 'understanding' crowd at his feet. He tells them the truth about his feelings, with intimate honesty and secrecy. The other noble characters speak from centre-stage, backed by the audience's dignitaries. The common audience literally backs Richard as they watch him fooling them with his acting. His wooing of Lady Anne in the third scene is a bravura display of his satanic art of deception.

Once he is crowned king, though, and has to occupy the centre of the stage himself he loses his proximity and his intimacy with his popular audience. From then on it is he who becomes the victim, acted on rather than acting, and losing the audience's subconscious alliance with him. Iago does the same in *Othello*, addressing the audience directly in soliloquy, visibly acting what he is not when he speaks to Othello or the other characters he is fooling. Vindice in *The Revenger's Tragedy* does it too, using the stage margins to confide in the audience while fooling the royal family. Hamlet stands on the margins of the stage, alone and apart from the court when we first see him in the play's second scene. Comedians, also using the marginal *platea* next to the audience rather than the central *locus*, do the same. Three-dimensional staging admits a radically different dynamic from two-dimensional in the intimacies it grants its characters, on the one hand with the audience, and on the other with the remoteness of authority. Othello stands centre-stage while Iago speaks from the margins.

If one soars like a hopeful eagle over the mass of debate about such matters, the largest prey in this contextualizing must be the still unsettled question of stage design, and in particular the entry doorways. In recent years, following Richard Hosley's work identifying plays written for specific playhouses, we have begun to register the architecture of the stage. Not all plays can be allocated in this way, but most of the surviving play texts can, like the plays produced for Henslowe by his teams of collaborative writers, or Shakespeare's for the Globe with its stage posts and the Blackfriars without them but with a balcony of musicians, or plays written for Beeston's Cockpit, detailed most likely in the plan and profile of the *frons scenae* by Inigo Jones. The consistency of the three-door *frons*, despite Johannes De Witt's drawing of a two-door Swan, gives substance to the idea that the three doors had specific roles, the flanking doors for oppositional entries like the Montagues and Capulets at the beginning of *Romeo and Juliet* or Oberon and Titania's first meeting in *A Midsummer Night's Dream*, with the central opening surrounded by the most colourful and potent audience members for spectacles and for trumpeted authority entrances.

I believe that the central doorway, whether curtained by an arras or hung with double doors, served not just as the authority position but as the emblem of harmony where pairs of lovers made their exit at the end of a play. That suits the concept of three-dimensional staging, where the centrally placed figures stand at the *locus* confronting the audience while the clowns and tricksters prowl round the periphery talking to them. But it also raises many other questions about blocking. We might think that an authority figure like the Duke in the opening scene of *Romeo and Juliet*, appearing through the central opening to quell the rioting mob in front of him, would have the visible benefit of standing in front (*sic*: 'front') of the most socially elevated members of the audience seated above and behind him in the lords' rooms. He is backed, literally, by authority. We might think that an audience carefully disposed all round the stage, the authority figures sitting above on the stage balcony and the *hoi polloi* standing opposite them at the lowest level in the yard, presented a proper image of Elizabethan social divisions.

But it must have created problems for the players. Addressing an audience grouped in front of you is easy for modern actors. The Elizabethan had far more complex problems. You did not readily turn your back on authority, any more than you kept your hat on in your master's or mistress's presence. *Romeo*'s Duke spoke to the mob with his back to the section of the audience whose status he reflected, and whose power his position on stage invoked. But what should have happened when he engaged in dialogue? How then did he relate to the lords above? How did he cope with the three-dimensional problem of talking through the back of his head? One of the most testing problems in all this matter of the *locus* is where Coriolanus should have stood and how he moved with his changing roles in that unique play about a headless state. We have a lot to learn about the techniques of acting in the round that were standard practices for the Elizabethans.

Learning about that is in part a matter of experimenting on the new Elizabethan stages now in use in London, Lenox, Mass., and Staunton, Virginia. Working in a circular auditorium with a three-door *frons* raises a multitude of incarnadined questions. In this complex process of experimentation to learn how the plays work best in three dimensions, given the imperfections of the surviving play texts, we need to take great care identifying the best way to read the too often enigmatic language of the texts. To Alan Dessen's point about how familiar and standardized was the theatre language that made the original stage directions so cryptic, we must add his other searching but much less readily answered question, as to whether a reference in dialogue to something on stage means that it has to be there to be gestured at, or that it does not have to be there because the words alone could summon it for our imaginations.

A pretty, and pretty demanding, test-case for all these questions of text and context, a litmus paper to identify the level of acidity in modern responses to all this pessimism, is a deservedly not very well-known play, *The Two Noble Ladies*. One of fifteen items in a manuscript that includes the equally unexciting *Edmund Ironsides*, British Library Egerton 1994, the play was written on twenty-two folio leaves, one of them serving as the cover, probably making a single gathering of twelve sheets. Two leaves are missing from the end section, along with the first half of one containing a section from Act 1. The paper it is written on postdates 1600, and the hand seems to be the anonymous author's, with some additions in another hand, including what seems to be a draft title page inserted on the verso of the title leaf. Its date is almost certainly

1620. The title page calls it 'The 2. Noble Ladys, / and / The Converted Conjurer'. In spite of that, the verso page says it is called simply

> The two noble Ladies: A Trage-comicall
> Historie often times acted with approbation
> At the Red Bull in St. Johns Streete
> By the Company of ye Revells.

and adds 'The Actors Names', a list of the characters with short descriptions, starting with 'the Souldan of Egipt' and 'the Califfe of Babilon'. If we can ignore the multivalent titling, making the play simultaneously a tragedy, a comedy, and a history, the verso is the more correct version. It is not two plays but one, the 'converted conjurer' being the play's alternative title. The two ladies are the virtuous daughters of, respectively, the Sultan of Egypt and the Califf of Babylon, and the play's conjuror at the end abjures his black magic for the better magic of Christianity. We can date the play to 1620 because the Queen Anne's Men at the Red Bull became known as the Revels Company after Anne died in 1619.

The manuscript, mainly written in a clearly readable English hand, seems to be authorial, since a number of corrections or stylistic adjustments appear to have been made in the process of copying. For instance, TLN 321 (Act 1 scene 4) reads 'then [yeild to] to such [foule] motions yeild my virgin eare'. The first 'yeild' is marked for cutting, the first 'to' is inserted under the line above, and 'foule' is also cut, so that the line's final version should obviously read 'Then to such motions yield my virgin ear', a perfectly sound line. The cuts might show that the line was being recomposed from the first draft rather than offering the author's second thoughts. This hand was clearly that of the originator of the whole play script.

A second hand also appears, chiefly making staging notes in the left margin. Enter what we miscall the prompter. Most of the stage directions, fairly precise in specifying what was wanted, appear boxed in the right margin in the author's hand, and the left-hand margin's annotator was clearly reinscribing them more concisely and in a more convenient location. Where the author specifies *'Enter the Califfe with Attendants and Souldiers'* on the right at TLN 802, the second hand simply puts on the left *'Ent Califfe'*. This writer specifies the names of several players for the mute and carry-on roles, using the names of hired men who we know were in the Red Bull company in 1620. At line 768, for the author's *'Enter a Lord of Babilon with his sword drawn'*, the second hand puts *'Ent. Anth Brew'*, meaning Antony Brew or Brewer of the Red Bull company. Identifying which mutes or bit-part players took the walk-on roles was the book-keeper's job. It was probably also someone more familiar than the author with the company's resources who struck out the author's description of a spirit with a shield on his breast emblazoned in golden lettering and replaced the word '*Golden*' with '*silver*' (TLN 1082). The verso title page entries with the names of the characters are in a third hand, by someone who took the script over to prepare it for the press. The press, I think understandably, chose not to print it.

So we have a playhouse manuscript that cannot be what we usually call a prompt book, because it has few of the notes such as warnings to make a player 'ready' found in other texts used for prompting, like *The Merry Milkmaids*.[13] Nor is it a regular playhouse book-keeper's transcript since it is still in the author's hand. He was unprofessional enough to use the speaker's full name at the start of each speech, not abbreviating them as the playhouse scribes did. He omitted the horizontal lines the book-keepers used to mark the breaks between acts and scenes. Sadly, the manuscript does not seem to be the allowed book of the play, since the Master of the Revels, George Buc, has not inscribed his licensing note at the end. Just possibly one of the lost end-leaves had the licence with its signature of the Master on it, but Buc seems normally to have taken care to write his licence on the last page of the play text, as he did with *The Second Maiden's Tragedy*. Writing it on a loose and empty page ran too much risk of the licence being misappropriated for use with another play.

The Two Noble Ladies is chiefly famous for the anti-realism of its staging, something we like to think we know about because of the author's stage directions in a scene where two soldiers are drowned in a river onstage, a nice challenge to any filmic director's imagination.[14] They drag one of the two heroines, Justina, to the Euphrates to drown her on the Califf's orders. She is a princess of Antioch, which Egypt has conquered, and the beloved of Clitophon, son of the Califf of Babylon. The Califf, his father, refuses to let them marry because she is a Christian, so Clitophon refuses to lead the Babylonian army against the invading Egyptians. He does not agree to fight until his father says they can marry, but as soon as he is off to battle the Califf sends his men away to drown her. Hence this scene, 3.3. A stage direction at TLN 1149 says '*Enter 2. Souldiers dragging Justina bound*'. They intrude on a scene between the conjuror of the title Ciprian and Lysander, the second of the two lovers, who stand aside to watch them. The dialogue says

> *1 Souldier.* Come, now w'are allmost at our journeys end;
> This is swift Euphrates, here cast her in.

Justina then has her last plea for pity and asks for time to pray, to which the second soldier replies 'Prate not of prayer'. Lysander as a bystander says 'O help to rescue yonder Innocent', but the conjuror says (literally) sit still and leave that to me. Then the two soldiers have this dialogue:

> *2 Souldier.* Come this way, this way, heare the streame is deepest.
>
> *1 Souldier.* I am enforc'd I know not by what pow'r
>   To hale her this way.
>
> *2. Souldier.* what strange noise is this?
>
> *1. Souldier.* dispatch, the tide swells high.
>
> *2. Souldier.* what feind is this?
>
> *1. Souldier.* What furie ceazes me?
>
> *2. Souldier.* Alas, I'm hurried headlong to the streame.
>
> *1. Souldier.* And so am I, wee both must drowne and die.

The staging of this apparently realistic drowning is explained clearly by the authorial stage directions in the right margin. An order for *'Thunder'*, copied by the book-keeper on the left, appears just before 2 Soldier says 'what strange noise is this?' That is followed by a direction *'Enter 2. Tritons with silver trumpets'*. At 'what feind is this?' the direction says *'The tritons ceaz the souldiers'*, and when the soldiers exclaim about being 'hurried headlong to the streame', the stage direction says *'The Tritons Dragge Them In* (meaning off-stage) *sounding their trumpets'*.

This is of course a show of the conjuror Ciprian's magic. The book-keeper noted none of it other than the thunder on the left, nor are there any actor names for the soldiers, so presumably he would expect them to have been coached separately with their lines and actions. Nor would the audience have been surprised at the supernatural intervention, because earlier in the same scene they had seen Ciprian conjure up a spirit to tell Lysander his future, after which an angel appears and tells Ciprian his. The angel's announcement in Act 3 anticipates the play's conclusion, which the author clearly saw as needing the discovery space and stage trap in fairly easily identified pieces of spectacle. In 5.2, the last scene but one, at TLN 1752, we have an authorial stage direction in the right margin. The conjuror says 'Let me see / this Christian Saint which I (in spite of hell) / am forc'd to worship'. The stage direction says *'Justina is discovered in a chaire asleep, in her hands a prayer book, divells about her'*. Ciprian the conjuror comments 'O how heav'nly sweet / she looks in spite of hells enchantments, and / charmes the fierce feinds at once with rage and wonder'. This looks like standard verbiage to explain what is made visible in the discovery space to most of the audience but is inaccessible to those on the margins or sitting in the lords' rooms over the stage.

The rest of the scene follows predictably. When Ciprian tries to kiss her she wakes, saying 'Forbid it heav'n', and a stage direction says she opens her prayer book and the demonic spirits *'fly from her'*. Ciprian declares he will turn Christian, she gives him her book, and the angel from Act 3, now described by the author as *'the patriarch-like Angell with his crossier staffe in one hand, and a book in the other'*, confronts the devils, whom the author orders to *'sinck roaring; a flame of fier riseth after them'*. The author wanted the trapdoor to be set as hell with flames ready to receive them. Shortly after Ciprian *'Throws his charmed rod, and his books under the stage'*, and again *'a flame riseth'*. This indicates some doubt in the author about the staging, because the word *'under'* in the manuscript replaces *'into a'*, as if he was not at first sure what would be available to receive the pagan magic.

He shows a similar uncertainty in the final scene, when the other noble lady, Miranda, the Sultan's warrior daughter, comes on stage to confront her love Lysander in single combat. Her entry is described in this stage direction: *'Flourish. Enter Herald, Miranda following him in her Owne Amazonian attire, an helmet on and the beavor down'*.

Lysander, half-recognizing 'This stature, gesture and this shape she own'd', says 'what ere you are graunt me to see your face, / before we fight'. When she shows him her face – 'Then shall Lysander see / he must be conquer'd by a woman' – the manuscript has two entries on the right on successive lines, *'She lets him take of her helmet. / She puts up her beavor'*. The beaver, as with the ghost of Hamlet's father, was an integral part of a metal helmet, through which the face can be seen, as Hamlet expects of Horatio, so the two directions must be the author's offer of alternative stagings. Lysander in fact responds to her voice, not her face, exclaiming 'ha! / her voice; 'tis shee'. It looks as if the author provided even a third possible way that the company might have devised to stage this key confrontation.

The manuscript is revealing more in the way that it shows how the author conceived his own idea of the staging than in how it was actually done at the Red Bull. It gives us two of the three steps in the process of production. We have the text of the words the author wanted spoken, and his directions for how he hoped it might be staged. We have the much more cryptic notes for action by the book-keeper. What we do not have is anything that can tell us exactly what the company did finally choose to stage. We cannot even be sure whether the manuscript is a quasi-allowed book, a maximal text containing all that the actors were supposed to say. *The Two Noble Ladies* does tell us how one author hoped his play might be staged, but little more. It even offers some of the author's alternative ideas about the staging. But the book-keeper's notes do not give much guidance about how it actually was staged in 1620. The rest is guesswork. What we need is a much closer knowledge of staging practices and of the genesis of these dreadfully variable kinds of play book that we seek to preserve in our fixated and too crystalline modern editions, over-plugged as they are with facile assumptions about the original staging.

Notes

1. Anthony B. Dawson's overview of shifts in editorial positions, 'Correct impressions: editing and evidence in the wake of postmodernism', in *In Arden: Editing Shakespeare: Essays in Honour of Richard Proudfoot*, ed. Ann Thompson and Gordon McMullan (London: Thomson Learning, 2003), 31–47, takes up broadly the position I use here.

2. Leah S. Marcus, *Unediting the Renaissance: Shakespeare, Marlowe, Milton* (London and New York: Routledge, 1996). I would question some of the points she makes, but her analysis of *Merry Wives* in particular stands up to scrutiny.

3. This term comes from the manuscript of Fletcher's *Bonduca*, to which the book-keeper who transcibed it added a note saying 'the booke where by it was first Acted from is lost: and this hath beene transcribd from the fowle papers of the Authors which were founde'. Daborne in 1613 sent a draft of a play to Henslowe saying 'I send you the foule sheet & ye fayr I was wrighting'.

4. *William Shakespeare. The Complete Works*, ed. Stanley Wells and Gary Taylor *et al.* (Oxford: Clarendon Press, 1988), xxxvii.

5. '[T]ouching the suppression of a Scandalous Comedie, Acted by the Kings Players, We have called before us some of the principall Actors & demanded of them by what lycence and Authoritie, they have presumed to Act the same, in answere whereunto they produced a Booke being an Orriginall and perfect Coppie thereof (as they affirmed) seene and allowed by Sir Henry Herbert knight Master of the Revells under his owne hand, and subscribed in the last page of the said Booke, they confidently protested, they added or varied from the same nothing at all' (Privy Council letter to the King's secretary, 21 August 1624, quoted in *Malone Society Collections*, I.4–5: 380–1).

6. Its title page, despite being not entered in the Stationers' Register till 21 April 1657, states: 'As it was publikely Acted 19.days togeather, with extraordinary Applause'. N. W. Bawcutt, *The Control and Censorship of Caroline Drama. The Records of Sir Henry Herbert, 1623–73* (Oxford: Oxford University Press, 1996), 210, notes it in part 5 of Herbert's diary.

7. I am grateful to Mariko Ichikawa for drawing this stage direction to my attention.

8. Bawcutt, *Caroline Drama*, 83.

9. Ibid., 153, 168, 199.

10. Antony Hammond, 'Encounters of the Third Kind in Stage-Directions in Elizabethan and Jacobean Drama', *Studies in Philology*, 89 (1992), 71–96, esp. 81.

11. Mary E. Hazard, *Elizabethan Silent Language* (Lincoln: University of Nebraska Press, 2000).

12. For a rewarding study of these three-dimensional positions in *Macbeth*, see Robert Weimann, *Author's Pen and Actor's Voice: Playing and Writing in Shakespeare's Theatre* (Cambridge: Cambridge University Press, 2000), 196–208. His analysis of the two positions in *Richard III* is in 'Performance-Game and Representation in *Richard III*', in *Textual and Theatrical Shakespeare: Questions of Evidence*, ed. Edward Pechter (Iowa City: University of Iowa Press, 1996), 66–85.

13. See Leslie Thomson, 'A Quarto "Marked for Performance": Evidence of What?', *Medieval and Renaissance Drama in England*, 8 (1996), 176–210.

14. George F. Reynolds, *The Staging of Elizabethan Plays at the Red Bull Theater, 1605–1625* (New York: Modern Language Association, 1940) is the only theatre historian to make much of the play.

5

Staging Evidence

Anthony B. Dawson

Othello as witness

This is a paper concerned with the relation of narratives, intention, and evidence, and I want to begin with a narrative of my own.[1] On 26 August 2002, National Public Radio ran an opinion piece by Ken Adelman in which he interpreted in some detail the council scene in *Othello* (1.3) to make an argument in favour of attacking Iraq.[2] He began by noting the contradictory nature of the evidence provided by the messengers at the beginning of the scene – 107 ships under weigh? 140? 200? or (later) only 30? 'Shakespeare's top security leaders and Othello don't lack facts', he says, 'they have lots of them – too many actually – and their facts are contradictory'.[3] From this he infers that facts are unimportant – getting 'the big picture' is what matters: 'Today's intelligence reports are, in the words of *Othello*, "oft with difference" on Saddam's precise ties with terrorism and the exact size and nature of his weapons of mass destruction. "Yet," as Shakespeare says, "they do all confirm the main thing,"[4] that he's the number-one threat facing American and all civilized, freedom-loving nations today.' And so, says Adelman, stop scrambling after facts, they only get in the way. Instead, 'President Bush and his national security team [should] do what Othello and his team did in Venice on their crises – get the big picture, push the details aside and use force to confront the danger and to protect their people. Myself? I stand with Othello on this one'.

It would be tedious to catalogue all the misrepresentations in this (for starters, Othello is not even in the room), so let me concentrate on only one issue. The worried senators are not unconcerned with facts, the most important of which is that, as quickly emerges, there is a clear threat on Cyprus. The scene dramatizes a process of putting together a detailed and accurate picture – in fact, just to hammer home the point, it does so twice: at the outset with the Turkish threat and later with the accusation and exoneration of Othello. So is Ken Adelman just a bad reader? Who in fact *is* Ken Adelman? Assistant to US Secretary of Defense Donald Rumsfeld from 1975 to 1977, Ambassador to the UN as well as director of arms control during the Reagan administration, Adelman and his wife run a company called 'Movers and Shakespeares' which uses 'the insights and wisdom of the Bard' in programs designed for corporate 'Team-Building, Executive Training, [and] Leadership Development'.[5] Their website carries testimonials from, among others, the Directors of the Center for Public Leadership at Harvard's Kennedy School of Government, a brace of US admirals, and a VP of AT&T. Adelman is also co-author of *Shakespeare in Charge: the Bard's Guide to Leading and Succeeding on the Corporate Stage*. So it appears that he is an important conduit for how Shakespeare is channelled into the political mainstream.

In his eagerness to use the Bard to bolster a weak argument, Adelman passes over the racial/religious politics of his analogy, the conflation of Turks and Iraqis. To mention that would no doubt be messy. Instead why not deploy Shakespeare as a WMP (weapon of mass persuasion) in a rhetorical battle, a kind of character witness who testifies to the validity of your position? Never mind what *really* goes on in the scene or the play. Behind the analogy, of course, is the powerful assumption that continuities between Shakespeare's time and our own are valid and can underlie far-reaching claims. (I think it is true that such continuities do exist, though not in the way that commentators such as Adelman assume, and that the efforts of the cultural materialist left to disclaim them is misguided.[6]) Both then, in *Othello* and now, so the analogy goes, a threat to the Christian West is posed by the Muslim East, driving the need to do something, perhaps to deploy a general whose racial profile complexly mediates the distance between East and West (Othello thus morphs into Colin Powell, who is mentioned in the broadcast as warning Adelman about accepting intelligence reports at face value). The earlier, fictional episode can stand as an exemplar, even a guide, to present action because of the self-evident nature of the link between them (Shakespeare's universality underpins the equation). And is it mere coincidence that of all Shakespeare's plays, the one cited should be *Othello*, the most far-reaching and disturbing of his many explorations of the dangers of what looks like evidence and of the illusory appeal of ocular proof?

The sequence at the beginning of the third scene, the one quoted by Adelman, is often cut or reduced in modern performance, though its flurry of conflicting messages is germane. Adelman is right to put some weight on this moment, but he misses the point: just because facts (or what look like facts) are hard to interpret does not mean that they are unimportant.[7] Adelman's view is that because data can be confusing, we shouldn't bother about facts at all (again this notion is echoed by a lot of materialist critics dedicated to indeterminacy). But the play makes clear that accurate interpretation *is* possible: indeed, what at first looks deceptive turns out to be 'certain' (1.3.43). The Turks have constructed a ruse – seeming to head toward Rhodes, only to meet up with an 'after fleet' (that's where the 'thirty sail' come in) and steer for Cyprus (1.3.35–7). The sceptical senators have already suspected this: ' 'tis a pageant to keep us in false gaze' (1.3.18–19) says one when told that 'the Turkish preparation makes for Rhodes' (1.3.14). Just as Adelman says, evidence of troop movements, in the view of strategists used to the cunning ways of the enemy, should not be taken at face value; aggressive intent cannot be so easily disguised. The Turk, in this view, is 'staging' the evidence, constructing a 'pageant' designed to mislead its interpreters. But the point is that the senators are soon proved right – they are apprised of a new set of facts that align with the hypothesis they have already formulated. The threat from the East is both duplicitous and real. Adelman wants to claim the same thing about the Iraqi case, but he ignores the relation between hypothesis and fact that the senators are careful to guard. Once their sceptical view of the international situation is established as the correct one, they realize the need for Othello to answer the Turkish menace, turning naturally to the man they think best can help them. Paradoxically, of course, the senators' choice falls on a man not, in the end, remarkable for his strategic rationality; indeed Othello shows in what follows that while he can undermine suspicion of his motives by a compelling mythic narrative (one that overrides the complexity of those motives), he can as easily fall victim to the power of a less exotic but equally powerful story. Here, perhaps, we can see the fiendish cleverness of Adelman's reading: he erases Othello's credulousness while capitalizing on his mythic credibility.

Worries about the foreign enemy are quickly set aside when Brabantio mounts his accusations (another point left unmentioned by Adelman), but as the careful Duke reminds the unhappy father, 'to vouch this is no proof'; it is all too easy for 'thin habits and poor likelihoods / Of modern seeming' to intrude themselves (1.3.106–9). The ensuing investigation, of course, exonerates Othello on the basis of his story and Desdemona's testimony. But here too the evidence is vexed: Othello is asked directly whether he drugged Desdemona, and his answer is to call for her and let her speak: 'If [they should] find [him] foul in her report', he says, then the senate should whistle him off to prey at fortune (1.3.117). But how can her testimony be trusted if he has successfully overcome her resistance through magic? The question is never asked, though it hovers behind the scene, reminding us, as the Duke says a moment later, that 'opinion [is] a sovereign mistress of effects' (1.3.224–5). That obscure phrase, glossed (in Riverside) as 'public opinion, the ultimate arbiter of what is to be done' suggests further that opinion (a key word in *Troilus and Cressida*, where it carries strong connotations of *interest*) produces the effects it arbitrates.[8] Opinion makes things happen, but, as the very existence of broadcasts like that I have been discussing attests, opinion is controversial and changeable.

There is then a warning here at the beginning of *Othello* about the complexities of reading evidence. At the same time, there is no doubt about the outcome of either investigation – the Turk really does intend to sack Cyprus, and Desdemona did freely choose her husband. The facts, despite Adelman's insistence on their irrelevance, add up. Sceptical rationality in the face of evidence is clearly salutary, as is understanding the possibility, even the likelihood, of deception. That indeed is what makes evidence an issue in the first place. But scepticism by itself may not be salutary at all – distrust of the usefulness and value of facts (and, as I said, this is an attitude that Adelman shares with a lot of recent cultural critics with very different political views) is a dangerous game that can be played by both sides.

Othello, of course, keeps staging and restaging the problem. That it rings multiple variations on the painful difficulties of interpreting evidence is well known, as is the hero's propensity to succumb to the seductiveness of the sort of compelling narrative that he deploys as proof of his own integrity. Unlike the sceptical senators, he fails to 'test . . . poor likelihoods' (107–8). But of course some 'facts' are harder to come by than others, and the temptation to rely on rhetorical persuasion is compelling. Othello's mythic narrative dramatizes the dint of stories, the force of words to sweep away facts, making them seem trivial and unimportant. This is the shadowy side of the Renaissance valorization of rhetoric. If Othello sweeps away facts, as Adelman suggests, Iago stays closer to them, or at least to a simulacrum. Indeed, Iago's mythic narrative is the more compelling for being, seemingly, so ordinary, so dependent on simple observation, gossip, and factoids. But it would be missing the 'big picture' and trivializing the tragedy to derive a lesson that, for example, to set store by facts is to side with Iago. *Movers and Shakespeares* trades in precisely this kind of reductionism, and to do so it has to run fast and loose with the very evidence it claims to rely on.

I begin with these ruminations on the uses of Shakespeare in the military and corporate marketplace because I see a continuity between some of the problems of evidence, intention, and interpretation that we face in a forum on theatre history, clearly a long away from the centers of power, and the larger social circumstances that surround and infiltrate it. No doubt the question of evidence in humanistic pursuits has less far-reaching consequences than in war or terrorism, but we live in a world where the status of evidence and we ourselves are constantly under surveillance. When Shakespeare appears as a witness in that world, we have a responsibility to listen and speak.

At the least, we can say that *Othello* both highlights the complexity of facts and explanation, and insists on the rightness of some interpretations and the falsity of others. At the end of the play, Emilia's testimony produces the truth for Othello. That sequence is very cannily managed, as Emilia's passionate words, Iago's attempts to silence her, the climactic allusion to the handkerchief, the startled horror of the onlookers, all converge to invert totally Othello's conviction. Why is Emilia's testimony at this point more credible than Iago's? Testimony, after all, is a weaker form of evidence than ocular demonstration,[9] though of course there has been no ocular demonstration, only the pretence of it (and indeed, in plays like *Much Ado about Nothing* and *Cymbeline* seeing itself makes a poor basis for believing). The final scene skilfully makes us forget our doubts and in doing so suggests the entanglement of evidence in intentionality. Suddenly Emilia's passionate desire to exonerate her mistress erupts into the situation – it is her *clarity* that matters, and the facts of the case rearrange themselves in the silent Othello's mind (he says nothing for a crucial seventeen lines as Emilia testifies and Iago threatens); a different interpretation that explains all of those facts and reverses Othello's earlier misreadings is made available, and he seizes on it. I think it is that convergence, skilfully staged of course by the play, that matters, though even at the end Othello is still trying to 'prove' an explanation that will satisfy but which seems beyond the reach of evidence: 'If that thou be'st a devil, I cannot kill thee', he says as he lunges at Iago who is, as he himself sardonically replies, hurt but not killed (5.2.287). Othello's desperate lunge for truth speaks of the limits of evidence – he can't *prove* that Iago is a devil, a frustrating fact supported by the long critical history of trying to understand this most enigmatic of villains. So the play dramatizes both a scepticism towards, and a plausible convergence of, evidence. Indeed, the latter is in many ways a product of the former: informed belief, i.e. what we mean by truth, arises out of sceptical rationality.

Toward the end of the great seduction scene (3.3), when Othello demands ocular proof, Iago is momentarily pressed, he has to stall for time, but it isn't long before he finds a way to circumvent the demand for 'satisfaction' ('Would I were satisfied!' [390]). Iago debases the very need for solid evidence, for 'facts', transforming it into perversity: 'How satisfied, my Lord? / Would you the supervisor grossly gape on?' (394–5). At this point we get a shift in the way the possibility of irrefutable evidence is represented:

> It were a tedious difficulty, I think,
> To bring them to that prospect; damn them then,
> If ever mortal eyes do see them bolster
> More than their own. What then? How then?
> What shall I say? Where's satisfaction?
> It is impossible you should see this,
> Were they as prime as goats . . . (397–403)

Let me pause over the slippery word, 'then'. Elsewhere in this book, Bruce Smith suggests the importance of prepositions as markers of stage movement.

At this moment, it is the adverb that does that work. Physical movement (an insinuating nod, a sidling, a brisk turning away) lies hidden in the word, but even more subtly, 'then' entails a logical slide and a psychic slip. It is fascinating to watch Iago actually manufacture the impossibility of clear knowledge, while using a word that implies the validity of reasoning from evidence to appropriate interpretation. He moves from an ambiguous subjunctive ('were'), through the interrogative (those four tantalizing questions), to a flat declarative, 'It is impossible'. 'Satisfaction' (erotic, logical, ethical) remains forever out of reach while at the same time it is promised – that's the trap – and then, supposedly, delivered in the next speech ('I lay with Cassio lately ...' [413 ff.]). Thus a transgression that is in fact open to the possibility of ocular proof is transformed into one that can only be inferred from external signs. Othello succumbs to this strategy, argues Katharine Maus, because in a bid to retain a 'fantasy of perfect transparency' (i.e. that Desdemona is transparent to him), he has to 'repress his awareness of his own limitations as an observer'[10] – although the force of her overall argument suggests that the play dramatizes evidence as an *insoluble* epistemological problem. Iago exploits and inverts those limitations, turning reasonable doubt into what appears to be a real basis for certain discovery (i.e. Othello's temporary doubt becomes a kind of permanent proof of Desdemona's guilt). Just when sceptical rationality is called for, Shakespeare provides it through Iago, but only as something strategically staged as a tactic to undermine itself.

In general, then, the play puts two contrasting views of evidence into circulation, both of which are limited, and both of which are still in play in the stories we tell about early modern theatre and those we hear about military adventuring: evidence is either transparent or deceptive. Arguments about interpretation frequently come down to claims about the transparency of one's own evidence and the deceptiveness of others'. A high-profile recent example is the ongoing controversy in Britain about the alleged 'sexing up' of dossiers designed to make the murky intelligence about Iraqi weaponry a transparent ground for action. One thing that Ken Adelman (and perhaps Iago) fails to consider is that even if the view that facts don't matter can be used as a rallying cry before an invasion, afterwards the awkwardness of facts can return to haunt those who ignored their importance.

Facts of course are not always easy to establish, nor do they speak for themselves. They become evidence only when they are made part of an intentional narrative or argument, and, as *Othello* makes clear, assessing intention is a vexed but necessary business. Keeping the dubieties of interpretation and proof in mind, but turning more directly to the craft of theatre history, I would like now to explore some of the ways that evidence is adduced and deployed by scholars and critics in their analyses of 'script' (specifically textual variation) and 'stage' (specifically early performance of *Troilus and Cressida*).

The testimony of texts

Patricia Parker, in her suggestive chapter on *Othello* and *Hamlet* in *Shakespeare from the Margins* claims that the scene at the end of *Othello* 'where Desdemona (both female character and boy actor) undresses for bed . . . would seem to promise "ocular proof" of the "body beneath"' but instead produces only 'an oscillation and radical instability of evidence' characteristic of those plays,[11] and indeed her critical method supports that general view in its intricate inter-weaving of verbal associations. But I would argue that the epistemological prob-lems thus put into circulation do not indicate a radical scepticism about the possibility of using evidence to arrive at true conclusions, nor about the actual stability of concepts like truth or identity. They indicate rather a recognition of deceptive possibilities. And I think there is lots of evidence to suggest that Elizabethans very easily distinguished between boy actor and role, and had no more trouble than we do bringing what William Archer called dual conscious-ness (and Diderot referred to as the 'paradox' of theatrical representation) to bear on what they witnessed on the stage.[12]

But the kinds of views underlying Parker's analysis are prevalent in present-day explorations of early modern 'script' and 'stage' and have affected the way we think about evidence in both textual study and theatre history. In textual study, pluralism is unquestionably dominant. Editions of multi-text versions of plays, such as the three-text *Hamlet*, the synoptic *Hamlet*, the 'Enfolded Hamlets',[13] various calls following on the separate Q and F editions of *Lear* and *Hamlet* for similar double versions of plays such as *Othello* and *Troilus and Cres-sida*, editions of the quartos, bad and good, in the Cambridge series, not to mention the vast amount of scholarship devoted to the linkage of the contin-gency of texts with the contingencies of performance, the insistence on col-laboration, the undermining of authorship, and much more – all this attests to the current distrust not only of certainty, but even of attempts to ascertain an accurate historical sense of the relations between various texts. It also, espe-cially in discussions of what used to be called 'bad quartos', eschews aesthetic evaluation, preferring a kind of democratic equality of all texts. This strikes me as a mistake, just because of the real, if *relative*, autonomy of the aesthetic field, which might indeed be said to have its own forms of intentionality. That there are institutional connections between, say, ideas of value and social position, does not mean that we can hollow out the aesthetic, marking it simply as a disguised form of the political (as Marx himself was aware).[14]

One conclusion that is often drawn from the observation of textual indeter-minacy is that identity was less stable in Shakespeare's day, that notions of authorship were more fluid, and characters conceived in discursive rather than internalized ways. Such thinking can even underpin such counterintuitive views as that not just gender but even biological sex was far from stable. When critics move from textual pluralism to claims about Elizabethan personhood, I want to ask whether the existence of textual variation, evidence for revision, indeterminate (or at least difficult to determine) relations between different versions of the 'same' work, whether such matters support the view that Elizabethans saw texts or actors or personal identities as 'radically unstable' (to return to Parker's formulation). Variable speech prefixes in printed play texts, for example, are now frequently seen as signs, not of compositorial error or authorial carelessness, but of the purely 'discursive' nature of 'personal (non) identity' to quote Peter Stallybrass and Margreta de Grazia.[15] That is, textual marks point to a sense of personhood significantly different from ours, identity, even self-identity, being a post-Enlightenment construct unknown to Elizabethans.

It is interesting what has happened to intentionality in this kind of move. It has been detached from individual consciousness and transformed into a social or cultural phenomenon – it is still there, determining the waywardness of textual designation of persons, but it is not really anybody's *doing*. In their influential article on the materiality of the Shakespearean text, Stallybrass and de Grazia quote Randall Macleod (a.k.a. Random Cloud) to show that the standard present-day spelling of Shakespeare's name is a result of typographical exigency. For them, this 'reflects not a personal investment in the question of identity but rather an economic one in the preservation of typeface' (274). This conclusion derives from assumptions about cultural intention and arises from the critics' desire for a particular reading of the early modern person. Certainly the relation between the adduced evidence and the conclusion is tenuous at best. Even if we accept the thesis that Shakespeare's name came to be spelt with a medial 'e' (not found in any of the surviving signatures) only as a result of printing house practices and the peculiarities of type, how does textual, or typographical, instability support the idea that Shakespeare (or anyone else – Jonson is a much stronger example) had no investment in the question of his own identity? If what is meant by the quoted statement is that early modern *readers* had no investment in the identity of the *author*, that is a slightly less tendentious claim, but easily refuted by data that Stallybrass and de Grazia themselves cite – the brief epistle to the quarto of *Othello* which asserts that 'The Authors name is sufficient to vent his work', as well as by evidence they do not cite, such as the 1609 epistle to *Troilus and Cressida*. There, we are told that the book before the potential buyer is 'a birth of your braine [i.e. Shakespeare's] that neuer under-tooke any thing commicall, vainly'; that indeed 'this authors commedies . . . are so fram'd to the life that they serue for . . . commentaries of all the actions of our liues'. Textual uncertainty, while widespread and real, does not easily support the views often derived from it, that authorship as a concept hardly existed (or was in the process of being invented) in early modern England,[16] that personal identity was radically different from our own sense of it, that indeed early modern people were captivated by indeterminacy.[17]

Not everyone would take such an extreme view as that of Stallybrass and de Grazia (in fact their article might even be read as a provocative joke), but most scholars would regard textual variants in such elements as speech prefixes as valid and worth preserving, under the assumption that different texts command equal respect as historical artefacts. Some, such as Leah Marcus, would go further and claim that trying to determine the relative authority of different texts is an ideologically suspect and anti-historical practice.[18] Faced with the vagaries of printed texts, many recent textual critics have taken the view that features such as squinting or absent punctuation, variant spelling, or multiple meanings of words that get lost when editions adopt modern spelling, indicate a particular, culturally defined cast of thought: they are signs of a conviction that knowledge is 'radically unstable'. Behind this, as I suggested earlier, is an unstated, maybe unconscious, conception of social intentionality. That is, interpreters ascribe a meaning to textual variation derived from a sense that seemingly random differences arise not from the intentions (failed or otherwise) of particular authors, scribes, or compositors, but from a more generalized kind of intentionality realized in the mistakes or differences that comprise the 'evidence'. Hence critics lament the enforcement of uniformity in modern texts, the banishment of wayward and shifting meanings inherent in the fluid orthography and uncertain stage directions of early modern texts. Today's editors, they claim, forgo what is intended (in a broad cultural sense) by the variable text, and hence shut down the possibilities of multiplicity made available to early modern readers and denied to modern ones.[19]

This argument rests on two assumptions, both of which seem far-fetched: first that modernization of spelling, punctuation, etc. somehow fixes meaning and does not allow for ambiguity – but there's plenty of ambiguity around in modernized versions of Shakespeare; and, second, that observed material differences, such as those noticeable in texts, unproblematically support conclusions about cultural attitudes or ways of thinking. But at the very least, such data are confused and ambiguous. Nevertheless, since the larger cultural claims are anchored, or such is the implication, in hard material facts, even including typefaces and ink, they can lay claim to a powerful explanatory weight. There are two distinct levels of intentionality on display in this process: on one level we have the scholar/critic who holds a certain view of early modern ways of knowing and wants to marshal evidence to support that view; and on another, we have the intentions he/she ascribes to the material facts deployed – that they were in a sense put there on purpose, by a mysterious process of cultural dissemination. I think that it makes more sense to talk about individual than about social intention and agency, even though individuals are of course typically situated in institutional settings.

Troilus before the Inns of Court

In this final section I want to hook what I have been saying about texts into questions of performance (the 'stage' side of our project's pairing), by addressing the relation of theatrical and textual evidence, and how they are used to reinforce each other. It is a big issue, one touched on by several of the chapters in this book, so I will tie it down to a couple of questions about *Troilus and Cressida*, a play that has inspired a number of ingenious narratives that seek to muster the scanty, and contradictory, evidence into a meaningful pattern.

The epistle prefaced to the second state of the 1609 quarto of *Troilus* declares that the play was 'neuer clapper-clawd with the palmes of the vulger', nor 'sullied, with the smoaky breath of the multitude'. While the title page of the same issue makes no mention of performance, that of the *first* state of the text declares unequivocally that the play was staged at the Globe.[20] It reads: 'THE / Historie of Troylus / and Cresseida. / *As it was acted by the Kings Maiesties* / seruants at the Globe' (italics in original). This, in concert with the Stationer's Register entry of February 1603, which reads in part, 'The booke of Troilus and Cresseda as yt is acted by my lo: Chamberlens Men', appears to provide clear testimony that the play *was* publicly performed by Shakespeare's company. Here we have a salient example of contradictory, even perhaps deceptive, evidence. Was the original title page an error or a deliberate lie? Or alternatively, are the epistle and the revised title page, which promises the delights of 'the conceited wooing of *Pandarus* Prince of *Licia*', a mistake, or, worse, a ruse designed to lure elite readers (Shakespeare's Pandarus, unlike Homer's, is not referred to as a Prince of anywhere, let alone Licia, nor can he be said to do any real 'wooing')? The epistle certainly seems aimed at potential buyers who pride themselves on not mixing their breath with that of ordinary public theatre patrons. Still, seeing the revised preliminaries as deceitful or wrong has not been the prevailing view, despite the many features of the epistle that would support such an interpretation – especially the privileging of reading over performance, with the consequent denigration of the stage and disparaging references to the vulgar. All in all the epistle seems to derive from a desire to produce a special cachet associated with this play text, one that the author of the epistle declares to be the wittiest of Shakespeare's comedies. Tellingly, however, the epistle-writer himself seems uncertain about the elitist values he espouses; at certain points he implies that the play was a *stage* success. Indeed the rhetoric of the epistle collapses the distinction between performance and reading that the writer is at pains to make. He praises Shakespeare's comedies for being exquisitely 'fram'd to the life' a phrase that suggests he is referring to performance as much as to written texts – 'wit' is the essence of both – and declares all such dull and heauy-witted worldlings, as were neuer capable of the witte of a Commedie, comming by report of them to his [i.e. Shakespeare's] representations, haue found that witte there, that they neuer found in themselues, and haue parted better wittied then they came: feeling an edge of witte set vpon them, more then euer they dreamd they had braine to grinde it on.[21]

Presumably those who 'come by report' and then 'depart' are theatregoers. Thus in seeing Shakespeare's plays (as in reading them) one encounters 'Commentaries, of all the actions of our liues'. Overall, then, the writer contradicts himself since he touts the play for never having been put before the vulgar public, but he also suggests that acquaintance with Shakespeare's comedies would cause his prospective readers to flock to the theatre to see them enacted. In that self-contradiction perhaps lies a clue to the braided nature of print and performance in Shakespeare's theatre. Readers and critics today often think of page and stage, printed and oral, as sharply demarcated, or at least assume that in the minds of early modern writers there was a fairly firm distinction between the two. But texts like the *Troilus* epistle call that assumption into question.

Beginning with Peter Alexander in 1929, a diverse set of critics, including Nosworthy, Honigmann, Taylor and Elton,[22] have argued that the right way to interpret the evidence of the double quarto is to conclude that the first title page was wrong or misleading – i.e. that the play in the form it was now being published had not been performed at the Globe, that the publisher realized this after the print run had begun, that an explanatory preface was quickly got up, and the new title page was composed to replace the original.[23] In other words, most interpreters have read the apparent intentions of the epistle straightforwardly. Alexander, basing his reading on the special characteristics of the text itself, suggested that the play was composed for the Inns of Court. It was its abrasive satirical style, its fondness for witty insult, and even, uncharacteristically for Shakespeare, its abuse of the audience, that made the suggestion plausible, even though there is no documentary evidence to support it. One reason for the popularity of the Inns theory might be the play's mocking exploitation of the divide between elite and popular culture. As in textual studies, where terms such as 'corruption' have been said to betray a scholarly anti-theatricalism tinged with distrust of the vulgar, so a similar (perhaps unconscious) attitude may be detectable in the way scholars have read the non-evidence for the early performance history of *Troilus and Cressida*. If the play is represented in the epistle as 'caviar to the general', should we assume it was *designed* to have a strictly elite appeal? In other words, does the Inns theory arise from a modern form of the snobbery discernible in the preface?

Whatever its source, the Inns theory combined rhetorical evidence from the play with a particular (and I would say tendentious) reading of external documentary evidence to construct an argument about early performance history. Part of the intention was no doubt to solve the problem of structure and genre posed by the play's oddity. The problem of structure is, in turn, intricately linked to a particular textual puzzle: the double appearance in the folio text of the play of a key passage – at the end of 5.3 and again, with slight variations, immediately before Pandarus' epilogue (in Q it appears only as the lead-up to the epilogue). Hence, one of the impulses behind the resort to the Inns of Court theory has been the intractability of certain textual problems and their complicated relation to the uncertainties of early performance. That is why textual critics such as Alexander, Honigmann, and Taylor have been prominent in exercising their wit on the matter. The passage in question runs as follows (here quoted from F in the 5.3 version):

> *Pand.* Why, but heare you?
> *Troy.* Hence brother lackie; ignomie and shame
> Pursue thy life, and liue aye with thy name.[24]

This bit of textual repetition has been adduced to support a theory of revision, one that, if true, would radically affect the original 'intention' of the play – in particular its generic shape. Put succinctly, the play's original design as tragedy (with the quoted passage intended for 5.3 and without the epilogue) was shifted to satire at some crucial point in its development, and that point was, so it is argued, the decision to specifically mark the play for performance at the Inns.[25]

Commentators have long noted that the doubled passage seems to fit better in what some have regarded as its 'original' position in 5.3, since what is Pandarus suddenly doing on the battlefield at the end? So, as developed in the wake of Alexander by J. M. Nosworthy a generation ago and, in a somewhat different way by Honigmann, we have a scenario something like the following: Shakespeare originally intended to write a tragedy for the public stage but in the course of writing abandoned this aim, perhaps taking advantage of an offer to provide an entertainment for the Inns,[26] and bent the play toward satire, by interpolating (Nosworthy's term) a number of comic sequences into his tragic plot, and, most prominently, by designing a scurrilous epilogue. Many scholars who have accepted this scenario (though not, for reasons to be explained below, Nosworthy or Taylor) argue that Shakespeare therefore moved the brief rejection of Pandarus from the end of 5.3 as it appears in F to its Q/F spot just before the end in order to provide a suitable transition to Pandarus' epilogue – suitable that is to the satire, though out of keeping with the fictional location and the solemn tone.

The Inns of Court, with their taste for invective, ridicule, and scorn, offered a convenient ground for the shift. Shakespeare, says Nosworthy, converted his 'half-written tragedy' into a 'burlesque', a view of the text developed in detail by Elton many years later (though Elton does not concern himself directly with the revision theory). After 1603, Nosworthy continues, Shakespeare returned to his original tragic intent with a performance at the Globe (he thus rejects the claims of the epistle writer and the implication of the revised title page). His view of the doubled passage is different from Alexander's (and that of many later commentators who regard the F text as deriving from 'foul papers') since he sees the appearance of Pandarus at the end of 5.3 as the later version, and argues that in remaking the tragedy Shakespeare 'dispensed with the now inappropriate Epilogue' (81). Gary Taylor, while rejecting some of Nosworthy's more outlandish notions, builds his analysis of textual provenance on this argument; he quotes with approval one bit of evidence cited by Nosworthy that I think worth attending to:

> The Epilogue . . . is certainly . . . addressed to the Inn of Court performance, in which the incongruity [of Pandarus on the battlefield] would have been unremarkable . . . A valediction in which a character confronts the audience with such sentiments . . . would normally be received with acclamation by a student audience . . . Nor have these lines any real meaning except in an Inn of Court setting. No character in his right mind would be likely to make his will ('my will shall *here* be made') on the apron at the Globe.[27]

This last claim bears thinking about – the rhetoric is strong, even imperious, but it may be objected that the word 'here' is taken rather too literally, especially if we compare other epilogues, like those of Puck and Prospero, where 'here' denotes a subtle combination of fictional locale and the stage itself. Metaphorically speaking, an imagined space that combines battlefield and public theatre might be a more suitable spot to gather up and bequeath disease than a private precinct. And even if we were to read 'here' literally, the notion of preparing a will in a raucous law school hall is almost as eccentric as doing so on a public stage! Pandarus addresses the audience as 'Brethren and sisters of the hold-door trade', but there were no 'sisters' resident at the Inns, a fact that no proponent of the Inns of Court theory has ever mentioned.[28] And why, finally, should we accept the idea that 'such sentiments' would *normally* be acclaimed by students is left entirely unclear. So the story designed to fit the evidence seems tenuous. Indeed, the whole scenario suggests that the various critics are caught like Othello in the grip of narrative, trapped by their own stories. After all, Pandarus' remarks include everyone in the act of pandering, certainly not a flattering address to the audience but not one confined to lawyers either. Nevertheless, on this basis, Taylor constructed an ingenious argument for the provenance of the two texts which has led, famously, to the play now frequently being read by students in the Oxford and Norton editions, either without the epilogue which appears in both Q and F (Oxford), or with it printed in italics as an 'extended conclusion' (Norton).[29] The attempt to sort out a textual crux has thus led to an elaborate theatre-historical narrative which then is used to support a questionable editorial decision.

A key problem with the mode of argumentation in this kind of analysis is that assumptions about textual provenance are used rather too loosely to support assumptions about theatrical provenance and vice versa. Mutually supportive they can and must be, but there is also a danger of circular logic.[30] Perhaps a more suitable model would be that of a loop, or a feedback mechanism of some kind, one that allows for details to augment a global view (what Adelman calls 'the big picture') and the global view in turn to make further sense of the details. Sorting out the different levels of intentionality might be a way to begin to clear the ground: to distinguish between, say, Shakespeare's revisionary intentions; those associated with both the personal expectations of the students at the Inns and the submerged elitism of scholars; those behind the writing of the epistle and the revision of the title page; those linked to theatrical production through, for example, the making of 'prompt books';[31] and the critical desire to sort out generic as well as textual problems. While postmodern theory has been salutary in that it has helped us get past interpretation of textual evidence in terms of a single, authorial intention, it leads to problems insofar as it tends to spawn distrust or outright rejection of intentionality *tout court*, or to subtend the substitution of broadly cultural intentions in the place of those of particularly situated social agents. It seems best to adduce multiple intentions in the interests of developing a 'thick description' of intentionality.

Concluding remarks

I think it fair to say that, over the past couple of decades, theatre history has expanded to include a wider range of material than it originally set out to encompass, and the border between it and cultural history, always uncertain, has become even more so. Given that, problems of evidence in the field are bound to become more complex and vexed. Recognition of this interpenetration is no doubt the reason to hold a series of conferences devoted to redefining theatre history. In an essay in the first volume in this series, Thomas Postlewait examined the evidence for Shakespeare biography, juxtaposing the documentary with the anecdotal (like the story of young William the deer-poacher) and appraising the truth value of each, taking into account the critique of documentary evidence mounted by a range of poststructuralist critics. His careful conclusion was that the two are inevitably linked, that despite efforts to squeeze out truth from fancy, sometimes that polarity does not correspond to the one between anecdotal and documentary (which, as the preface to *Troilus and Cressida* suggests, can itself be self-contradictory and will only yield a meaning within a narrative). '[D]espite their logical opposition', he remarks, they share 'a kind of doppelgänger relationship' (23).[32] Accepting this means accepting a much wider context for evidence than is traditionally allowed into historical research. This is not, however, out of keeping with recent historiography. Writing in *PMLA*, James Wilkinson has shown that, while the remains of the past constitute a huge domain of which the evidence traditionally used by historians is a small subset, in recent years the range of what counts as evidence has widened enormously.[33] Stories, such as those told of the lad Shakespeare, are part of the historical record, even if they are proven 'untrue'. They indicate attitudes or feelings, desires or fears.

Hence there are varieties of evidence, and much of human enquiry into the past is 'forensic' – that is, it depends on 'circumstantial' evidence. Michael Bristol, drawing on a number of philosophical accounts, makes this point; while he notes that forensic enquiry is 'aimed primarily at persuasion',[34] this does not mean that its evidence is not reliable. He suggests that the relation between the explanatory power of a given hypothesis and the kinds of evidence used to support it can be rigorous, even though it is not 'veridical' (that is, in some ways incontrovertible). While the term 'circumstantial evidence' suggests a lack of credibility, Bristol shows that it frequently functions as a perfectly adequate guide to highly plausible conclusions. The key requirement, as Bristol points out, is a persuasive 'explanatory relationship between the evidence assembled and the hypothesis proposed' (39). This approach is useful, especially if one wants to adjudicate between alternative hypotheses, such as whether 'Shakespeare did or did not revise his plays'. It is a little harder to apply Bristol's model to interpretive moves where different levels of evidence are adduced and hypotheses are not strictly formed or tested – as for example in the attempts to explain the conundrum of the texts and early stage history of *Troilus and Cressida*. But in principle, the possibility of persuasive accounts based on a convergence and concatenation of circumstantial evidence is not only real but valuable and productive.

Still, there are dangers. In a recent article in *The New Yorker* entitled 'The Unknown',[35] Jeffrey Goldberg describes the debates about evidence currently circulating at the Pentagon and the CIA. (The particular occasion was the relation between the Iraqi regime and Al Qaeda, but the issue is much broader and more serious than any one issue.) The main concern is with the interpretation of ambiguous data. The apparent unwillingness on the part of operatives to draw conclusions beyond what can be closely linked to what is known is coming under increasing fire by strategists (Ken Adelman provides an example) and Defense Department philosophers such as Donald Rumsfeld. Rumsfeld is excited by the prospect of getting beyond what is characterized as the 'poverty of expectations' (about what an enemy might be up to) and the 'failure of imagination' involved in not subjecting the evidence to alternative hypotheses. The head of the CIA, George Tenet, agrees, encouraging his analysts to 'lower the threshold of what is credible'; since 'nothing is crystal clear', it behoves them to move 'away from linear thinking' (45). One member of the Pentagon team, intriguingly named Douglas Feith, describes this movement in intelligence gathering in terms that seem appropriate to literary criticism, insisting, through an analogy with different moviegoers coming away with different readings of a particular film, on the necessity for multiple interpretations (an injunction to read the evidence according to personal desire). This move to a kind of post-structuralist pluralism in the international intelligence world, which clearly has grave consequences for policy and even military action, is highlighted by former CIA director, Robert Gates, who remarks that the ambiguity of evidence 'has to do with "intentions"'. If, he says, 'the stakes and the consequences are small, you're going to want ninety-percent assurance'. When the stakes are high, however, 'you have to be prepared to go forward with a lot lower level of confidence in the evidence you have' (47). Guessing at intentions is sufficient if there is enough at stake. This takes us back to Adelman's justification for war founded on the council scene in *Othello*, and to *Troilus*, a play that probes the foundations of war much more insistently than *Othello* and one that, as we have seen, tends to attract strong explanatory (and questionable) narratives just because of the paucity of evidence. That policy-makers might be ready to go ahead on the basis of what looks like a deconstructive turn in the assessment of information is indeed worrying. Keeping an eye on interpretive intention seems salutary not just in our restricted field but in the much larger one in which we are situated.

With this in mind, I would like to wrap up with a number of propositions that arise, some rather indirectly, from what I have been saying. In doing the work we do, it would be helpful, I think, to keep them in mind:

1. All evidence is in some way staged; i.e. it only becomes evidence when it is made part of an argument or interpretation, usually one that is embedded in some kind of narrative. Hence it is in a strong sense always rhetorical.
2. That is to say, evidence is inevitably linked to intention as well as persuasion. There is no evidence without intentionality.
3. When adducing, deploying, or assessing evidence, therefore, intentions need to be taken into account – whether it is the intentions of the interpreter, or of those who produced the data in the first place, or both.
4. One aspect of the evidence we examine and make use of in theatre history and textual criticism is aesthetic. The interpretive process cannot ignore the

aesthetic, but rather needs to acknowledge what might be called aesthetic intentionality.

5. When approaching the problem of evidence with specific reference to 'script and stage in early modern England', what the above propositions mean is that some account of intention (either authorial or collaborative) is unavoidable when scripts are in question – whether the plays themselves, their preliminary matter, or related documents.

(a) A corollary of this is that the possibility of deliberate deception might need to qualify any claim – as it does, for example, if we consider the epistle to *Troilus and Cressida*.

6. Renaissance dramatists such as Shakespeare and Jonson were fully aware of, and often dramatized, the conundrums associated with evidence, but they also avoided the totally destabilizing effects of such an awareness that we associate with postmodernism. They had a healthy regard for truth as supported by evidence, even as they were deeply aware of its potential for deception. Moreover, they were aware of the importance of reckoning with the intentionality of evidence.

7. This means, finally, that in assessing the use of evidence by present-day cultural critics, whether in the academy or the Pentagon, who may be inclined to see the fluid instability of identity as characteristic of early modern or of contemporary culture, we ought to be very attentive to the sorts of intentionality (or indeed the absence of any intentionality) that such critics assume or infer.

Notes

1. While this might sound like a revival of long-discredited new historicist practice, I am mainly concerned with the ways that explanatory narratives exploit data for persuasive purposes.
2. I am indebted to Coppélia Kahn for drawing my attention to this broadcast. As she says, 'it is crucial to establish a critical perspective on the invocation of Shakespeare's name in complex political contexts fraught with contingencies' (private communication).
3. I quote from the transcript of the talk available at http://www.npr.org/programs/atc/transcripts/2002/aug/020826.adelman.html. It should be noted that NPR does not vouch for the exact accuracy of the transcriptions in their electronic archives.
4. I'd guess that the misquotation here indicates a tin ear more than it does a deliberate twisting of textual evidence. The text actually reads: 'yet do they all confirm / A Turkish fleet...' (*Othello* 1.3.7–8). All quotations are taken from *The Riverside Shakespeare*, 2nd edn (Boston: Houghton Mifflin, 1997).
5. http://www.moversandshakespeares.com/index.html.
6. In fact, in a weird twist, the extreme right, represented here by Adelman, has adopted a position very similar to that of strong cultural materialism – that Shakespeare sup-

ports, or is complicit with, the brute exercise of power – indicating that a belief in Shakespeare's universality can lead to similar conclusions as a denial of it.

7. His own failure to properly take note of the 'facts' of the text is an ironic reminder of this.

8. On the force of the term in *Troilus and Cressida*, see Frank Kermode, '"Opinion" in *Troilus and Cressida*', in *Teaching the Text*, ed. Susanne Kappeler and Norman Bryson (London: Routledge & Kegan Paul, 1983), 164–79. M. R. Ridley's gloss (Arden 2nd edn, London: Methuen, 1962) on the Duke's phrase, followed by Ernst Honigmann (Arden 3rd edn, Walton-on-Thames: Thomas Nelson, 1997) is that public opinion 'determines what is to be done'.

9. Coke declared that witnessing was the least reliable evidence, 'seeing such variety amongst witnesses . . . as few of them agree together' (quoted in Karen Cunningham, *Imaginary Betrayals: Subjectivity and the Discourses of Treason in Early Modern England* (Philadelphia: University of Pennsylvania Press, 2002), 48.

10. Katharine Maus, *Inwardness and Theater in the English Renaissance* (Chicago: University of Chicago Press, 1995), 120–1.

11. Patricia Parker, *Shakespeare from the Margins: Language, Culture, Context* (Chicago: University of Chicago Press, 1996), 266.

12. See my discussion of this question in Anthony B. Dawson and Paul Yachnin, *The Culture of Playgoing in Shakespeare's England: a Collaborative Debate* (Cambridge: Cambridge University Press, 2001), 18–20, 32–4.

13. I refer to *The Three-text Hamlet: Parallel Texts of the First and Second Quartos and First Folio*, ed. Paul Bertram and Bernice W. Kliman (New York: AMS, 1991); Jesús Tronch-Pérez, *A Synoptic Hamlet: a Critical-Synoptic Edition of the Second Quarto and First Folio Texts of Hamlet* (Sederi: Universita de València, 2002); and Kliman's new project on 'enfolding'.

14. Adorno's paradoxical comments on this issue are apropos: 'Take a look at the widespread inclination (which to this day has not been mitigated by education [we might say that nowadays it has been *exacerbated* by education]) to perceive art in terms of extra-aesthetic or pre-aesthetic criteria. This tendency is, on the one hand, a mark of atrocious backwardness . . . On the other hand, there is no denying that the tendency is promoted by something in art itself. If art is perceived strictly in aesthetic terms, then it cannot be properly perceived in aesthetic terms'. T. W. Adorno, *Aesthetic Theory*, trans. C. Lenhardt (London and NY: Routledge & Kegan Paul, 1984), 9.

15. Margreta de Grazia and Peter Stallybrass, 'The Materiality of the Shakespearean Text', *Shakespeare Quarterly*, 44 (1993), 273.

16. The example of early Christian authors such as Augustine and Jerome should be enough to put that tired notion to rest – see Mark Vessey, '"Erasmus' Jerome: the Publishing of a Christian Author', *Erasmus of Rotterdam Society Yearbook*, 14 (1994), 62–99.

17. This last (implicit) claim is itself a weapon in an ideological battle against up-tight positivists and essentialists, but as we saw earlier in relation to Ken Adelman's reading of *Othello*, indeterminacy can be used against those who would wield it for political purposes.

18. See, for example, Leah Marcus, *Unediting the Renaissance: Shakespeare, Marlowe, Milton* (London: Routledge, 1996).

19. In a recent seminar on text at Stratford that I attended, two of the ten or so papers took exactly this line.

20. The two versions of the text, both published in 1609 by Richard Bonian and Henry Walley and printed by George Eld, are identical, except for the addition of the epistle and the altered title page.

21. *Shakespeare's Plays in Quarto*, ed. Michael J. B. Allen and Kenneth Muir (Berkeley and Los Angeles: University of California Press, 1981), 705.

22. See J. M. Nosworthy, *Shakespeare's Occasional Plays: Their Origin and Transmission* (London: Edward Arnold, 1965); E. A. J. Honigmann, 'The Date and Revision of *Troilus and Cressida*', in Jerome McGann ed., *Textual Criticism and Literary Interpretation* (Chicago: University of Chicago P, 1985) 38–54, and *Myriad-Minded Shakespeare* (New York: St. Martin's Press, 1989) ch. 7; Gary Taylor, '*Troilus and Cressida*: Bibliography, Performance and Interpretation', *Shakespeare Studies*, 15 (1982), 99–136; and William R. Elton, *Shakespeare's Troilus and Cressida and the Inns of Court Revels* (Aldershot: Ashgate, 2000). These critics often disagree, but all read the text, though for different reasons, as unsuited to the public stage. Taylor argues that the play must have been produced at the Globe some time, but without the epilogue; for him Q represents the text Shakespeare originally wrote for the play's 'premiere' at the Inns.

23. Some scholars, including Taylor, have speculated that the epistle was originally written back in 1603, shortly after the play itself, and was then 'found' with the Q MS at a late stage in the printing, thus necessitating the change in the title page.

24. As the passage appears in the final scene, both Q and F read 'broker' for 'brother' and there are other minor variants.

25. Some too, including Taylor, have seen the play as having a satiric intent from the outset. This view has recently been bolstered by the lengthy study by Elton (see n. 20), who lays out in detail a large number of parallels, some rather less convincing than others, between *Troilus* and texts known to have been used at the Inns. At the same time, the witty satirical style of the play has also been adduced as evidence of its immersion in the so-called war of the theatres, a view recently given renewed currency in a book by James Bednarz, *Shakespeare and the Poets' War* (New York: Columbia University Press, 2001).

26. Honigmann is sceptical about the Inns theory and speculates about an early performance at Cambridge; he suggests that Shakespeare originally planned a tragedy climaxing in the death of Troilus but then changed his mind. See 'Date and Revision' and *Myriad-Minded Shakespeare* (cited in n. 22).

27. Nosworthy, *Shakespeare's Occasional Plays*, 81, as quoted in Taylor, '*Troilus and Cressida*', 103–4.

28. I make these points in my recent edition of the play in the Cambridge Shakespeare series.

29. For an extended critique of Taylor's theory of original (for the Inns) and revised (for the Globe) versions, see Phebe Jensen, 'The Textual Politics of *Troilus and Cressida*', *Shakespeare Quarterly*, 46 (1995), 414–23. It should be noted that Taylor later apparently abandoned his theory of an Inns of Court performance, even though he did not alter his views about the provenance of the MSS behind Q and F which depended, to a large degree, on the Inns of Court theory. See Stanley Wells and Gary Taylor, *William Shakespeare: a Textual Companion* (New York: Oxford University Press, 1987), 438, where the note on 'Additional Passage' B. 21 explicitly repudiates the idea.

30. I have discussed this problem more extensively, with particular reference to different examples from *Troilus and Cressida*, in 'Correct Impressions: Editing and Evidence

in the Wake of Post-modernism', in *In Arden: Editing Shakespeare*, ed. Ann Thomson and Gordon McMullan (London: Thomson, 2003), 31–47.

31. A vexed term, as William Long and Paul Werstine have clearly shown. See William B. Long, 'John a Kent and John a Cumber: an Elizabethan Playbook and its Implications', in *Shakespeare and Dramatic Tradition: Essays in Honor of S. F. Johnson*, ed. W. R. Elton and William B. Long (Newark: University of Delaware Press, 1989), 125–43; and Paul Werstine, 'Narratives About Printed Shakespeare Texts: "Foul Papers" and "Bad" Quartos', *Shakespeare Quarterly*, 41 (1990), 65–86.

32. 'The Criteria for Evidence: Anecdotes in Shakespearean Biography, 1709–2000'. Professor Postlewait very kindly sent me his paper in advance of publication.

33. 'A Choice of Fictions: Historians, Memory, and Evidence', *PMLA*, 111 (1996), 80–1. In this article Wilkinson goes on to suggest the 'advantages of indirection – of choosing to exploit flawed evidence whose greatest virtue may reside in its irreducible imperfections' (81).

34. Michael D. Bristol, 'How Good Does Evidence Have to Be?', in *Textual and Theatrical Shakespeare: Questions of Evidence*, ed. Edward Pechter (Iowa City: University of Iowa Press, 1996), 24.

35. 10 February 2003, 40–7.

Part III
What is a Play?

6

Drama in the Archives: Recognizing Medieval Plays

Claire Sponsler

My title contains an obvious nod towards Natalie Zemon Davis' influential book about 'fiction in the archives', a 1987 study that examined records of royal pardon cases for the stories told in them by people desperate to save their lives after having been convicted of homicide. In Davis' hands, these legal documents revealed the considerable literary talents of ordinary people and in so doing asked us to reconsider our assumptions about the boundaries that supposedly separate not just 'the real' or 'the historical' from 'the fictional', but also literary from documentary texts.[1] Although it is situated primarily within the context of debates among historians about the nature of historiographic evidence, Davis' account makes an apt point of departure for a rethinking of the drama of pre-Reformation England – and particularly a rethinking that takes as its central concern the question I wish to pose, which is how we know a medieval play when we see one – given that the most important scholarly undertaking of the field in the twentieth century has been a return to the archives. That return came in the form of a systematic attempt, sponsored by the Toronto-based *Records of Early English Drama (REED)* project, to identify and publish all extant external references to early drama in England.[2]

It is no exaggeration to say that *REED's* findings have radically revised scholarly assumptions about medieval drama. *REED* has shown, for instance, that there was no such genre as Corpus Christi plays, but rather episodic biblical dramas that could be performed on Corpus Christi but also at Whitsun; that folk drama, like Robin Hood plays, were the most frequent kinds of performance and often took place on holy days and in religious settings; that drama was a central part of the life of towns and parishes all over England; that the distinction between 'medieval' and 'Renaissance' drama can no longer be maintained (the biblical plays of Coventry, Chester and York lasted until 1575 or 1580 and 'medieval' morality plays flourished alongside sixteenth-century school plays); and that the commercial theatre, in the form of companies of travelling players, existed well before the age of Shakespeare.[3]

REED has also shown that surviving play texts do not accurately reflect kinds and amounts of early drama: the large-scale biblical cycle plays such as York's, which have been taken as the quintessential form of medieval drama, in actuality represent only a small fraction of extant performance records (David Bevington estimates it at 16 per cent), and morality plays were even rarer.[4]

In the midst of all these surprises, perhaps most unexpected of all is what *REED* has not discovered: new texts of plays. After years of diligent archival work, the recognized corpus of Middle English drama still consists of the same long-known handful of texts from northern and south-eastern England (and Cornwall). It is worth pausing to recall what those texts are. Along with some fragments and single pageant manuscripts, four extant sets of plays from the north have been identified: the York register (c. 1463–77), the Towneley manuscript (c. 1500), two pageants from Coventry (both of them revisions by Robert Croo dated 1534), and the five antiquarian Chester manuscripts (1591–1607).[5] The plays from the south-east, while more diverse than those from the north, are for the most part contained in three manuscripts: there are the Digby plays (*Mary Magdalen*, end of the fifteenth century; *The Killing of the Children*, c. 1512; a farcical *Slaughter of the Innocents*; *The Conversion of Saint Paul*, 1500–25; and a fragment of *Wisdom*, c. 1470–5; all in Bodleian MS Digby 133, owned in the mid-sixteenth century by Myles Blomefeld, a collector of books); the Macro plays (*Castle of Perseverance*, 1400–25; *Mankind*, 1474–9; and a complete *Wisdom*, all in Folger MS V.a.354, which was owned at some point by a monk named Hyngham of Bury St Edmunds); and the N-Town play (a compilation of plays originally of separate and earlier origin brought together by the scribe-compiler in or after the last decade of the fifteenth century, in Cotton Vespasian D.8; the N-town play is also sometimes referred to as *Ludus Coventriae* because of a flyleaf note giving it that name, and is also sometimes called 'the Hegge manuscript' based on the name of a family that once owned the manuscript).[6]

What these manuscripts suggest is that in most cases the scripts of Middle English plays survived only under unusual circumstances, often involving antiquarian interests, and only at a point past the time when the plays had presumably been performed. Before the end of the fourteenth century, as Alexandra Johnston has noted, and indeed for much of the fifteenth century as well, nearly all the evidence for the existence of theatre in England is incidental, and that evidence for the most part does not include scripts of plays.[7]

One reason for the lack of surviving scripts is that many early plays probably existed in forms that were bad candidates for preservation, such as part sheets, roles, or performance copies not often of a status deemed worth preservation in civic or literary records. Another reason is that dramatic texts were treated as ephemera, and were assumed to have fulfilled their cultural function once the performance was over, no matter how elaborate or expensive that performance had been. Thus we get incidental mention of performances in account books, chronicles, and other public and private records, but only occasional preservation of their verbal texts, which can occasionally be found quoted in chronicles or other accounts of the performance. It is also possible, however, that more medieval plays have survived than we currently acknowledge and that they lie hidden within manuscripts that conceal their distinctively performative features. Why might that be the case? There are at least two answers: because, as scholars have long noted, early drama was produced within a culture in which a pervasive theatricality blurred the boundaries between representational forms such as liturgy, literature, and play; and because, as scholars have been slower to recognize, that blurring of boundaries was transferred to the physical appearance of the plays that were copied into surviving manuscripts.

Both kinds of boundary-blurring have typically been treated as problems to be surmounted in order to identify performances and extract them from the tangle of cultural activities in which they are enmeshed. At least since the time of Karl Young, who in his monumental *Drama of the Medieval Church* considered as dramas only those texts that contained rubrics explicitly describing costume and action, scholars have relied upon explicit mention of stage properties, costumes, and other signs of staging in order to identify early plays.[8] But agreeing upon what constitute signs of a performance has proven hard. Lawrence Clopper, for instance, has raised questions about references to saints' *ludi* that are often taken to signal plays, but that in his view point to games, processions, or other non-dramatic activities associated with the saint's day rather than plays proper.[9] If terminology and genre definitions are a problem for the identification of medieval dramas, as Clopper shows, so too are scribal techniques that do not always differentiate speaking parts or include stage directions, with the result that plays do not always look distinctively like plays.[10] The upshot of all this is that, as Ian Lancashire has said, sometimes 'what is and what is not dramatic is not obvious'.[11]

The problem of recognizing medieval plays takes on added importance in the case of John Lydgate, monk of the great Benedictine abbey of Bury St Edmunds, who was the most prolific and best-known writer of fifteenth-century England. The so-called mummings and entertainments that form a not insignificant part of his prodigious output are the fullest extant texts of royal and civic ceremonies in England before the sixteenth century and offer crucial access to the processes whereby such performances were created and then preserved in written form. Despite this substantial body of work, Lydgate looms small in standard histories of medieval and early modern drama. A recent assessment of Lydgate's performance pieces as 'primarily monovocal, allegorical, descriptive, "read" texts', devoid of such dramatic elements as verbal exchanges, mimesis and interaction among characters – and thus not really categorizable as drama at all – aptly sums up prevailing opinion.[12]

Lydgate deserves a closer look, however, for what his works reveal about the mutable nature of medieval performance – especially its fluid relations with other cultural forms – and about what the artefacts within which it was transmitted both reveal and conceal about early performance practices. Recent trends in theatre history have rightfully insisted upon the materiality of the text and have called for attentiveness to the documentary practices through which dramatic texts have been preserved and disseminated. In the case of Lydgate's mummings, such attentiveness asks for a rethinking of what constitutes 'drama' in late medieval England, what shape its relations with other forms of cultural activity took, and why and how dramatic texts entered into the written record.

Lydgate presents a uniquely useful opportunity for such a rethinking, given the extraordinary fact, rarely encountered within the corpus of medieval drama, of a known writer of verses designed for performance whose work has been preserved by a known scribe. Nearly all of Lydgate's performance pieces are available to us today thanks to John Shirley, the fifteenth-century scribe who included them in three anthologies compiled between the late 1420s and the late 1440s. Not only did Shirley copy these pieces but he also carefully attributed many of them to Lydgate, briefly noting their performance contexts and mentioning the occasions and audiences for which they were designed. This information is crucial, since while internal evidence implies some sort of performance context, without Shirley's rubrics few of these texts would today be identified as performances of any kind. Take away Shirley, and we would have little reason for thinking that Lydgate had ever turned his hand to writing verses for performances.[13]

The larger issue that Shirley's transmission of Lydgate's performance pieces touches on is the nature of the textual evidence for drama before the sixteenth century: what do the ways in which plays are recorded in manuscripts tell us about early performances? Should the canon of early theatre be expanded to include texts that do not look like plays but that may have been part of some sort of public performance? And perhaps most importantly, should we reconsider the tendency of theatre historians to view 'medieval drama' as a distinct and identifiable cultural category rather than an activity that merges – both in practice and in the documents that record that practice – with other creative activities produced within a broadly performative culture?

The remainder of this chapter will focus on seven short texts that at least since Henry MacCracken included them in his edition of Lydgate's minor poems have been identified as mummings.[14] Six of these texts, which for the sake of convenience I will refer to as mummings (even though only four of the texts are described by Shirley as having been associated with mummings), were apparently composed in a flush of energy between 1427 and 1429, when Lydgate was at the peak of his career as a public poet, with the major projects of the *Troy Book* and the *Siege of Thebes* behind him and the *Fall of Princes* yet to come. These six mummings survive uniquely in the Shirlean MS Trinity College Cambridge R.3.20 and in John Stow's copy of R.3.20 made in the sixteenth century, now MS BL Additional 29729. A seventh mumming was copied into Shirley's last anthology, MS Bodley Ashmole 59, which is datable by internal evidence to between 1447 and 1449. Each of the mummings is accompanied by a headnote in which Shirley identifies the genre of text that follows, assigns it to Lydgate, describes its occasion, and gives other details about it. Three of the mummings, according to Shirley's headings, were designed as Christmas entertainments for the young Henry VI and his mother Katherine; the four others were civic entertainments.

Shirley's importance as a preserver and disseminator of English literary texts is well established. A number of Middle English poems are known only from his manuscripts, and attributions and contexts are available for other texts only on the basis of information contained in his headings and marginal glosses. Shirley is especially crucial for establishing the Lydgate canon, as Derek Pearsall has noted, and is the sole authority for a number of Lydgate's minor poems, including all of the mummings.

Although there is agreement about Shirley's crucial role as a disseminator of texts, the precise nature of his scribal activities has been a matter of debate, with one camp viewing him as a commercial publisher who ran a scriptorium in London and the other seeing him as an antiquarian who copied books chiefly for his own pleasure.[15] Margaret Connolly, however, in a recent book-length study, argues convincingly that Shirley was neither commercial publisher nor antiquarian book-lover, but rather a compiler working within a context shaped by the 'culture of service' that he encountered in the course of his career in the household of Richard Beauchamp, the Earl of Warwick, with which Shirley had been associated since at least 1403. Connolly believes that Shirley compiled his anthologies with the assumption that they would be read by 'bothe the gret and the commune' of that household, as Shirley states in the preface to the first of his anthologies. Moreover, Connolly asserts, Shirley was no antiquarian collector of authors from the past, but instead filled his manuscripts with the writings of contemporaries and especially the work of one particular living poet – John Lydgate.[16]

Shirley's three large anthologies indeed all contain a substantial number of poems by Lydgate, along with other verse and prose pieces in French, English, and Latin. MS BL Additional 16165, compiled in the late 1420s, contains fourteen pieces by Lydgate, including *A Procession at Corpus Christi*, out of some forty-five texts that encompass works by Trevisa, Chaucer, Halsham, Edward of York and Richard Beauchamp. MS Trinity College Cambridge R.3.20, which was compiled in the early 1430s and which contains six of the mummings, is even more obviously centred on Lydgate, with, in its current form, twenty-six pieces by Lydgate out of some seventy-five texts (the actual proportion of work by Lydgate included in this anthology is even larger than these numbers suggest, since twenty-seven of the non-Lydgatian pieces are short, anonymous poems in French; the other named authors in the anthology include Chaucer, Suffolk, Hoccleve and Brampton). Shirley's last anthology, MS Bodley Ashmole 59, compiled in the late 1440s, contains thirty-five pieces by Lydgate out of around eighty texts, among them works by Gower, Scogan and Chaucer.[17]

What do the contents of these three anthologies tell us about Shirley's motives in compiling them and about his reasons for including poems by Lydgate? The first thing we can say is that with the exception of the *Temple of Glas* (which appears in Additional 16165), all of the Lydgate texts in the three anthologies are short – deliberately so, it seems, since Shirley copies, for example, extracts from the *Fall of Princes* but not the entire poem. Secondly, almost all of the Lydgate poems in these anthologies appear only once and are not recopied in Shirley's later anthologies. Combined with this lack of repetition, the emphasis on short pieces suggests that Shirley's aim was to collect and preserve Lydgate's shorter works, including those like the mummings that were occasional in nature and that might otherwise have disappeared; having once done so, Shirley apparently had no reason for recopying these same poems again elsewhere. The choice of texts, while apparently designed to gather together and save Lydgate's short, ephemeral texts from oblivion, also seems to have been geared to the tastes of Shirley's intended audience – particularly so in the case of Trinity R.3.20 – that is, readers within the Beauchamp household that formed the milieu for Shirley's efforts when in the 1420s he first turned his hand to copying literary texts.[18]

Why Lydgate? Connections seem part of the reason. Although there is no direct evidence that Shirley knew Lydgate, because both men moved in the same aristocratic and civic circles it is highly likely that they were acquainted. Shirley (c. 1366–1456) was roughly the same age as Lydgate (c. 1370–1450), and like Lydgate had close ties with the Lancastrian affinity, through his attachment to the household of the Earl of Warwick, who was appointed tutor to Henry VI in 1428. Records show Shirley in Warwick's retinue in France and England from 1403 until the late 1420s, when he appears to have settled in London where, while still maintaining connections with the aristocratic world of Warwick, he gradually developed associations with the city's merchant class.[19]

If personal acquaintance was one impetus for Shirley's copying of Lydgate's poetry, as it seems also to have been in the case of other authors Shirley included in his anthologies, so was an apparent desire to further Lydgate's career, particularly in terms of assuring that the poet received his due from contemporary readers and patrons. Stow's copy of what was presumably Shirley's preface to Trinity R.3.20, now missing, suggests that Shirley had an interest in promoting Lydgate and includes not only praise for the poet but also a pitch for rewarding him financially for his poetic efforts.[20] The same preface also locates Lydgate within an imagined social milieu, describing him as a maker of 'many a roundeel and balade', which he has 'sayd' 'with hys sugred mouthe', and calling him a purveyor of 'morall mater and holynesse / of salmes and of ympnes expresse / of loue and lawe and of pleyinges / of lordes of ladies of qwenes of kynges'. With these words, Shirley depicts Lydgate as a writer of instructive yet pleasing courtly poetry that could be expected to suit the tastes of readers within the Beauchamp household.

Shirley's decision to include the six mummings among the poems he copied in these anthologies obviously squares with his preservationist motives, and we can perhaps guess that he also assumed that the mummings would find favour with readers within the Beauchamp household, some of whom might even have watched them first-hand if their social orbit intersected that of the king and queen or the prominent Londoners for whom the mummings were, according to, Shirley designed. Whether or not Shirley's assumption proved accurate, that the mummings were apparently never recopied until they came into Stow's hands in the sixteenth century – despite the fact that Trinity R.3.20 was used in the production of at least two London manuscripts after Shirley's death – suggests that they were of little interest to anyone else beyond that original audience.[21]

If external evidence suggests that Shirley's motives in copying the mummings included the goals of the preservation of short texts and the pleasing of a coterie audience of readers, what does evidence in the manuscripts themselves tell us about Shirley's designs for the mummings and his understanding of their importance? The textual evidence points to the fact that when Shirley copied Lydgate's mummings, even as he took pains to make a record of the occasion of their original performance context, he had little interest in presenting the details of that performance.[22] As many have observed with frustration, the texts of the mummings simply do not tell us much about the performances themselves. While concerned to note the specific occasion on which the mumming was performed and for whom – as his headnotes show – Shirley is not particularly interested in recording any of the performative aspects of the mummings, even in places where the verses suggest that dramatic action may have taken place.[23] That is, Shirley rarely gives any particulars of staging – no mention of costumes, special effects, gestures, actions, vocalizations or musical accompaniments, at least some of which would likely have accompanied these performances – beyond occasional indication of characters to whom the presenter gestures or audience members whom he addresses.

Perhaps the absence of information about the actual productions occurs because Shirley did not witness or have access to full information about the performances, although given Warwick's close ties to the young Henry, members of his household – including Shirley – might well have been present at the royal mummings.[24] Or perhaps the lack of detail about the performances reflects the fact that, as Gordon Kipling has argued, Lydgate's role in the mummings was that of a 'deviser' who was responsible merely for the written text or 'device' (that is, the design instructions) for the performance, which is what we find recorded in Shirley's manuscripts.[25] Or perhaps Lydgate was, as Clopper has argued, 'a presenter not a playwright', whose art 'is presentational rather than representational' with characters who seldom speak in their own voices, little interaction between characters, and a predisposition towards 'reading' rather than performing.[26]

Whether Lydgate can be called a playwright, as Glynne Wickham and others have claimed, or whether he should be seen as a presenter or deviser, as Clopper and Kipling suggest – distinctions that may in any event be less important that the fact of Lydgate's involvement in some way with civic and court performances – Shirley's copies of Lydgate's verses for mummings remain important for what they can tell us about the problem of recognizing medieval plays. Whatever the exact nature of Lydgate's role in creating the mummings – deviser, presenter, or playwright – his verses formed part of a performance, if we believe Shirley's headnotes.[27] But Shirley's presentational tactics offer virtually no glimpse of those performances. That they do not may derive from the difficulties of recording aural and gestural material within the medium of writing,[28] or from Shirley's ignorance of the performances themselves, or from the nature of the texts he is copying (which, as Kipling argues, may not be scripts but 'devices'). The lack of detail about the performance context may also, however, be the result of Shirley's larger project of collecting Lydgate's works for *readers*, a project that led Shirley to blur the already fuzzy late medieval boundaries between written text and performance, poetry and play.

Despite some ambiguity, the terms Shirley uses to describe Lydgate's authorial role seem consistent with this project of creating a readerly compilation that seeks less to preserve the original circumstances of a text's production than to make it available to readers as part of Lydgate's corpus of poetic work. Although it has been argued that Lydgate might well have participated in at least one of the royal mummings, and although another performance poem by Lydgate includes a rubric pointing to the appearance of 'An ymage in poete wyse seying thees thre balades',[29] in Shirley's headnotes the mummings are consistently described as having been 'made' by, or in the case of the *Mumming at Hertford* 'devised' by, Lydgate, not performed or spoken or presented by him. Other fifteenth-century documents use the term 'maker' to refer to orchestrators or organizers of mummings,[30] but while Shirley's headnotes do not make clear whether Shirley uses 'made by' to refer to Lydgate in a similar way as the mastermind behind the whole performance or more restrictedly as merely the author of the accompanying text, Shirley's use of the verb 'devise' seems to tilt towards the latter. 'Devise' had a range of meanings, of which the most relevant for Shirley's usage include the acts of designing, planning, fashioning, shaping, constructing, or composing something.[31] In a more technical sense, 'deviser' could be used to designate the person who specified the visual and verbal subject matter (the 'device') for a painting, pageant, or sculpture.[32] 'Devise' could also in a more general sense mean *imagine*; the technical and general senses of the term 'devise' need not be mutually exclusive, as is suggested by Shirley's headnote to the *Legend of St George*, which seems to conflate both technical and general meanings in its description of that text as the 'devyse of a steyned halle . . . ymagined by Daun Johan . . . and made with the balades' at the request of the armourers of London. 'Making' and 'devising' were not necessarily unrelated activities, as is suggested by Chaucer's description in the *Knight's Tale* of Theseus' employment of every available craftsman 'to maken and deuyse' the tournament, and Shirley's headnotes seem to envision both terms as encompassing Lydgate's role in producing the mummings.[33]

If 'making' could be used to describe the hands-on labour of mounting a performance, it could also apply to the labour of crafting a written text. 'Made by' is in fact the phrase Shirley most often uses to describe Lydgate's authorial activities in regards to his non-dramatic poems and seems to have been used by Shirley to designate original compositions as distinct from verses that Lydgate translated or compiled, although the distinction is hardly precise: Lydgate's translation of 'So As the Crabbe Goth Forward', for instance, which is preceded by the French original, is described by Shirley as having been 'made in our englishe langage' by Lydgate and 'Gaude Virgo Mater Christi' is described as 'þe translacyoune . . . made by' Lydgate.[34]

Although we cannot know for certain what Shirley had in mind when he designated Lydgate a 'maker' of verses, it is probable that he was reflecting the notion of courtly 'makyng' that informed understandings of late medieval literary activity. As Anne Middleton has described it, courtly 'makyng' involved the creation of work that was 'conceived as a performance in the current scene of polite amusement and secular ritual'.[35] Deliberately recreative and highly aestheticized, courtly 'makyng' produced texts that served the ideological needs of and socially reproduced the late medieval aristocracy. As Lee Patterson has observed, the courtly 'maker' 'offered a ritualistic rehearsal, with minute variation, of familiar tropes of socially valuable modes of speaking and feeling' that 'played an important role in the project of aristocratic self-legitimization'.[36] What is perhaps most important in regards to Shirley and Lydgate is that courtly 'makyng' implied that the texts thereby created were public and hence in some sense performative. When Shirley used the phrase 'made by' to express Lydgate's authorial role, he presumably signalled that the accompanying poem was, like courtly poetry in general, designed for public airing, whether in the form of a text offered as a gift (as appears to have been the case for the 'Ballade on a New Years's Gift of an Eagle', which Shirley says was 'gyven vn to' Henry VI and his mother Queen Katherine, and was perhaps read aloud on that occasion), a pictorial display (such as the 'Ballade on the Image of Our Lady', which contains internal clues suggesting it accompanied a painting), or a mumming or disguising.[37] But since virtually all of Lydgate's poetry was produced by that poet in his role as courtly maker, it seems likely that it would not have occurred to Shirley to note any difference in degrees of performativity among the various texts he copied.

Like the terms Shirley uses to describe Lydgate's creative activities, the labels he applies to the texts of the mummings suggest the porosity of borders between different kinds of writing even while they tend to conscript the performances into the world of texts designed for reading. Although he mentions in the headings to all six of the Trinity R.3.20 texts (but not in the heading to *Bishopswood*) that they accompanied disguisings or mummings, Shirley also uses more overtly writerly terms to refer to the texts he copies. Two of the mummings are described as 'balades' (a balade was a poem in rhyme-royal stanzas – seven lines in iambic pentameter, rhyming ababbcc – and was Lydgate's favourite verse form), two as letters 'in wyse of balades', another as a 'bille', and the remaining two as 'devices'. All of these terms point to texts – ballads, petitions, and letters – that could be delivered orally, by recitation or declaiming. While these terms are performatively charged, they are also textually loaded and call attention to the way that these verses, in Kipling's words, 'represent themselves self-consciously as texts, as actual documents used in performance'.[38] While Kipling reads this textual self-consciousness as evidence of Lydgate's limited role in creating these dramatic performances, it can also be seen as a part of Shirley's efforts to collect Lydgate's courtly makings (i.e. his publicly performed works) and convert them into texts for private reading.

When we turn from Shirley's headnotes to the texts that follow, we see once more both genre blurring and a tendency to privilege the writerly and readerly. Several of the mummings contain rubrics or glosses that seem, although not unambiguously, to point to dramatic actions. The *Mumming at Hertford*, for instance, introduces the reply of the wives to their husbands' complaint with the line: 'Takethe heed of thaunswer of the wyves'. And marginal glosses in Latin and English in the same text (e.g., 'i. demonstrando vj. rusticos', 'demonstrando the Tynker', 'distaves') seem to mark the appearance of the various actors of the mumming. The *Mumming at London* similarly introduces the appearance of its characters with phrases like 'Nowe komethe [or 'shewethe'] here' and then the name of the character. More frequently, however, the text and glosses stress reading over performance. In the *Mumming for the Mercers*, extensive glosses in English and Latin explain the various classical gods mentioned in the text (e.g. 'Mars is god of batayle'). The *Mumming at London* and the *Mumming for the Goldsmiths* contain similar explanatory glosses that appear to be in Shirley's hand, such as a comment describing Julius Caesar as 'a bakars seon' (*Mumming at London*, line 67). In the *Mumming at Windsor*, Shirley engages in dialogue with Lydgate's text, writing next to a misogynist comment of Lydgate's: 'A daun Iohan, est y vray?' In general, Shirley's glosses seem geared towards information that aids understanding of the written text rather than imaginative recreation of the performance; they are notes intended to enhance the reading experience, not to recapture a lost performance context.

Finally, it is worth noting that the mummings are virtually indistinguishable in appearance from the poems that surround them. Like most of those poems, the mummings consist of verses of rhyme royal or octosyllabic couplets, with occasional interruptions to indicate the entry of characters but with few or no stage directions, speech tags, or other signs of the performance they presumably once accompanied. They look like what in Shirley's hands they have become: poetry designed for private reading.

To gain a sense of what is missing from Shirley's transcriptions, it helps to turn to Suzanne Westfall's reconstruction of what the *Mumming at Windsor* might have been like as a performance. According to Shirley, this mumming was performed for Henry VI at Christmas; most likely just after Henry's coronation in London and before his departure for Paris, where he would be crowned King of France in the upcoming year. The mumming describes how France was converted in Clovis' time through St Clotilda, emphasizing that the golden ampulla from which Clovis was anointed will soon be Henry's 'by tytle of right'. Westfall believes that although there is no external evidence showing that chapel members performed in disguisings before the reign of Henry VII, it is possible that they participated in Lydgate's three mummings for the royal household, given that those mummings contain features reflecting production values common to chapel performers; as a member of the clergy, Westfall observes, Lydgate would have been familiar with the capabilities of choristers and thus in a position to employ them in his mummings.[39] The *Mumming at Windsor*, in particular, seems to have required the participation of a chapel, Westfall believes. Since Shirley's headnote, unlike those for the other two royal mummings, does not mention a herald or *poursuivant*, but only says that it was 'made by Lidegate daun Iohn', Westfall argues that the mumming was spoken by Lydgate, who recited the fourteen verses and then informed the court that they could see the story enacted. (Westfall believes that the complex visual, mechanical, and aural effects of the mumming required the audience's full attention.) Westfall suggests that Clovis' conversion was accompanied by a flash of light as in the Digby *St Paul* and perhaps an angelic chorus (musical effects are implied when the angel presents the hermit with the shield and when the dove presents the ampulla). Mechanical effects would have been required to have God, the angel, and the dove descend; staging seems to call for a font for the baptism scene, height for heavenly characters, and a place from which to operate the effects; costuming demands were extravagant; special effects of gunpowder and a dove on a wire bearing the ampulla would have been needed; music would have included the typical use of harmonic singing to imply heaven.

None of this is specified by Shirley and has to be inferred from the text itself. While Westfall's reconstruction remains conjectural and would not satisfy those who demand that a text include dialogue and agonistic interaction between characters in order to qualify as a play, it nonetheless exposes a good deal of action, role-playing, and spectacle hidden within the text that Shirley presents.[40]

What, then, do Shirley's copies of Lydgate's mummings tell us? First, they demonstrate that dramatic texts do not always signal their performativity. If Shirley had not used headnotes to identify the mummings as such, there would be little to suggest that they were anything other than non-dramatic poems. This lack of visible difference between poetic and dramatic texts is not unique to Shirley's manuscripts. In a recent essay on early French drama, Carol Symes argues that the appearance of a text 'may have little to do with whether or not it was performed or regarded as a play'.[41] Particularly before 1300, formats of plays were as fluid as for non-dramatic texts and were altered to suit the pattern of the whole codex; different versions of pieces suggest they could be changed to suit different textual contexts or the needs of different readers. Moreover, layout and rubrication indicate that the generic definition of a play was in flux throughout the Middle Ages. Since plays were recorded through scribal techniques borrowed from other sources – musical, didactic, scholastic, and poetic – many do not look like plays. At the same time, texts regarded by us as plays are not always accompanied by a dramatic apparatus in their manuscript contexts, while texts not regarded by us as plays are laid out and rubricated in the same way, and are juxtaposed with identified plays, thus suggesting that they might have been performed.[42]

Shirley's copies of Lydgate's mummings also reveal cultural attitudes towards drama. Shirley's reason for identifying these seven texts as mummings seems motivated less by a desire to show that Lydgate was a dramatist than by an intent to provide the fullest possible information about the circumstances surrounding the creation of his poetry and to locate Lydgate's poetic efforts within a circle of influential patrons. Shirley thus treats the mummings the same as he does Lydgate's other occasional poetry, using headnotes to emphasize that the poem was crafted at the request of or for presentation to one or another exalted patron.[43] It seems that for Shirley, the mummings are worth preserving because they attest to Lydgate's importance as a poet writing for the powerful. What makes the mummings important for theatre history – the fact that they were part of performances of some sort – seems to have been for Shirley largely incidental and irrelevant, or even perhaps an impediment, to his apparent project of assembling and championing all of Lydgate's shorter verses, and to make them ready for use by private readers. If we take Shirley as a promoter of Lydgate's poetry, as scholars have been inclined to do, then the elision of markers of performativity in the transcription of the mummings might have something to do with not just a blurring of the lines between dramatic and poetic texts but a deliberate effort to co-opt them for a specifically literary, that is, writerly and readerly, aesthetic.

One reason such erasure of signs of performativity might have been desirable has to do with relations between literature and theatre in the late Middle Ages. Seth Lerer has suggested that the many theatrical allusions in the *Canterbury Tales* are part of Chaucer's attempt to stake out a place for his new kind of poetry against the then dominant cultural forms of courtly spectacle and civic religious drama.[44] Chaucer's search for authorial autonomy, in Lerer's view, takes him away from these public theatrics towards a place where spectators become solitary, private readers and performances become fictions. Unlike Chaucer, Lydgate did not define himself as a poet in opposition to theatricality, and in fact appears to have embraced it, judging by the frequency with which he turned his hand to the crafting of pieces designed for public performance. As Patterson's analysis of Lydgate's poetic identity argues, Lydgate's early career was founded on the production of a courtly public poetry whose chief function was to assert the stability and values of a class on whose margins Lydgate lived but from which he was excluded. In the process of producing his poetry, Lydgate constructed for himself the role of poet-propagandist, becoming, as Patterson puts it, 'a monk providing his sovereign with the monastically-generated materials needed to sustain royal authority'.[45]

But Lydgate's status as a public poet writing for elites, while no doubt part of what drew Shirley's attention in the first place, inevitably clashed with Shirley's aims in his anthologies. It is certainly possible that Shirley lacked the techniques or the information to replicate qualities of performance on the manuscript page. It is also possible that he did not know enough about the original performances to reproduce them and was working from exemplars that contained only the written text. But it is consistent with Shirley's larger purposes in his anthologies, and especially in Trinity R.3.20, to envision a more decisive downplaying of theatrical features in order to refashion Lydgate for literary and readerly culture. Shirley takes what were originally courtly or civic ephemera – entertainments designed for one-time performance on a specific occasion and destined for no textual afterlife – and converts them into enduring poetry that will be continually accessible to private consumption through the act of reading. It was presumably a similar impulse that prompted Robert Reynes, a churchwarden from the village of Acle in Norfolk, to copy play extracts into his commonplace book in the late fifteenth century as a way of remembering and making available for repeated reading performances that would otherwise be fleeting.[46] If Shirley is to be credited with making us aware of Lydgate's involvement in the production of drama performances, he is also answerable for obscuring the exact details of his role as writer of performance texts; the better to preserve the mummings for readers, Shirley subordinates drama to a literary poetics by flattening the no longer necessary and now distracting visual, mimetic and aural aspects of the performances. Like the fifteenth-century scribe who copied the verses from Queen Margaret's entry into London into a copy of Gower's *Confessio Amantis*,[47] Shirley thought of Lydgate's verses as literary even though, like Margaret's entry, they originally formed part of a performance. In both cases, verses that once had a performative context have been resituated within the frame of literate culture, converting them from spectacle to book. In the end, then, scholars are justified in viewing Lydgate's mummings – at least in the form in which they have come down to us – as 'read' texts, because that is what Shirley made them.

That phrase 'in the form in which they have come down to us' seems to me to be the place to end this essay. *REED*'s return to the archives demonstrated the pervasive nature of theatricality in medieval culture, but *REED*'s extractionist tendencies have deflected attention away from a consideration of what manuscript context can tell us about early drama. Shirley's copies of Lydgate's mummings usefully point to the complex processes that a visual and aural cultural form like medieval drama underwent as it entered the written record – the only medium through which we now have access to it. The example of Lydgate's mummings should urge us to bridge the gap between extensive references to performance and sparse play texts that defines the current state of medieval drama scholarship by reminding us that early dramas often entered the written record in ways that stripped them of their identifying marks. It is unlikely that we will find significant new numbers of texts that have visible markers of drama (speech tags, stage directions, mention of stage properties or costumes, dialogue), and appear to conform to modern notions of the dramatic (sufficient impersonation, agonistic dialogue, mimesis). But the indeterminate appearance of Lydgate's mummings suggests that there are dramatic texts still to be recovered by scholars alert to the fluid nature of medieval performances and attuned to the materiality of their manuscript context.

Notes

1. Natalie Zemon Davis, *Fiction in the Archives: Pardon Tales and Their Tellers in Sixteenth-Century France* (Stanford: Stanford University Press, 1987).
2. The history of the *REED* project has been recounted by Theresa Coletti, 'Reading *REED*: History and the Records of Early English Drama', in *Literary Practice and Social Change in Britain, 1380–1530*, ed. Lee Patterson (Berkeley: University of California Press, 1990), 248–84. For a discussion of *REED*'s impact – or lack thereof – on early modern drama scholarship, see Peter Holland's essay in this collection.
3. Alexandra F. Johnston has summarized these outcomes in ' "All the World Was a Stage": Records of Early English Drama', in *The Theatre of Medieval Europe*, ed. Eckehard Simon (Cambridge: Cambridge University Press, 1991), 117–29, esp. 118–19.
4. See David Bevington, '*Castles* in the Air: the Morality Plays', in *The Theatre of Medieval Europe*, ed. Eckehard Simon, 97–116, esp. 106.
5. The York register was made when the city required participants to record their texts with the city; not every guild did so and some apparently performed versions different from the texts in the register; see Richard Beadle, 'The York Cycle', in *The Cambridge Companion to Medieval English Theatre*, ed. Richard Beadle (Cambridge: Cambridge University Press, 1994), 85–108, esp. 89–91. Records from Coventry show cycle plays as early as 1420, but do not specify the cycle's content or how many plays it included: Hardin Craig, ed., *Two Coventry Corpus Christi Plays*, 2nd edn, EETS es 87 (Oxford: Oxford University Press, 1957), xi–xiv, put it at ten, but Lawrence M. Clopper, *Drama, Play, and Game: English Festive Culture in the Medieval and Early Modern Period* (Chicago: University of Chicago Press, 2001), 173, counts eight, and from their contents concludes that Coventry's play was chiefly a passion play with some additional material. The Towneley manuscript, named for its seventeenth-century owners, appears to contain a cycle of plays from one town, which in the past was identified as Wakefield from references in the manuscript (two pageants have the name 'Wakefield' written in rubrics at the head of their texts and there are what seem to be local allusions in some of the plays); various idiosyncrasies in the manuscript have called that into question, as Barbara Palmer notes in ' "Towneley Plays" or "Wakefield Cycle" Revisited', *Comparative Drama*, 21 (1988), 318–48. The five non-identical manuscripts of the Chester plays were copied by antiquarian scribes from the city 'Regenall', apparently a city register of scripts from which plays could be chosen to put together a cycle that might vary each year; see David Mills, *Recycling the Cycle: the City of Chester and its Whitsun Plays* (Toronto: University of Toronto Press, 1998). The York and Towneley plays show a variety of stanzaic forms and do not read as integrated wholes, while the Chester plays more consistently use an eight-line rime couée and show greater coherence, suggesting that there was one playwright who worked through the entire Chester cycle; see the discussion in Clopper, *Drama, Play, and Game*, 181–2.
6. In addition to these extant texts, several plays survive in miscellaneous manuscripts: the Norwich *Grocers' Play* (two versions dated 1533 and 1565); the Brome *Abraham and Isaac* (late fifteenth century); the Croxton *Play of the Sacrament* (c. 1461); *Dux Moraud* (c. 1425–50), a player's part for a moral play about incest; and some fragments (including the Ashmole fragment, which may be from a play of Saint Lawrence). For a discussion of the southern plays, see John C. Coldewey, 'The Non-cycle Plays and the East Anglian Tradition', in Beadle, *Cambridge Companion*, 189–210. The southern plays have been edited by: Donald C. Baker, John L. Murphy

and Louis B. Hall, Jr., *The Late Medieval Religious Plays of Bodleian MSS Digby 133 and E Museo 160*, EETS 283 (Oxford: Oxford University Press, 1982); Mark Eccles, *The Macro Plays*, EETS 262 (Oxford: Oxford University Press, 1969), and Stephen Spector, *The N-Town Play: Cotton MS Vespasian D.8.*, 2 vols, EETS ss 11–12 (Oxford: Oxford University Press, 1991), all of whom discuss ownership of the manuscripts.

7. Alexandra F. Johnston, 'What If No Texts Survived? External Evidence for Early English Drama', in Marianne G. Briscoe and John C. Coldewey, eds, *Contexts for Early English Drama* (Bloomington: Indiana University Press, 1989), 1–19, at 3.

8. Karl Young, *Drama of the Medieval Church*, 2 vols (Oxford: Clarendon Press, 1933). Young's reliance on rubrics was noted by E. Catherine Dunn, 'French Medievalists and the Saint's Play: a Problem for American Scholarship', *Mediaevalia et Humanistica*, 6 (1975), 51–62, at 55.

9. Clopper, *Drama, Play, and Game*, esp. 300–6.

10. Donald C. Baker has also noted the problem of recognition: 'When is a Text a Play? Reflections upon What Certain Late Medieval Dramatic Texts Tell Us', in Briscoe and Coldewey, *Contexts for Early English Drama*, 20–40.

11. Ian Lancashire, *Dramatic Texts and Records of Britain: a Chronological Topography to 1558* (Toronto: University of Toronto Press, 1984), xxxiii.

12. Clopper, *Drama, Play, and Game*, 165.

13. Which of Lydgate's poems should be taken as being linked to performances remains a matter of debate. To cite just one example, Alan H. Nelson, *Medieval English Stage: Corpus Christi Pageants and Plays* (Chicago: University of Chicago Press, 1974), 4–5, 173–4, regards the 'Procession of Corpus Christi' as a description of a series of plays, while Clopper, *Drama, Game, and Play*, 164, n. 67, disagrees, on the grounds that no Corpus Christi procession for which we have documentation consists of a chronological set of Old and New Testament figures and that Lydgate's term 'fygures' refers to literary *figurae*, while 'shewed' probably means only 'presented' or 'demonstrated'. Clopper concedes, however, that the reference to 'diuers likenesses' points to visual representations of some sort, perhaps a series of images such as in 'Bycorne and Chichevache'.

14. Henry N. MacCracken, ed., *The Minor Poems of John Lydgate*, 2 vols, EETS os 192 and es 107 (Oxford: EETS, 1911, 1934), 2: 668–701.

15. The former interpretation derives from Aage Brusendorff and Eleanor Hammond in the 1920s and rests on an entry in the rental of St Bartholomew's Hospital, compiled in 1456, which states that Shirley rented a large tenement in the middle of the courtyard with four shops; this view has been challenged by Richard Firth Green, among others. See the discussion in Margaret Connolly, *John Shirley: Book Production and the Noble Household in Fifteenth-Century England* (Aldershot: Ashgate, 1998), 2–3.

16. Connolly, *John Shirley*, 191.

17. For a list of the contents of the three Shirlean manuscripts, see Connolly, *John Shirley*, 30–1, 70–4, and 146–9.

18. As Connolly notes, it makes sense to look to the Beauchamp household, Shirley's known milieu in the 1420s when he began copying literary texts, for an understanding of his motives and intentions for his anthologies; see *John Shirley*, 33.

19. For Shirley's biography, see Connolly, *John Shirley*, 15–63. See Derek Pearsall, *John Lydgate* (London: Routledge & Kegan Paul, 1970), 160–71, for Lydgate's connections with Warwick.

20. See Connolly, *John Shirley*, 84–5.

21. Some of Lydgate's other public performances had a longer life. His poem describing the entry into London of Henry VI in 1432, for example, was the basis for Edward

VI's coronation entry on 19 February 1547; see W. R. Streitberger, *Court Revel 1485–1559* (Toronto: University of Toronto Press, 1994), 180–1. P. H. Parry, 'On the Continuity of English Civic Pageantry: a Study of John Lydgate and the Tudor Pageant', *Forum for Modern Language Studies*, 15 (1979), 222–36, argues that Lydgate's mummings developed features that were still current in the sixteenth century.

22. In his headings, in addition to describing the genre of the following text, Shirley also mentions the occasion on which it was performed and by or before whom. The *Mumming at London* was, his heading says, 'þe deuyse of a desguysing to fore þe gret estates of þis lande, þanne being at London'. The *Mumming at Hertford*, which Shirley states was devised at the request of 'þe Countre Roullour Brys slayne at Louviers', was 'putte to þe kyng holding his noble feest of Cristmasse in þe Castel of Hertford'. The *Mumming at Eltham* was made by Lydgate 'at Eltham in Cristmasse, for a momyng tofore þe kyng and þe Qwene'. The *Mumming for the Mercers of London* was 'brought by a poursuyaunt in wyse of mommers desguysed to fore þe Mayre of London, Eestfeld, vpon þe twelfeþe night of Cristmasse, ordeyned ryallych by þe worþy merciers, citeseyns of London'. The *Mumming for the Goldsmiths* was 'mommed' by the goldsmiths 'in right fresshe and costele welych desguysing to þeyre Mayre Eestfeld vpon Candlemasse day at nyght, affter souper'. The *Mumming at Windsor* was made by Lydgate for 'Kyng Henry þe Sixst, being in his Castell of Wyndesore, þe fest of his Crystmasse holding þer'. Lydgate's seventh mumming, the *Mumming at Bishopswood*, was, according to Shirley 'sent by a poursyvant to þe Shirreves of London, acompanyed with þeire breþerne vpon Mayes daye at Busshopes wod, at an honurable dyner, eche of hem bringginge his dysshe'. See MacCracken, *Minor Poems*, 2: 668–701.

23. In *Bishopswood*, birds sing, perhaps providing an opening for musical accompaniment, and Vera is described as 'coming down' to bring spring and also to present various gifts (of propserity, victory, honour, and peace) to the assembled estates, although this figure, if present, is given no spoken lines. In *Eltham*, Bacchus, Juno, and Ceres are all described as sending gifts to the king and queen through wine, wheat, and oil brought by 'marchandes þat here be' (l. 5); it is not certain that these and the other gods who are mentioned in the poem are represented in any way, although the repetition of their names as well as a line near the end saying that Bacchus, Juno, and Ceres 'bere witnesse' (l. 82), strongly imply they are. The *Mumming at London* opens with the lines 'Loo here þis lady that yee may see, / Lady of mutabilytee, / Which þat called is Fortune', and each of the other ladies (Prudence, Rightwysnesse, Fortitudo, and Attemperaunce) is similarly introduced in the text; while Shirley's headers refer to them coming in or showing themselves, suggesting that actors impersonating them are entering one by one, the text merely says they can be 'seen here', making it less certain they were being impersonated. In *Windsor*, the only suggestion that anything has been represented or performed comes near the end in lines saying 'So lyke it nowe to þy Magnyfycence, / þat the story of the flour delys / May here be shewed in þyne heghe presence' (ll. 93–5). In the *Mumming for the Mercers*, Jupiter is described as sending his poursuivant out of Syria and across Europe to land finally in the port of London; three ships he encounters along the way are also vividly described perhaps suggesting they figure as stage properties in the performance; the final verse of the mumming refers to 'certein estates, wheche purveye and provyde' who wish to visit and see the mayor before they 'firþer flitte' if he will admit them. The *Mumming for the Goldsmiths* describes how David and the twelve tribes of Israel come to 'þis citee' (l. 5), bringing royal gifts to the mayor; two stanzas later, David is said to have now descended with the tribes to

present his gifts, suggesting they entered on a ship from which they have now come down with the gift of the 'ark of God' which they have brought 'into this toune' (l. 25). The mumming addresses 'O yee Levytes' who carry the ark and orders them to sing and to show their melody with 'hevenly armonye' (ll. 30–3). Finally, in *Hertford*, the text refers to the king's 'poure lieges' (l. 4), the rustics who have come to complain about their wives; the text implies that the six wives spoke their complaint directly and that someone, perhaps the presenter, spoke for the king when he rendered his judgement at the end.

24. Shirley was in Calais in the spring of 1427, but may have returned to England by the time of the *Mumming at London*, which was probably performed for the Parliament that opened on 13 October 1427; Shirley had been one of John Throgmorton's clerks at the Exchequer since at least July 1426 and by 13 October 1426 had been appointed under-sheriff of Worcestershire, a post taken over by another Beauchamp retainer by 3 November 1427 (see Connolly, *John Shirley*, 23). Following Warwick's appointment as Henry VI's tutor on 1 June 1428, there would have been little need for Warwick's servants to travel to the continent and there is no evidence that Shirley ever did so again. During the period of the mummings, Shirley appears to be have been in or near London and in contact with Warwick's household (Connolly, *John Shirley*, 52–3).

25. Gordon Kipling, 'Lydgate: the Poet as Deviser', in *Chaucer and the Challenges of Medievalism: Studies in Honor of H. A. Kelly*, ed. Donka Minkova and Theresa Tinkle (Hamburg: Peter Lang, 2003), 73–101.

26. Clopper, *Drama, Play, and Game*, 165.

27. Wickham discusses the Hertford mumming as the script of a comedy in *The Medieval Theatre*, 3rd edn (Cambridge: Cambridge University Press, 1987), 162; Walter F. Schirmer views the mummings as 'primitive forms of stage play', in his *John Lydgate: a Study in the Culture of the XVth Century*, trans. Ann E. Keep (Berkeley: University of California Press, 1961), 100.

28. For a recent reflection on the problem of reproducing the aural and visual (as well as the gestural) in writing in the medieval period and beyond, see J. A. Burrow, *Gestures and Looks in Medieval Narrative* (Cambridge: Cambridge University Press, 2002), esp. 182–3.

29. The rubric appears in 'Bycorne and Chychevache', in MacCracken, ed., *Minor Poems*, 2: 433. Three of the mummings refer to delivery or presentation of the text during the performance by a 'poursyuant' or 'herald'.

30. See, for example, *The Brut, or the Chronicles of England*, ed. Friedrich W. D. Brie, 2 vols, EETS os 131, 136 (London: Kegan Paul, Trench, Trübner, 1908), 2: 360, line 32: 'þe Duk of Surrey, þe Duk of Excestre . . . & oþir moo of hir afinite, were accorded to make a mummyng vntoþKing . . . and þere þay cast to sle þe King yn hir revelyng', and *The Historical Collections of a Citizen of London in the Fifteenth Century*, ed. James Gairdner, Camden Society, ser, 2, vol. 17 (Westminster: Camden Society, 1876), 108: '. . . certayne personys, called Lollers . . . hadde caste to have made a mommynge at Eltham, and undyr coloure of the mommynge to have dystryte the kyng and Hooly Chyrche'.

31. See the *Middle English Dictionary*, s.v. 'devisen', (4): 'To design or plan (sth.)' and (5): 'To form (sth.), fashion, shape, or construct; compose (a letter, poem, etc.); portray (sth.)'.

32. See the discussion of 'devising' in Kipling, 'Lydgate: the Poet as Deviser', esp. 78–9.

33. The *Knight's Tale*, in *The Riverside Chaucer*, ed. Larry D. Benson, 3rd edn (Houghton Mifflin, 1987), l. 1901.

34. MacCracken, *Minor Poems*, 2: 464–7 and 1: 288–9, respectively. Shirley's rubric for 'A Seying of the Nightingale' similarly blurs distinctions between authorial originality and the recycling of received material in claiming that the verses were 'ymagyned and compyled' by Lydgate (1: 221–34). On two occasions Shirley indicates that Lydgate 'wrote' the following verses, and on one of those occasions, Shirley combines the acts of writing and making, saying that Lydgate 'wrote & made' a poem for Queen Katherine; see 'A Ballade, of Her That Hath All Virtues' ('. . . whiche þat Lydegate wrote at þe request of a squyer') and 'That Now Is Hay Some-tyme Was Grase' ('. . . a balade which Iohn Lydgate the Monke of Bery wrott & made at þe commaundement of þe Quene Kateryne'), 2: 379–81 and 2: 809–13.

35. Anne Middleton, 'Chaucer's "New Men" and the Good of Literature in the *Canterbury Tales*', in Edward Said, ed., *Literature and Society* (Baltimore: Johns Hopkins University Press, 1980), 15–56, at 32.

36. Lee Patterson, '"What Man Artow?"': Authorial Self-Definition in *The Tale of Sir Thopas* and *The Tale of Melibee*', *Studies in the Age of Chaucer*, 11 (1989), 117–75, at 119.

37. See MacCracken, *Minor Poems*, 2: 649–51 and 1: 290–1.

38. Kipling, 'Lydgate: the Poet as Deviser', 92.

39. Suzanne Westfall, *Patrons and Performance: Early Tudor Household Revels* (Oxford: Clarendon Press, 1990), 35–7. Glynne Wickham, *Early English Stages, 1300–1660* (London: Routledge & Kegan Paul, 1959–81), 3, 130–1, notes that, during the time of Chaucer and Lydgate, 'the histrionic techniques of poet and preacher alike were being so regularly exercised that at any moment it would become possible for actors to collaborate with both in acting out the story, thereby relieving them of the need to assume any voice other than that of the expositor who introduced and concluded the active, three-dimensional *exemplum*'.

40. Thomas Pettitt's brief reading of 'Bycorne and Chychevache' similarly draws to the surface latent hints within the text that seem to echo folk plays (in length, number of performers, use of a presenter, self-presentation of the characters, and grouping of speeches around a simple plot) and hence to point to fully-fledged dramatic enactment; see his 'Early English Traditional Drama: Approaches and Perspectives', *Research Opportunities in Renaissance Drama*, 25 (1982), 1–30, at 12–13. One of the manuscripts of 'Bycorne and Chychevache', Trinity College, Cambridge MS R.3.19, in fact identifies the poem as 'þe maner of straunge desguysinges, þe gyse of a mummynge', though Shirley's copy in Trinity R.3.20 instead identifies it as 'þe deuise of a peynted or desteyned clothe' designed for a great hall.

41. Carol Symes, 'The Appearance of Early Vernacular Plays: Forms, Functions, and the Future of Medieval Theater', *Speculum*, 77 (2002), 778–831, at 778.

42. For instance, the *Courtois d'Arras*, which modern scholars call a play, has no dramatic apparatus (stage directions or character designations) in its four extant manuscripts and circulated as a lai or fabliau (see Symes, 'Appearance', 782), while *Dame Sirith* (c. 1300), never identified as part of the canon of English drama, perhaps should be. See also the Anglo-Norman *vita* of Saint Catherine preserved in John Rylands Library MS French 6 (c. 1250), which has some speech tags, but is a narrated text; Clopper, *Drama, Play, and Game*, 305, calls it a *ludus*, not a play, but its status seems ambiguous.

43. Although the reliability of Shirley's information has been questioned, Pearsall, *John Lydgate*, 77, believes that 'where he can be checked', Shirley 'is very accurate in his attributions'.

44. Seth Lerer, 'The Chaucerian Critique of Medieval Theatricality', in *The Performance of Middle English Culture: Essays on Chaucer and the Drama*, ed. James J. Paxson, Lawrence M. Clopper and Sylvia Tomasch (Cambridge: D. S. Brewer, 1998), 59–76.
45. Lee Patterson, 'Making Identities in Fifteenth-Century England: Henry V and John Lydgate', in *New Historical Literary Study: Essays on Reproducing Texts, Representing History*, ed. Jeffrey N. Cox and Larry J. Reynolds (Princeton: Princeton University Press, 1993), 69–107.
46. See Cameron Louis, ed., *The Commonplace Book of Robert Reynes* (New York: Garland, 1980).
47. See Gordon Kipling, 'The London Pageants for Margaret of Anjou: a Medieval Script Restored', *Medieval English Theatre*, 4 (1982), 5–27, at 11.

8
Re-patching the Play

Tiffany Stern

Introduction: history and criticism

The collection of pieces of evidence must always be one of the fundamental purposes of theatre history; therefore, thinking out new ways to get at evidence – using the archaeological findings from the Rose theatre, for instance – is of primary importance.[1] Naturally, the nature and variety of the material examined defines the uses to which it can be put. Recent archive work has been devoted to collecting data out of manuscript records – account books, wills, lawsuits, contracts, birth and death registers – and has therefore led to a proliferation of fresh documentary-based criticism concerning the way, for instance, actors' guild membership affected their ability to hire apprentices.[2]

Accounts and legal documents of the kind recently gathered are extremely likely to be accurate and can be used without too many fears that they have been mediated. But the movement towards collecting 'primary' factual early modern material seems to have led to an unconscious movement against gathering 'new' evidence of the 'secondary' and necessarily fragmented kind: stories and jokes out of sermons, jest books, travel journals, pamphlets, poems etc., evidence that is unlikely to be strictly 'true'.[3]

So here, to show the kind of evidence that can still be found in secondary texts, is a moment from an early modern jest book that has not previously been discovered by theatre historians.

Of two who went to see two playes.
Two Gentlemen went to see *Pericles* acted, and one of them was moved with the calamities of that Prince that he wept, whereat the other laughed extreamely. Not long after the same couple went to see the Major of Quinborough, when he who jeered the other at *Pericles* now wept himselfe, to whom the other laughing, sayd, what the Divell should there bee in this

merry play to make a man weep. O, replied the other, who can hold from weeping to see a Magistrate so abused?
The Jest will take those who have seene these two plaies.[4]

The teller of the story relates, after the event, an exchange at which he may well not have been present – if, indeed, it happened at all: anecdotal jests rely on exaggeration and invention rather than fidelity to real events. Yet despite the lack of direct facts, the tale provides evidence for a variety of points. That two members of an audience intentionally contrasted two plays shows the critical and comparative way in which spectators might judge theatrical events; that men might expect to weep at tragedies provides information about audience reaction, gender, and emotion. Neither play is discussed in terms of playwright, suggesting, here, the importance of play over author, while the assumption in the last line of the joke – that the person who reads this jest book is likely to be a theatergoer – identifies a link between certain types of 'reader', certain types of book, and playhouse audiences. A theatre historian concerned with repertory would note that both plays were performed by the King's Men. Did the two spectators have a loyalty to one particular playhouse and was single-theatre allegiance normal? An editor of the *Mayor of Queenborough* would learn the title by which the play was conventionally known in the 1630s (earlier it had been called *Hengist King of Kent*). The anecdote is, moreover, a 'new' reference to a Shakespeare play, and serves to illustrate that data about the most famous plays of the most famous playwright of the early modern period has by no means all been gathered.

So returning to the hunt for secondary evidence is important. Indeed, probably only the suggestion, often made, that most evidence about the early modern theatre has already been found, has stopped scholars from looking for more. A brief look at the recent history of theatre history will reveal the impressive works of scholarship that gave the subject its sense of 'completeness', and will also show which early modern secondary sources have not been consistently examined for theatrical material.

Towards the end of the nineteenth century, E. K. Chambers embarked on his twenty-year project, *The Elizabethan Stage*, which was finally published in four volumes in 1923. Not an academic, Chambers spent each working day at the civil service where he had a job in the Education Department. He had little leisure to go to rare-book libraries, and could not do much in the way of original research.

After a heavy day at his office, [Chambers] would retire to his study immediately after dinner in order to make a little progress. His library when it came to be sold was found to be not considerable. The work that he did at this time, when visits to the British Museum were infrequent, is an impressive tribute to the resources of the London Library.[5]

Chambers' research, that is to say, was defined – and confined – largely by the holdings of the London Library, a private subscription library in Piccadilly. What the theatre historian could do was limited by the, largely secondary, information available to him. A wonderful accumulator and assessor and reorganizer, Chambers actually did little to add to the sum of playhouse knowledge. Rather, he made a 'fresh attempt at synthesis' using information discovered in the Victorian and Edwardian periods.[6] Yet the completeness, the rationality, and the measured weighing of evidence that typifies Chambers' approach, gave his work the appearance of being absolutely comprehensive. In fact, the little 'new' material that Chambers was able to supply was taken from close reading of play texts themselves: as Chambers' interest in staging had arisen from an interest in plays, this is hardly surprising.

The companion to Chambers' work, Gerald Eades Bentley's seven-volume *Jacobean and Caroline Stage*, was published piecemeal between 1941 and 1968. Bentley had more opportunity for research than Chambers, though the Second World War made access to English libraries (he was an American) difficult, a fact that is reflected in the content of the early books. The *Jacobean and Caroline Stage* inherits Chambers' focal interests, and is divided into plays, authors, actors, and playhouses. The volumes also use evidence similar to the kind favoured by Chambers: plays themselves, once again, provide the main sources of secondary material.[7]

Perhaps now at least one 'new' (because largely unexplored) source for early modern theatre references is clear. Of the roughly 50 350 printed books published between 1580 and 1660, about 700 are plays. They can be assumed in general to have been looked through for theatrical references; this does not, of course, mean that all have been found. But surprisingly few of the remaining printed 'non-play' texts – amounting to roughly 49 450 books – have ever been looked at specifically by theatre historians. Even early modern authors known to allude to the stage in their writings – Brathwait, Peacham, Rowlands, Breton – have never had their complete works read through for theatrical references. The printed non-play is a huge untapped resource of theatrical data, particularly when the non-play is written either by a playwright or by a writer known to have been interested in the theatre.

My own researches, so far, have led me to look over some 10 000 rare books; from them I have now gathered well over 1000 'new' references, many of which are repetitions of standard tropes, some of which are considerably more telling. Using 'new' material from a variety of sources – early modern 'non-plays', prologues and epilogues, page-layout, and later sources – the next section suggests that a modern interest in primary and documentary evidence may have led theatre historians not simply away from fragmentary, secondary, and anecdotal evidence about the early modern theatre, but also away from the fragmentary nature of the plays themselves.

The play as patch-work

Theatre histories often explore the context surrounding the creation of the play. Was there one author or many? Did the physical make-up of the theatre or the company shape the production of the work? Each of these topics importantly helps define the world that brought about the text. But despite the huge interest in what shaped the play, the nature of the play itself is less often questioned. The unity of a play is often taken as a given; articles on the revising of play texts tend to assume that one whole and complete text was equally revised over by its author. Why, it is then asked, did playwrights bother to write long plays that would have to be cut and rewritten in the playhouse itself? By exploring the fragmentary nature of the text, an answer to that question can be suggested.

The designation 'playwright' seems to have come into being in the 1610s.[8] With its implications of writing plays as a trade – playwright obviously relating to such jobs as cartwright and wheelwright – 'playwright' was probably, as a title, originally pejorative. There were other more common and neutral words to describe the profession. One – the most usual – was 'poet', telling in itself with its implication that all plays are or should be in verse. Another less hierarchical term was 'play-maker', a simple description of the task of writing plays. A fourth title has not been critically noticed, or at least not for what it implies. When Thomas Dekker writes about 'a Cobler of Poetrie called a play-patcher' he alerts the reader not only to another term of abuse for a playwright, but also to another definition of what the playwright does.[9]

On one level the phrase 'to patch' a play implies that the writer is ransacking his commonplace book, gathering together disparate material from various sources to turn into theatrical events. The suggestion then is that a play is a collection of fragments taken from elsewhere and loosely held together; playwrights are 'men only wise enough, / Out of some rotten old worme-eaten stuffe / To patch up a bald witlesse *Comedy* . . .'[10] Other references suggest that there was something 'patch-like' in the very way a play was written in the first place. When 'Constantia Munda' accuses playwrights of defaming the female sex she writes 'Every fantasticke Poetaster which . . . can but patch a hobling verse together, will strive to represent unseemely figments imputed to our sex . . . on the publique Theatre'.[11] Here the very method of creating the play seems to be, somehow, 'patchy'. The noun 'play-patcher' and the verb 'to patch a play' take the glamorous edge off 'poet' and may reflect a worry that the worst plays combine borrowed phrases, ragged second-rate verse, and prose. But 'play-patcher' also points in the direction of a truth about the theatre. There was a sense at the time that plays were not whole art-works in the way that poems were. Plays had the bit, the fragment, the patch in their very natures.

The way that spectators 'used' plays at the time confirms – and perhaps encourages – the sense of the fragmentary. If plays were themselves written out of odds and ends from commonplace books, they certainly resolved almost immediately back into them. It was normal for audiences to plunder the performances they attended, removing particular types of text for future use elsewhere in non-play contexts. A stock of jokes was always valuable:

> So there be among them that will get jestes by heart, that have gathred a Common-place booke out of Plaies, that will not let a merriment slip, but they will trusse it up for their owne provision, to serve their expence at some other time.[12]

Other naturally separable fragments were 'amorous discourses'. These were flirtation-aids for the verbally insecure who could 'Court th' attracting beauties of the age / With some con'd stuffe brought from the Cockpit stage'.[13] Even the language of lawyers, wrote Thomas Trescot resignedly in 1642, consisted often of 'but a few shreds and scraps dropt from some *Stage-Poet*, at the *Globe* or *Cock-pit*, which they have carefully bookt up'.[14] Sections of plays, that is to say, habitually became detached from their contexts to thrive in others. Such sections might well outlive the full play; indeed, the more 'removable' a passage is, the less reliant on context, the more likely it is to appeal. Short quotations and 'easily extractable' passages went straight into tablebooks and tavern-chatter; 'Hamlet: Revenge!' survives from the *Ur-Hamlet*, though the rest of the text is lost; from Shakespeare's *Hamlet* what seems to have become immediately part of the currency of quotation was not 'to be or not to be' but the more generally applicable 'hic et ubique?' or its paraphrase, 'here and everywhere'.[15]

Here is another fragment from Shakespeare's *Hamlet* in a form just different enough from any printed *Hamlet* to suggest its origins in a theatrical commonplace book. It adds to the sense that, were Shakespeare's play lost, surviving references would provide a startlingly lopsided picture of the text itself, for what seems to have been of value to Shakespeare's audience are parts of the play a modern reader might think least striking. In print, but hidden away in a volume on that offers a *Helpe to Discourse* (advice on how to improve one's conversation), this Shakespeare reference has not been noticed before.

Q *What birds are those that are called prophets twice borne?*
A. The Cocke: first an egge from the Hen, after a Cocke from the Egge: they foretell seasons and changes of weather, according to the Verse:

Some *say for* ever gainst that season comes,	sayes F that Q1, Q2, F
Wherein our Saviours birth is celebrated,	
The Bird of dawning singeth all Night long,	
And then they say no spirit *dares walke*	
abroad,[16]	dare stir Q1 can walk Q2, F
So *sacred* and so *hallowed* is that *tune.*	gracious . . . hallowed Q1
	hallowed . . . gracious Q2,
	F time Q1, Q2, F
W. Shaks [italics and editorial notes mine][17]	

Here the within-play context of the passage is irrelevant enough for the vital word 'time' to be mis-remembered / transcribed as 'tune', changing the nature of the observation from one about a religious moment to one about bird-song. Even very remarkable plays, in other words, could easily disintegrate into fragments that had only a tenuous connection to the whole; in the passage above, the name of the author is supplied but not the speaker of the passage (Marcellus) or the title of the play. This extract illustrates not just how plays were listened to, but what plays were a resource for; tellingly, the very same passage is also extracted during performance by Edward Pudsey in his commonplace book, now in the Bodleian Library.[18] Plays appear to have been enjoyed partly for their removable *mots* and 'sententiae'; they provided books like the *Helpe to Discourse* with proverbs and textual beauties as well as jokes, flirtatious phrases, and, as here, nature tips. Playwrights concerned to publish their plays, meanwhile, like Ben Jonson, highlight with the use of quotation marks parts of the text they thus identify as separable.[19] Plays, in other words, had the sense of the fragment in their very make-up and were to a certain extent written to be resolved into commonplace books. For a play that was not published, indeed, quotation was the way it would be promulgated amongst the audience – and thus the mark of its success.

So the term 'play-patcher' simply confirms that some plays were understood not anyway to have been written as single complete entities. Beyond the commonplace-book aspect, a look at the printed layout of surviving texts raises the suggestion that some plays were transcribed, kept, learned, revised, and even written, not as wholes, but as a collection of separate units to be patched together in performance.

A brief glance at almost any printed early modern play will reveal that certain of its sections are typographically different from others. Usually, songs, for instance, are printed in different type from the body of the play; in addition they are frequently headed with a generic description, 'the song' or 'a song', even though what they are is perfectly clear from the context. So in the folio *Twelfth Night*, TLN 939–41, the Duke's 'I prethee sing', is followed by an italic heading 'The Song.', followed by, also in italics, the actual song, 'Come away, come away death'. Headings like 'the song' or 'the letter', which serve no useful purpose for a modern reader or actor, are generally removed by editors when preparing the text for publication. Sometimes, however, all that remains in the printed text is the heading: the body of the song no longer exists. John Marston's *What you Will* of 1607 (1.1) provides one such example:

> Jacomo: . . . looke Sir heares a ditty.
> Tis foully writ slight wit cross'd here and there,
> But where thou findst a blot, their fall a teare.
> The Song.
> Fie peace, peace, peace, it hath no passion int.[20]

What was the song that Jacomo found so lacking in passion? And how can it have been lost from the play text? The 'lost song' indicates something about the nature of the manuscript text that came into the printer's hands. What must have been the case with Marston's text is what the layout of the printed text of William Habington's *The Queene of Arragon* (1640) reveals. For *The Queene of Arragon* on first appearance seems, too, to contain lost songs. Here is one song heading, again, without the attached text, from sig. D3a of that play:

> Queen: Play any thing.
> *During the Song, Enter Ascanio, Lerma, Sanmartino, &c.*
> Ascanio: Cease the uncivill murmur of the drum.[21]

Yet the song in this instance is not in fact lost: it is printed at the back of the play book together with the other song to be sung mid-play and the epilogue.[22] As the layout of Habington's text indicates, the manuscript playbook on which this text is based contained merely the song-heading; the actual songs were kept separately. That this was common practice is made clear by texts belonging to different theatrical companies that do the same thing. Heywood's *The Rape of Lucrece* (1608), for instance, boasts on its title page that it is printed 'With the severall Songes in their apt places'; when it comes to it, however, some of the songs are also gathered together in the back pages: the printer seems to have forgotten to distribute them through the play in time.[23] 'Lost songs' can be attributed to the fact that the words to the ditties were on other pieces of paper – perhaps with the music also inscribed on them – that have not survived.

In a world in which every actor had to hold in his head some forty-odd parts for the different daily plays in repertory, the advantages of not having to learn what can be read from a sheet of paper are obvious. There is every reason to think that some songs (and, indeed, some letters) were kept on separate pieces of paper to be handed over and read on stage when needed; this was in fact the way songs and letters were handled for the next couple of centuries. If, however, songs are textually different from the rest of the play, then they are obvious sites for revision and rewriting by other authors. Heywood's *Rape of Lucrece* offers one such example, for the songs already referred to as collected at the back of the play were 'added by the stranger that lately acted *Valerius* his part' as the title page also makes clear. Webster is less sanguine about other people's songs in his writing (which does not prevent their being put into his text). During proof correction of the quarto for *The Duchess of Malfi*, he appears to have demanded that a note be added next to the song 'Armes, and Honors, decke thy story', 'The Author disclaimes this Ditty to be his'.[24]

The 'separate song' offers one reason why songs so easily go in and out of plays. The songs in the manuscript of *The Mayor of Queenborough* are not in its printed text; the 'Willow song' is absent from the 1622 quarto of *Othello* but present in the folio.[25] Indeed, in a note appended to his manuscript volume of six plays, William Percy tells 'the Master of children of Powles' specifically to remove songs if the text requires shortening:

> if any of the fine and foremost of these Pasturalls and Comoedyes conteynd in this volume shall but overreach in lengh [sic] . . . then in tyme and place convenient, . . . let passe some of the songs.[26]

If songs are on different pieces of paper, then even the character to whom the song is given is potentially changeable. It is worth observing here that moments of textual difference often occur around songs; that the songs in *Twelfth Night*, for instance, seem to have been taken from Viola and given to Feste.[27] Here, then, is one clear line of fluid text: 'songs' in general are more extractable, movable, revisable units of play than other pieces of text. This may be connected, too, to the function of song as song. Even if removed, even if never sung on stage at all, the severed song easily becomes part of other contexts, either living in the aural world – Richard Ligon was struck by hearing in 1650s Barbados a tune out of Shakespeare's *2 Henry IV* – or living in the world of poetry.[28] When Thomas Carew includes 'Songs in the Play' in his *Poems* of 1651, he gives his songs a chance of surviving outside his plays, while suggesting, too, that songs belong as much to the generic type 'poem' as they do to 'play'.[29] How much a part of 'the play' is the song then? By including songs from Beaumont and Fletcher's *The Nice Valour* in his commonplace book, one anonymous writer at least shows that he was prepared to isolate songs as removable fragments of text like the sententiae already discussed.[30] Because of the way the play could exist as a divided text, certain definable sections of it easily fit into different kinds of book.

What other bits of the play might sometimes have been written on separable pieces of paper? Again the clue is in the layout of printed texts. Prologues and epilogues in early modern printed texts are regularly placed where they do not textually belong; typically they follow on one from the other, both preceding the text itself (in performance, of course, if both are present, the one opens the play and the other concludes it). They, too, usually have a separate generic heading, 'the prologue', 'the epilogue', they, too, are generally printed in different type from the main text. Again the suggestion is that they were not always written into the play book itself. At the start of *Thorny Abbey* the Fool enters 'with a Paper in his hand for a Prologue'; he has a text on its own sheet.[31] While, for Beaumont and Fletcher's *Complete Works* of 1679, the printers give a grateful thank-you to the 'gentleman' who has recently provided them with 'several Prologues and Epilogues, with the Songs appertaining to each Play, which were not in the former Edition'; somehow the gentleman has come by a sheaf of papers containing materials absent from the play manuscripts in the printing house.[32] By extension, stage orations, like songs, could easily have different authorship from the body of the play. James Shirley provides a list of the prologues he has written for Fletcher plays while in Ireland, while Richard Brome, defending the accusation that he had breached his contract with Salisbury Court, insisted that he worked hard and had made 'many prologues and epilogues . . . songs, and one induction' for company plays.[33]

As with songs, stage orations flourished in books of poetry, sometimes even when 'lost' from their play. Once again, *The Mayor of Quinborough* furnishes an example. Two manuscripts for the play survive which predate its 1661 printed text. Of the differences between manuscripts and printed book (neither of the manuscripts was the direct source for the book), one is that the printed text lacks the songs, another is that it lacks the epilogue. Meanwhile what calls itself a prologue to *Queenborough*, different from that in either printed or manuscript text, had already been separately published in *Wit Restor'd in severall Select Poems* (1658): 'Loe I the Maior of Quinborough Town by name, / With all my brethren saving one that's lame; / Are come' (actually this passage opens the fourth act of the printed and manuscript plays).[34] As this shows, prologues and epilogues age more regularly than the play to which they are attached, and are also more regularly lost. Shakespeare's texts offer several examples of this. The 'bad' quarto of *Henry V* was printed in 1600 – within a year of first performance – without the prologues, epilogues, and chorus. Were they in fact subsequently written for the play, or had they already been detached from it?[35] The prologue for Shakespeare's *Troilus and Cressida*, meanwhile, did not feature in either of the variant first (1609) quartos of the text, nor was it part of the original folio setting of the play; it was acquired at the very last moment in the folio's publication process to fill what had become, for other reasons, an empty recto.[36]

That prologues and epilogues were only ever impermanently attached to their plays is made clear in a variety of ways. One is the regularity with which they would be replaced – revised or revived plays usually have new 'revision' prologues.[37] Another is the regularity with which they would be lost altogether; many plays are printed without either that seem to have had at least one of them originally. 'Remember well,' enjoins Time in *The Winter's Tale*, TLN 1600–2, 'I mentioned a sonne o'th'Kings, which Florizell / I now name to you', but as the play stands we have never met Time before and are in no position to remember what he has said. Reference to a lost prologue? Perhaps. Both *Hamlet* and *Othello* include jibes about the regularity with which a prologue precedes a tragedy; both plays are, themselves, published without. As ever, there is some suggestion that changes and revision are more likely to happen to prologues and epilogues than to other parts of the play text; but as with songs, stage orations, detached from the play, do not necessarily die – they often become part of some generically different text. Books of poetry frequently include prologues and epilogues, but even a jest book can provide a home for a prologue that is as much a joke as an introduction to a play. Here, for instance, is a prologue which survives in a book of 'bulls' or quips; a prologue, more-over, that is named for its playhouse but not its play: there is no knowing the text of which this was once part:

A Bull Prologu, to a foolish Audience.

You who sitting here,
doe stand to see our Play;
Which must this night,
be acted here to day.
Be silent, 'pray,
though you alowd doe talke,
Stirre not a jot,
though up & down ye walk . . .[38]

Prologues and epilogues had a different rate of survival from the rest of the text for a particular reason that is covered much more fully in a forthcoming article.[39] Here it is in brief.

Whenever a special occasion occurred for which explanation or apology was necessary, a special prologue would be written: prologues survive in books of poetry for 'Ezekiel Fen at his first Acting a Mans Part' and for 'A young witty

Lad playing the part of Richard the third: at the Red Bull'.[40] These might be spoken and therefore written at any time during the life of the play but they seem to be for single performances (when Ezekiel Fen performs next it will no longer be the first time he has acted a man's part; the witty lad only performed *Richard the Third* once as a novelty). This variety of prologue and/or epilogue usually survives away from the text it flanked; printed plays tend to include prologues and epilogues 'for court' and prologues and epilogues for public performance (rather than a particular actor). Of these, court prologues are, like special-occasion prologues, for single performances, as plays were habitually acted only once at court. In other words, every prologue and epilogue looked at so far is for one performance only.

How often, then, were regular prologues and epilogues – the prologues and epilogues for general performance – usually spoken? The prologue to Jonson's *Bartholomew Fair* gives a hint: it makes articles of agreement between the spectators at the Hope theatre and the playwright on a specific day, 'the one and thirtieth day of *Octob.* 1614'.[41] As it stands, the prologue is relevant only for one performance. Bearing this in mind, the one-day nature of other stage orations becomes more apparent. There are prologues that, as with Shakespeare and Fletcher's *The Two Noble Kinsmen*, stress that the text they introduce is a 'virgin' unsullied by criticism; others simply broadcast their connection to the first performance: 'The DIVILL is an Asse, That is, to day, / The name of what you are met for, a new Play'; 'Wee promis'd you a new Play by our bill'; 'The worst that can befall at this new Play, / Is, we shall suffer, if we loose the day'.[42] As Christopher Brooke explains at the opening to his 1614 poem *Ghost of Richard the Third*, 'An *Epistle* to the Reader is as ordinary before a new *Book*, as a *Prologue* to a new Play'.[43] Stage orations of the kind printed with plays, at least from roughly after 1600 (fewer survive from before then, and all are more generally written), seem to have been the preserve not of all performances but of first performances.

Why this may be relates to other facts about plays when they were 'new'. A new play's first performance appears to have been known as its 'trial'; what was being tried was not the actors, however, but the play itself. On the first performance the audience would judge the play and decide whether to give it approval for further performance or whether to damn it; if it 'pleas'd not the Million' (*Hamlet*, TLN 1479), it would not, generally, be played again. Playwrights were terrified of the trial and many, as the induction to John Day's *Isle of Gulls* (1606) makes clear, would be sure to have 'a prepared company of gallants' present on the first day to applaud the play's best bits. 'Our Author . . . is unfurnisht of . . . a friendly audience' explains Day's prologue. 'Then', is the answer, 'he must lay his triall upon God and good wits'.[44] From, again, some point after 1600, first performance trials are regularly referred to. 'That you should authorize [the play] after the Stages tryall was not my intention', writes

Nabbes; Heminges and Condell maintain that, whatever the reader of Shakespeare's folio plays thinks, the texts 'have had their triall alreadie' (A3a).[45] The large number of published play texts that insist that they have 'passed the censure of the stage with a general applause' or were 'the object of . . . Commendations . . . being . . . censured by an unerring Auditory' testifies to the importance of passing the trial in the life of the play.[46]

Epilogues usually also refer to the judgemental process, begging an unsure audience to approve or 'pass' the play by giving it a 'plaudite'. Indeed, the audience seem sometimes to have been asked at the end of the first day, not only to make their feelings clear by clapping or hissing, but also to shout 'ay' or 'no', a process that continued until the nineteenth century. Dibdin explains how theatre audiences of the 1820s were asked at the end of first performance:

> 'Ladies and Gentlemen, under the sanction of your kind approbation' &c. &c. The Ayes or the Noes generally interrupt the remainder; and the author is sent home, either over-elated at transitory success, or . . . blamed, depressed, and . . . ashamed.[47]

Just the same process seems to be taking place for the epilogue of Walter Mountfort's 1633 *Launching of the Mary*:

> Yf then this please (kinde gentlemen) saye so
> Yf yt displease affirem yt wth your No.
> your, I, shall make yt live to glad the sire
> your, No, shall make yt burne in quenchles fire.[48]

Any such prologue and epilogue, begging that the play be saved, fearing that it may be damned, has a very particular relationship to the text to which it is latched. Prologues and epilogues seem to exist to promote and protect the play in its minority, and to plead that the play should live. The uncertain survival of prologues and epilogues, then, may be traced to the fact that their connection to the play was a one-day one. Other stage orations make the immediacy of the one-day relationship clear by highlighting the fact that the trembling playwright is actually present in the theatre on this special day, 'listening behind the arras, to hear what will become of his play'.[49] From his hidden position, he waits to hear what the audience conclude:

> You'd smile to see, how he do's vex and shake,
> Speakes naught but if the Prologue does but take,
> Or the first Act were past the Pikes once, then –
> Then hopes and Joys, then frowns and fears agen.[50]

All of this relates to (or brings about) another theatre possibility that, again, informs the nature of the play text. If the audience were the judges of the first performance 'trial', then they could potentially get the text changed and altered to suit them, blackmailing the author to make the alterations they requested rather than have his play damned altogether. Much as a film is screened to a trial audience whose criticisms affect the cut eventually released to the general public, so early modern hissing and mewing may itself have revised certain plays after the first performance: *Every Man Out of His Humour* 'had another *Catastrophe* or Conclusion, at the first Playing: which . . . many seem'd not to rellish . . . and therefore 'twas since alter'd'; Cowley's hastily mounted *The Guardian* was reworked 'After the Representation' and the author 'changed it very much, striking out some whole parts, as that of the *Poet* and the *Souldier*'.[51] A play in its first performance really might be longer or rougher than that same play in any subsequent performance (one explanation for Gurr's 'maximal' and 'minimal' texts is that 'maximal' were given at first performances and were cut by audience approval and disapproval into 'minimal' for subsequent performances).[52] Hardly surprisingly, a first performance cost more to get into, the audience, presumably, paying for the extra power they would have over this specific variety of text.[53]

The whole relates to another fact, as ever, hard to date. By the 1630s prologues and epilogues for most plays make clear that at least part and perhaps all of the author's payment depends on receiving a portion of the revenue from the second or third day of playing, the so-called 'benefit' performance. By that time, too, many prologues describe themselves as preceding a second performance: 'Every labour dyes, / Save such whose second springs comes from your eyes', maintains *The Costly Whore* in 1633; Jasper Mayne's 'unbought Muse did never feare / An Empty second day, or a thinne share'.[54] But the epilogue to Armin's *Valiant Welshman*, published much earlier, in 1615, also expresses the worry that the play may be sent to its tomb, and voices the hope that he, the Bardh-epilogue will instead be allowed to give 'second birth' to the work.[55] One reason, then, why the playwright might have meekly accepted the ignominy of critical judgement from an audience is, as a 1632 epilogue explains, '[the poet's] promis'd Pay / May chance to faile, if you dislike the Play'.[56] Play-revision occurring after the first performance probably relates to the financial necessity of a play's survival to a second performance; the advent of benefits is, however, frustratingly hard to date. The earliest clear contemporary reference to a benefit is 1611, when a Dekker prologue jibes at a playwright who is only concerned that 'he *Gaines*, / A Cramd *Third-Day*'.[57] Years later, in *The Playhouse to Be Let*, Davenant was to state that playwrights 'in the times of mighty *Tamberlane*, / Of conjuring *Faustus*, and the *Beauchamps* bold, / . . . us'd to have the second day', and there are Henslowe accounts that may (but may not) indicate benefit performances taking place in 1601.[58]

Several Shakespearian prologues and epilogues seem to refer to some of the issues covered in this argument. Epilogues that suggest they do not yet know whether the play has 'taken' or not include 'I charge you (O men) for the love you beare to women . . . that betweene you, and the women, the play may please', *As You Like It* (TLN 2788–91), and ''Tis ten to one, this Play can never please / All that are here' (*Henry VIII*, TLN 3450–1). *2 Henry IV*, in addition, goes on to promise that 'our humble Author will continue the Story (with Sir John in it) . . . unlesse already he be kill'd with your hard Opinions' (TLN 3344–7). There is even, perhaps, the suggestion that the author is prepared to countenance revision in the light of audience criticism in *A Midsummer Night's Dream*'s 'Gentles, doe not reprehend. / If you pardon, we will mend' (TLN 2214–15).

Here the point is simply to raise more questions about the fragmentary and changeable text. While many critics have promoted the idea of the 'fluid' play text, and many others have argued against that idea (would the actors really be prepared to learn and relearn a different text for the same play?), identifying lines of fluidity – songs, prologues, epilogues – at least gives revision a logic. It also raises some fundamental questions about textuality. If a play sometimes existed as separate sheets that only came together in performance itself, and even then, only on certain specific performances, then what is the 'whole' play: what is written, what is played, what is performed the first day, or what is performed on subsequent days?

To confuse the subject yet further there is another, different piece of paper that also relates loosely to the playtext. This paper was probably, like the others, kept with the play but, unlike them, was seldom spoken. It also seems uniformly not to have survived – or at least, not in original form. It is the playbill.

Often ignored because it was not part of the spoken performance, the bill nevertheless has some claim to be part of 'the text' of a play, depending on what the text is taken to be. Giving details such as title, venue, 'lure', and, sometimes, authorship, the bill is as much a product of the play as the title page; indeed, there is every reason to believe that some of the more lurid title pages for plays are made out of the content of the bill. Is the title page/playbill 'part' of the play? Modern editing shows some ambivalence towards the question. A concern with accuracy of title – *Henry VIII* or *All is True*, for instance – contrasts with a willingness to confine information actually provided by title pages to textual notes. '*The Tragedie of King Richard the third. Conteining, His treacherous Plots against his brother Clarence: the pitiful murther of his innocent Nephewes: his tyrannicall usurpation: with the whole course of his detested life, and most deserved death*' is not a summary of the play that most editions broadcast.[59] Yet this may well have been what early modern Londoners who were literate read: it may have drawn them to the theatre, and, later, made them buy the printed quarto; it may have been what some of them thought the play was 'about'.

The bill was the first and sometimes only form in which a passer-by might encounter a play; as it was printed (the stationers' register includes the names of the four men who had the successive right to print players' bills from 1587–1642: John Charlewood, John Roberts, William [and Isaac] Jaggard, Thomas [and Richard] Cotes), all plays visibly belonged to the world of the printing house. And, as all plays for all playhouses had their bills produced by the allowed bill-printer, so advertising for all plays may have looked similar: the printing house brought the separate companies and playhouses together.

Even more than songs, prologues, and epilogues, the bill had a full life away from the play text as non-play literature. Playbills were advertisements, and their context was the world of other advertisements. Together with lawless posters or 'siquises' (so called because they usually began 'si quis . . .', 'if anyone . . .'), libels, and with the title pages to books that were also hung as advertisements, playbills clung to the doorposts of the houses of London, bringing the theatre visibly into the heart of the very city that had rejected it.[60] Indeed they were so present and so predictably a part of London life that Breton's hour-by-hour account of what happens in the morning of a London day includes the fact that by 'Nine of the Clocke' the 'Players Billes are almost all set up'.[61] Bills were varieties of text that embraced a mixture of permanence and changeability in their nature. Guessing from the one surviving English rope-dancing bill printed by the printers of the players' bills, and from the earliest surviving French playbill, it seems probable that bills were printed with 'gaps' for variable information. They were, that is to say, fixed and fluid, again, along definable lines. The rope-dancing bill, for instance, which appears to be for travelling players, has blanks for 'changeable information', here, place of performance. The blanks can be filled in manuscript; the rest is permanent. The rope-dancing bill reads:

> *[ms: At 9 a Clok]*
> At the *[ms: Rose in winestreet]*
> this present day shall bee
> showne rare dancing on the
> Ropes, Acted by his Majesties
> servants, wherein an Irish Boy of eight
> yeares old doth vault on the high rope,
> the like was never seene: And one Mayd
> of fifteene yeares of age, and another
> Girle of foure yeares of age, doe dance on
> the lowe Rope; And the said Girle of foure
> yeares of age doth turne on the Stage,

and put in fourescore threds into the eye
of an Needle. And other rare Activityes
of body, as vaulting and tumbling on
the Stage, and Egges dancing upon a
Staffe, with other rare varietyes of
Dancing, the like hath not beene seene in
the realme of England. And the merry
conceites of Jacke Pudding.
If God permit.
Vivat Rex.[62]

Stock playbills could, too, have had gaps around the lure or the title: a variety of fixity and variability is a hallmark of a text of this kind.

So now to the whole play as it might have existed in the box of playhouse 'books'. It may have been made up of a loosely tied bundle of papers, consisting of a book of dialogue (or several if the play were submitted piecemeal as some of Daborne's were),[63] some separate sheets containing songs and letters, other separate papers containing prologues and epilogues (unless kept elsewhere as no longer relevant), and finally, perhaps, a separate bill/title page providing the lure that attracted the audience. That is not to say that all plays existed like this. After all, some kind of 'complete' text was submitted to the Master of the Revels – though what kind and at what stage is queried by this argument. Nevertheless, substantial bits of play seem to have existed as separate but definable fragments, each raising the possibility of different authorship, and each capable of having other existences in other books, other places, and other contexts, being as much poems, jests, and advertisements as they were sections of the play. Even as bits of play text they may have differed in their level of permanence. Most permanent was, perhaps, the dialogue of the play, least permanent, perhaps, the prologue and epilogue. So plays could also have, internally, different levels of fixity.

The last point to be made is to do with the treatment of the 'book' by the playhouse. For though the full dialogue may have existed in one place, that is not what actors were given. Plays were disseminated as fragments: what actors had to learn from were called 'parts', the very word drawing attention to the fact that they were 'not whole'. These parts were made up of the speeches the actor was going to say with a 'cue' consisting of the one-to-three words preceding each speech. The speaker of the cue for professional productions was not generally named, and the length of the gap between one speech and another was not indicated. The actor, then, received his character as a roll or book of connected fragments, providing him with everything he would say but nothing that would be said to or about him beyond the cues. Of course, performance filled those gaps, but again that makes the play the 'thing performed' rather than the 'thing learned'; as parts were learned in full before group rehearsal, what the actor committed to memory was a context-limited fragment. Even for the actors, then, the play was fragmented, but along standard lines; indeed, if a play were never printed, then the only way that it was ever 'published' (in the sense of broadcast) was as 'parts' rather than as a whole.

A look at some surviving professional theatre 'parts' from the early modern period, the Restoration, and eighteenth century, shows just what an actor characteristically had to work with. The later examples confirm the normality of the surviving early modern professional 'part' and show the consonance of professional theatre parts over time. Questions about the fixed and changeable nature of a play's dialogue will relate, of course, to the nature of the text from which the actor learned.

Here follows a section from the part of 'Orlando' from Robert Greene's *Orlando Furioso*. It is the earliest surviving British professional theatre part and dates from the 1590s; damage to the left of the text has rendered the part harder to read than it was originally.

—————————————————————— Angelica
ah. my dear Anglica
syrha fetch me the harping starr from heaue*n*
Lyra the pleasant mystrell of the s[h]phears
that J may dau*n*ce a gayliard wth Angelica
r<u> me to Pan, bidd all his waternimphes
come wth ther baggpypes, and ther tamberins.
—————————————————————— for a woema*n*
howe fares my sweet Angelica?
—————————————————————— for hir honesty
Art thou not fayre Angelica
  s
<w>hos<e>browes a[re] faire as faire Jlythia
that darks Canopus wth her siluer hewe.
—————————————————————— art Angelica
Why are not these, those ruddy coulered cheek*es*
wher both the lillye, and the blusshing rose
sytt*es* equall suted, wth a natyue redd[64]

The part of 'Ignoramus' (1662) is similar. Again, the piece is for professional performance, again, the cues vary from one to three words; again, their speaker is not, typically, named:

—————————————————————— persona.
oh how they linger! I must not let him pass

nor know I how to keep him while she come;
'save you Sir
——————————————————— mittimus.
a poore man sir, spent my whole estate in law,
————————————————————— away.
I beseech your councell.
————————————————————— legem pone.
this greedy Cerberus must have a morsel,
and I have nothing left, but one poore souz.
perhaps he may fasten on't –
indeed sir I am a very poore man.
————————————————————— nihil dicit
a slender fee sir, I beseech your councell.
————————————————————— the case[65]

Finally, here is a section from the opening of a part for Scrub in Farquhar's
Beaux Stratagem. Dating from the 1730s, this particular part belonged to the
great eighteenth century actor Macklin:

> *Act 2*^{d}
> Enter L.D.P.S. [Left Door Prompt Side]
> at ————————————— Scrub
> Sir!
> ————————————— Week is this
> Sunday, an't pleasure your Worship.
> ————————————— Scrub.
> Sir!
> ————————————— of your Razor   *{Exit*[66]

That plays were learned in this form seems to have affected the way they
were revised and is likely also to have affected the way they were written. Revising fully over an entire text will have been the least desirable of all methods
of revision – for that will then have obliged the prompter to recall each separate actor's part, and rewrite it, before asking the actor to learn over again what
he had already committed to memory – but in a slightly different form. A look
at Shakespeare's *Hamlet* in 'good' quarto (1604/5) and in folio reveals a
different attitude to revisions. The cuts and changes made to *Hamlet* between
the earlier (quarto) text and the later (folio) one are not made to all parts – so
not all parts have to be returned to the prompter or relearned. In fact only
eight parts are altered: Hamlet, Gertrude, Claudius, Horatio, Laertes, Rosen-
crantz, Guildenstern and Osric (the five leads and the three clowns). The first
point, then, is that revision in *Hamlet* seems to have happened along 'strands'

in a play rather than over the whole text. If songs, prologues and epilogues can be seen as 'strands' in a text too, then another picture of just what a play is emerges. Rather than being one entire text, a play appears to have a linear rope-like structure: it is made up of different independent threads each of which can be pulled or removed.

Another part-based element of the revision in *Hamlet* is that almost all alterations are within-speech, as in the example below.

> O throwe away the worser part of it,
> And leave the purer with the other halfe,
> Good night, but goe not to my Uncles bed,
> Assume a virtue if you have it not,
> ~~That monster custome, who all sence doth eate~~
> ~~Of habits devil, is angel yet in this~~
> ~~That to the use of actions faire and good,~~
> ~~He likewise gives a frock or Livery~~
> ~~That aptly is put on~~ refraine to night,
> And that shall lend a kind of easines
> To the next abstinence, ~~the next more easier:~~
> ~~For use almost can change the stamp of nature,~~
> ~~And either the devil, or throwe him out~~
> ~~With wonderous potency:~~ once more good night,
> And when you are desirous to be blest,
> Ile blessing beg of you, for this same Lord
> I doe repent; but heaven hath pleasd it so
> To punish me with this, and this with me,
> That I must be their scourge and minster,
> I willb estowe him and will answere well
> The death I have him; so againe good night
> I must be cruell only to be kinde,
> This bad beginnes, and worse remaines behind.
> On word more good Lady.
>   (Q2, I4a–b; F 2540–55)[67]

Within-speech cuts do not disturb cues; other actors' parts are thus not affected by the alteration (and so do not have to be called back to be changed or relearned). Play revisions often take this form, happening in small fragments throughout the speeches of a play, rather than, as a modern reviser might expect, over entire scenes. If cued parts offer the explanation for this, then they also offer a new way of conceiving the 'solidity' of a text for, by implication, a speech is more changeable in its middle than in its cue-line.

Plays, then, should not always be regarded like epic poems in which each bit of text has the same worth. Rather, each variety of fragment could have a different anticipated lifespan, and a different relationship to the full text: the play could be made up of patches of varying fixity and, as has been said, the audience listened to the play partly with an ear for its 'reusable' bits. The fragments that make up a text and that a text resolves into shape the way it is written, revised, and learned affect the way it survives. Larger questions, too, attend on the patchiness of the play. In a play that can be, as I have argued, at its root fragmentary rather than whole, where is the author – and, perhaps, more disconcertingly, where is – and what is – the text?

The future

Of late, modern criticism has seriously questioned Victorian ideas of authorship and characterization. The unity of the play text itself, however, has hardly been queried. Even in the 1980s when play revision came to the fore as a subject, the use of Shakespeare's *King Lear* as a test case, which was an unusual 'full play revision', hid the fact that more common play revision was bitty, slight and confined to certain parts, or to the elements of the play that were generically different, like songs.[68] Indeed, what is intriguing in an age so interested in 'deconstruction' is why the text as fragment has not been more seriously considered already. There are at least two reasons. One is that editing has become increasingly important over the years – and it is in the nature of editing to make play texts look as complete as possible. Another is because of current ambivalence towards the 'fragment' as discussed above. Here, then, is a direction to be explored further.

It is by no means the only direction. The power of the 'heap' of information as used in the above argument is to show general trends happening across theatres and across periods. The demerits of that system are the same as its merits: that evidence gathered from different sources and periods leads to statements that are generalized, which means that they may not be true to a certain play text, a particular author, or a specific theatre. Nevertheless, it is only writing that examines 'trends' that can find a home for sources not clearly attributable to one theatre or author: the anecdote from a poem that flanks Randolph's poetry, for instance, that mentions the playwrights who

> But Midwives are, not Parents to a Play . . .
> Their Brains lye all in Notes; Lord! how they'd look
> If they should chance to loose their Table-book![69]

All the researchers of unattributable (or multi-attributable) information can do is provide a substantial collection of material to show how broadly true their observations may be. Which introduces the most awkward and irresolvable problem arising from the nature of much evidence of the early modern period, but particularly printed evidence of the kind employed in this argument. That is that each year of the early modern period provides more books than the previous year; there are considerably more books printed after 1600 than before. Also, more books have lasted from after 1600 than before: books are more likely to survive as part of a collection, and the habit of book collecting, which increased as wealth increased, became more common as printed matter became more available after 1600. For both reasons, book evidence will of necessity provide more examples from after 1600 (the date itself is a rough one, used for convenience). Combined with that is a separate problem that, again, hovers roughly around 1600: that is that the mode of discourse, particularly the telling of anecdotes, also changed around the turn of the seventeenth century, and writers on every subject simply become more ready to tell stories as time goes on. It will be noticed that most of the sources used here were published (though not necessarily written) post-1600. That means that their relevance to pre-1600 plays is always open to question. There can be no answers to these important caveats; rather, there can be a suggestion about the use of this kind of research.

Each different modern method of interpretation offers a way of 'clustering' material around a certain topic; each discovers points that other kinds of clustering ignore. That is why balance is important, and to provide balance there should be as many different approaches as possible. And there are. The movement towards separating evidence into small clearly defined units – chapters in this volume look at particular companies, and single plays – is met by another towards making the units as large as possible – other chapters in this volume look beyond the theatre for evidence of 'theatricality': pageants, public speeches, etc. My argument deals with broad sweeps of time and evidence, and so is more closely aligned with the second movement than with the first. It can be related to other general trend-based work like Alan Dessen's brilliant staging discoveries – discoveries that can only be made by collecting together as many stage directions from as many plays as possible.[70] Every topic, in highlighting one element of theatre history, of necessity deselects another kind. A chapter on strolling players may obscure gender issues; a chapter on gender may obscure architecture. All are therefore necessary both in themselves and as correctives: each counters the partiality of another.

A final point is that the inferences this chapter has made from what looks like old-fashioned historical research very much reflect the age – this age – in which they are drawn. The method 'deconstructs' the text along certain lines and then, up to a certain point, 'de-authors' it. So the conclusions put forward as being gathered objectively and without an agenda also seem to be, disturbingly, historically contingent. Perhaps this merely shows the truth of the observation that all research is a product of its time. Or perhaps what has happened is what David Scott Kastan suggests should (and will) take place more and more in the post-theory world: that literary studies will return 'to history, albeit a history that must itself be inflected by . . . theoretical initiatives'.[71]

The return to history undoubtedly is a feature of what will happen next. Rare books and even manuscripts are permanently available to be studied on the Internet; whereas before only scholars in easy reach of a few copyright libraries were able to produce book-based research, now anyone attached to a university that subscribes to EEBO (Early English Books Online) or LION (Literature OnLine) has most major books of the sixteenth to eighteenth century at his or her fingertips. This chapter started out by suggesting that the material available shaped the interpretations produced: with more material more widely available, theatre history will become increasingly filled with new evidence and all the new possibilities that implies.

Will the 'new' historical work be different in its nature from old historical work? Anthony Munday, in the 1580s, compared 'the writers [of plays]' to

> Tailors, who having their sheers in their hand, can alter the facion of anie thing into another forme, & with a new face make that seeme new which is old. The shreds of whose curiositie our Historians have now stolen from them, being by practise become as cunning as the Tailor to set a new upper bodie to an old coate; and a patch of their owne to a peece of anothers.[72]

Perhaps the theatre historian, even across time, is only another version of the play-patcher anyway.

Notes

1. For a description based on archaeological discoveries, see R. A. Foakes, 'Henslowe's Rose/Shakespeare's Globe' in this volume.
2. See, for instance, the new material gathered in William Ingram, *The Business of Playing* (New York: Cornell University Press, 1992). David Kathman's 'Biographical Index to the English Theatre' website (*http://www.clark.net/pub/tross/ws/bd/kath.htm*) will be a primary source for 'new' biographical information. John Astington's *New Dictionary of National Biography* entrance for Andrew Cane, forthcoming, is an example of how biography can affect our understanding of the theatre: it shows that important actors could hold two discrete professions and looks at how being a goldsmith impinged on Cane's acting life.
3. The tremendous and enormous exceptions to that are in the new evidence provided in the works of Andrew Gurr.
4. A. S. Gent, *The Booke of Bulls, baited with two centuries of bold jests* . . . (1636), 137–8.
5. F. P. Wilson, 'E. K. Chambers', in *Shakespearian and other Studies* (Oxford: Clarendon Press, 1969), 212.
6. E. K. Chambers, *The Elizabethan Stage*, 4 vols (Oxford: Clarendon Press, 1923), 1: viii.
7. Gerald Eades Bentley, *The Jacobean and Caroline Stage*, 7 vols (Oxford: Clarendon Press, 1941–68).

8. *OED* dates the first recorded use of 'playwright' to 1687, but in fact the word was extant by 1617. See John Davies, *Wits Bedlam* (1617), F7a: 'of all *Glory*, purchas'd by the small, / A *Play-wright*, for his *Praise*, payes most of all!'; Henry Fizgeffrey, *Notes from Blackfriars* (1617), F7a: Crabbed (Websterio) / The Play-wright, Cart-wright'. Ben Jonson publishes poems 'To Play-wright' and 'On Play-wright' in his *The Workes of Benjamin Jonson* (1640).

9. Thomas Dekker, *Newes from Hell* (1606) in *The Non-Dramatic Works of Thomas Dekker*, 5 vols, ed. Alexander B. Grosart (1884, New York: Russell and Russell, 1963), 2: 146.

10. George Wither[s], *Abuses* (1613), 224.

11. Constantia Munda, *The Worming of a mad Dogge* (1617), 3.

12. Barnaby Rich, *Faultes Faults, and nothing else but Faultes* (1606), B4b. There are many such references. For an earlier one see John Marston, *Scourge of Villanie* (1598), H4a: 'H'ath made a common-place booke out of plaies, / And speakes in print, at least what ere he sayes / Is warranted by Curtaine plaudites'. Dekker's gull in *The Guls Horne-Booke* (1609) reproduced in *Non-Dramatic Works*, 2: 254, is advised to 'hoard up the finest play-scraps you can get, upon which your leane wit may most savoury feede, for want of other stuffe'.

13. Thomas Beedome, *Poems Divine and Humane* (1641), G5a. Again, this is one of many references. John Stephens, *Satyrical Essayes Characters and Others* (1615), 276, describes a lawyer's clerk who 'dares attempt a mistresse' only 'with Jests, or speeches stolne from Playes'; even Robert Burton in *The Anatomy of Melancholy* (1621), 581, bemoaned the 'silly gentlewomen' who 'are fetched over ... by a company of gulls ... that have nothing in them but a fewe players endes and complements'.

14. Thomas Trescot, *The Zealous Magistrate* (1642), C3b.

15. For the first, see Thomas Lodge, *Wits Miserie* (1596), 56: 'He ... looks as pale as the Visard of ye ghost which cried so miserally at ye Theator like an oister wife, Hamlet, revenge'; Samuel Rowlands, *The Night Raven* (1620), D2a: 'I will not cry Hamlet Revenge my greeves'; *Sir Thomas Smithes Voiage and Entertainment in Rushia* (1605), K1a: 'his fathers Empire and Government, was but as the Poeticall Furie in a Stage-action, ... a first, but no second to any Hamlet; and ... now Revenge, just Revenge was coming with his Sworde drawne against him ... to fill up those Murdering Sceanes'. For the second, see E. S., *Anthropophagus: the Man-Eater* (1624), 14: 'These ambi-dexter Gibionites [flatterers], are like the Sea-calfes, Crocodiles, Otters ... Aristotle & Plinie speake of ... for they are like Hamlets ghost, hic & ubique, here and there, and every where, for their owne occasion'; Wye Saltonstall, *Picturae Loquentes* (1631), E4a: 'Hee's as nimble as Hamlets ghost heere and everywhere'.

16. All texts at this point contain a version of these two lines (here quoted from the first folio): 'The nights are wholsome, then no Planets strike, / No Fairey talkes, nor Witch hath power to Charme', TLN 161–2. Henceforth all quotations from Shakespeare's folio will be provided from Charlton Hinman's *The Norton Facsimile: the First Folio of Shakespeare* (New York: W. W. Norton, 1968), using the through-line-numbering (TLN) of that edition.

17. W. B., *A Helpe to Discourse* (1623), 249–50. The misquoted 'tune' is repeated in all subsequent reprintings of the book.

18. MS Bodleian Eng. Poet. D. 3, reproduced in *Shakespearean Extracts from Edward Pudsey's Booke*, collected by Richard Savage (Stratford on Avon: John Smith, 1888), 52: 'Against yᵗ tyme wherin oʳ savio's birth is celebrated yᵗ cock singeth al night long; then no spirits dare stir abroad, the nightes bee wholsome; no planets, ffayries or witches hurt'.

19. See Ben Jonson's *Sejanus* (1605). More on this subject can be found in Mark Bland, 'The Appearance of the Text in Early Modern England', *TEXT*, 11 (1998), 91–127.

20. John Marston, *What you Will* (1607), B1a. Other examples of 'lost songs' can be found in William Bowden, *The English Dramatic Lyric* (New Haven: Yale University Press, 1951), 87–94.

21. William Habington, *The Queene of Arragon* (1640), 2.1. D3a.

22. Ibid., I2b–I3a.

23. *The Annals of English Drama 975–1700* by Alfred Harbage, rev. S. Schoenbaum, 3rd edn, rev. Sylvia Stoler Wagonheim (London and New York: Routledge, 1989) records that *Rape* was a Queen Anne's production and that *Queen of Arragon* was performed by both amateurs and the King's Men. Other plays with songs grouped aside from the main body of the text include Middleton's *Mad World* (1640 ed.), played by Queen Henrietta's Men, which has a single song at the back, Thomas Dekker's *The Shoomakers Holiday* (1600), an Admiral's Men play, which has the songs placed at the front of the text before the prologue, Philip Massinger and Nathan Field's *The Fatall Dowry* (1632), a King's Men's play, which also has the songs at the front, but has no prologue. A song is slightly misplaced within the text by the printer of *Love's Cure* in Francis Beaumont and John Fletcher's *Comedies and Tragedies* (1647), 134; it, too, may be a King's Men's play.

24. John Webster, *The Works*, ed. David Gunby, David Carnegie, Antony Hammond and Doreen DelVecchio (Cambridge: Cambridge University Press, 1995), 1: 527. My thanks to David Carnegie for this example.

25. See Thomas Middleton, *Hengist, King of Kent; or the Mayor of Queenborough*, ed. from the manuscript in the Folger Shakespeare Library by R. C. Bald (New York and London: Charles Scribner's Sons, 1938), xxxiii. The 'Willow song' is absent from the quarto of *Othello* (1622), though the surrounding text still suggests the expectation that it should be sung. For a provocative discussion of this textual crux, see E. A. J. Honigman, *The Texts of Othello and Shakespearian Revision* (New York: Routledge, 1996), 11–14.

26. MS Huntington HM 4, fol. 191.

27. See F. W. Sternfeld, *Music in Shakespearean Tragedy* (London: Routledge and Kegan Paul, 1963), 29, 173.

28. Richard Ligon, *A true and exact History of the Island of Barbados* (1657), 12: 'Dinner being neere halfe done . . . in comes an old fellow . . . and plaide us for a Noveltie, The *Passame sares galiard*; a tune in great esteeme, in Harry the fourths dayes; for when Sir *John Falstaff* makes his Amours to Mistresse *Doll Tear-sheet*, *Sneake* and his Companie, the admired fiddlers of that age, playes this tune, which put a thought into my head, that if time and tune be the Composits of Musicke, what a long time this tune had in sayling from *England* to this place.'

29. Thomas Carew, *Poems, with a Maske* (1651), 83. For other varieties of textual disturbance around songs see Tiffany Stern, 'Letters, Verses and Double Speech-Prefixes in *The Merchant of Venice*', *Notes and Queries*, 244 (1999), 231–3.

30. MS Huntington HM 116 L10–F3, fol. 125.

31. Reproduced in *A Choice Ternary of English Plays*, ed. William M. Baillie (Binghampton, NY: Medieval and Renaissance Texts and Studies, 1984), 45.

32. Beaumont and Fletcher, *Fifty Comedies and Tragedies* (1679), A1a.

33. Gerald Eades Bentley, *The Profession of Dramatist in Shakespeare's Time* (Princeton, NJ: Princeton University Press, 1986), 257.

34. Sir John Mennes, *Wit Restor'd in severall Select Poems* (1658), 162.

35. The chorus' reference to Essex's projected Irish triumphs (present only in the folio 1623 text) would seem to date the inserts to between March and September 1599, suggesting early removal. See Andrew Gurr's introduction to his *Henry V* (Cambridge: Cambridge University Press, 1992), 7.

36. See Peter W. M. Blayney, *The First Folio of Shakespeare* (Washington, DC: Folger Library Publications, 1991), 21.

37. For some examples of revised plays with new stage-orations, see Bentley, *Dramatist*, 137.

38. A. S. Gent, *The Booke of Bulls* (1636), C4b–C5a.

39. Tiffany Stern, ' "A Small-beer Health to his Second Day": Playwrights, Prologues, and First Performances in the Early Modern Theatre', *Studies in Philology* (forthcoming, 2004).

40. Henry Glapthorne, *Poems* (1639), 28; Thomas Heywood, *Pleasant Dialogues and Dramma's* (1637), 247. Shakespeare's *Richard III* is published without a prologue.

41. Ben Jonson, *Ben Jonson*, ed. C. H. Herford and Percy Simpson, 11 vols (Oxford: Clarendon Press, 1925–52), 6: 15.

42. Jonson, *Jonson*, 6: 163; Lodowick Carlell, *Arviragus and Philicia* (1639), A3a; James Shirley, *Poems* (1646), 149.

43. Christopher Brooke, *Ghost of Richard the Third* (1614), π4b.

44. John Day, *Isle of Gulls* (1606), A2a.

45. Thomas Nabbes, *Tottenham Court* (1636), A3b.

46. Thomas Middleton, *The Family of Love* (1608), in *The Works*, ed. A. H. Bullen, 8 vols (London, 1886), 3: 7; Philip Massinger, *The City Madam*, in *The Plays and Poems of Philip Massinger*, ed. Philip Edwards and Colin Gibson, 5 vols (Oxford: Clarendon Press, 1976), 4: 19.

47. Thomas Dibdin, *The Reminiscences of Thomas Dibdin*, 4 vols (London: Colburn, 1827), 1: 7–8.

48. Walter Mountfort, *The Launching of the Mary* (1633), ed. John Henry Walter (Oxford: Oxford University Press, 1933), 124. See also R. A., *The Valiant Welshman* (1615), I4b: 'Bells are the dead mans musicke: ere I goe, / Your Clappers sound will tell me I, or no.'

49. Shirley, *The Duke's Mistress* (1638) in *Dramatic Works and Poems of James Shirley*, ed. William Gifford, 6 vols (London: John Murray, 1833), 4: 274.

50. Prologue to *The Scholars* in Francis Beaumont, *Poems by Francis Beaumont* (1653), 75. See also Brome, *The English Moor* in *Dramatic Works*, 3 vols (London, 1873), 2: 86, who wants no one to claim he 'skulks behind the hangings . . . affraid / Of a hard censure'; Jonson and Brome who stand together 'behind the Arras' to watch the reception of the 'new sufficient Play', *Bartholomew Fair*, Jonson, *Ben Jonson*, 6: 13, 15, Henry Glapthorne who, in *Ladies Privilege* (1640), J2b, is described as standing 'pensive in the Tyring-house to heare Your Censures of his Play'. For other examples and more on the subject, see Tiffany Stern, 'Behind the Arras: the Prompter's Place in the Shakespearean Theatre', *Theatre Notebook* (2001), 110–18.

51. Jonson, *Ben Jonson*, 3: 602. Abraham Cowley, *Poems* (1656), [a]1b.

52. Andrew Gurr, 'Maximal and Minimal Texts: Shakespeare v. the Globe', *Shakespeare Survey*, 52 (1999), 68–87.

53. For inflated first performance charges see, for instance, Jasper Mayne's poem on Ben Jonson in *Jonsonus Virbius* (1638), 31: 'when thy Foxe had ten times acted beene, / Each day was first, but that 'twas cheaper seene'. For more on first performance admission prices before the interregnum see Chambers, *Elizabethan Stage*, 2: 532; entrance charges for new plays during the Restoration period are referred to in

Samuel Pepys, *The Diary*, ed. Robert Latham and William Matthews, 11 vols (London: Bell and Hyman Ltd, 1970–83), 2: 234: 'to the Opera . . . and it being the first time, the pay was doubled'.

54. *The Costly Whore* (1633), H4b; Jasper Mayne's *The City Match* (1639), B1a.

55. R. A., *The Valiant Welshman* (1615), I4b.

56. Richard Brome, *Novella* in *Works*, 1: 179.

57. Thomas Dekker, *If This Be Not a Good Play, the Devil Is In It* (1612), in *The Dramatic Works of Thomas Dekker*, ed. Fredson Bowers, 4 vols (Cambridge: Cambridge University Press, 1953), 3: 121.

58. William Davenant, *The Dramatic Works of Sir William D'Avenant*, ed. James Maidment and W. H. Logan, 5 vols (Edinburgh: W. Paterson, 1872), 4: 31. Henslowe gave a financial gift to Day 'after the playing of the second part of Strowd' – see Bentley, *Dramatist*, 131.

59. William Shakespeare, *Richard III* (1598), title page.

60. For the hanging of book title pages see R. B. McKerrow, 'Booksellers, Printers, and the Stationers' Trade', in *Shakespeare's England*, 2 vols (Oxford: Clarendon Press, 1916), 2: 212–39 (231). More on this subject and the subject of playbills will be provided by Tiffany Stern, '"On each Wall / And Corner Poast": Playbills, Title-pages, and Advertising in Early Modern London', forthcoming.

61. Nicholas Breton, *Fantasticks: Serving for a Perpetuall Prognostication* (1626), E4b–F1a.

62. Reproduced in William Van Lennep, 'Some English Playbills', *Harvard Library Bulletin*, 8: 2 (1954), 235–241, where it is wrongly attributed to Jaggard's printing house. It was in fact printed by Cotes and therefore dates to some time in or after 1627.

63. Daborne letter to Henslowe, 25 June 1613: 'J have took extraordynary payns wth the end & altered one other scean in the third act which they have now in parts', in W. W. Greg, *Henslowe Papers*, 3 vols (London: A. H. Bullen, 1907), 3: 73.

64. MS Dulwich College I, Item 138. Reproduced as facsimile with transcript in W. W. Greg's *Dramatic Documents from the Elizabethan Playhouse*, 2 vols (Oxford: Oxford University Press, 1969), 2, and against the text of the 1594 quarto to *Orlando Furioso* in Greg's *Two Elizabethan Stage Abridgements* (Oxford: Malone Society, 1922).

65. Part of 'Ignoramus' for Ferdinando Parkhurst's play *Ignoramus or The Academical-Lawyer* in the Houghton Library. Title continues 'Acted at the Cock-pitt in Drury Lane; And also before . . . The King and Queen . . . on . . . 1st of November 1662'.

66. Macklin's part of Scrub in George Farquhar's *The Beaux Stratagem*, for Drury Lane, 9 May 1738? Harvard theatre Collection MS (TS 1197.54.5).

67. Other within-speech cuts occur at 1.2.60; 2.2.210; 2.2.393; 2.2.320; 3.2.205; 3.4.72; 3.4.73; 3.4.190; 4.1.39; 4.7.88; 4.7.99; 5.1.100. For more on the subject of parts and revision in *Hamlet*, see Tiffany Stern, *Rehearsal from Shakespeare to Sheridan* (Oxford: Clarendon Press, 2000), 106–10.

68. Shakespeare's *King Lear* became the model for the critical study of revision after the publication of *The Division of the Kingdoms: Shakespeare's Two Versions of King Lear*, ed. Gary Taylor and Michael Warren (Oxford: Oxford University Press, 1983). How actors could relearn a play with changes as substantial as those in *Lear* is a mystery to me, and I can only conjecture that the two *Lear* texts were performed by different players.

69. Ric. West, 'To the pious Memory of my deare Brother in Law, Mr Thomas Randolph', in Thomas Randolph, *Poems* (1640), B4b.

70. See Alan Dessen, *Elizabethan Stage Conventions and Modern Interpreters* (Cambridge: Cambridge University Press, 1984); Alan Dessen, *Recovering Shakespeare's Theatrical*

Vocabulary (Cambridge: Cambridge University Press, 1995); and Alan Dessen and Leslie Thomson, *A Dictionary of Stage Directions in English Drama, 1580–1642* (Cambridge: Cambridge University Press, 1999).

71. David Scott Kastan, *Shakespeare After Theory* (New York and London: Routledge, 1999), 28.

72. [Anthony Munday], *A Second and Third Blast of a Retrait from Playes* (1580), 105–6.

Part IV
Women's Work

9
Slanderous Aesthetics and the Woman Writer: the Case of *Hole v. White*

Carolyn Sale

In 1607, a group of citizens from Wells, Somerset, attempted to publish a 'wicked Libell in Ryme' that celebrated a series of slanderous street shows in which the citizens had taken John Hole, a local constable, as their principal target. The libellous 'ryme' in question, 'My Loving Friends That Love to Play', never made it into print. If it had, it could not have identified its author in either its front matter or its contents. The 'ryme' survives, however, in the records for the resulting Star Chamber trial, *Hole v. White*. This chapter is about the signatureless character of the 'Ryme' and the 'histrionicall shewes' that the poem celebrated. If it had made it into print, 'My Loving Friends That Love to Play' would have had no author in the law's terms, that is, no person to whom its slander could be traced back. The surviving records for the trial show that in its attempt to establish an 'author' the prosecution resorted to a rhetoric of 'procurement', 'advisement', and 'direction' to trace the slander back to a 'first cause' or 'first maker'. 'My Loving Friends That Love to Play' boasts of the defendants' success at shielding or screening the 'first cause' or 'first mover' of the slanderous campaign in its chorus: 'yett I doe lyve in quiett rest and thinke my holinge game the best'.[1] It is nevertheless possible for us to read the surviving records for evidence that the 'first mover' or 'first cause' of the slanderous activity in Wells and the 'contriver' of the slanderous street shows was a woman, Thomasine White. Reading the trial documents for the very thing that the defendants attempted to obscure, Thomasine White's hand in the affair, we recover for British theatre history a woman's involvement in early modern provincial theatrics as originator or 'author'. The recovery of this woman's hand has a particular frisson for those of us who wish to write the history of women's involvement in theatrical practices in England as Thomasine White claimed to be illiterate. The scrawl with which she signs her deposition – which is something more than an 'x' or cross, but certainly not a fully-fledged signature – is thus a tantalizing metonym; it registers White's material involvement in the slanderous campaign, but just barely. To make her part in the affair legible, we have to read through the defendants' feints – a feint of which it, as a register of her imputed inability to read and write, may itself be a part. We also have to read the documents for the impact upon them of the legal fiction of coverture.

In his 'Bill of Complaint' to the King, John Hole alleged that the slanderous campaign began as a response to his objections, as constable of the peace, to the community's celebration of the annual May Games on the first Sunday in May 1607. Hole claimed that these celebrations, whose traditional carnivalesque fare included a Lord and Lady of the May, a Robin Hood, a 'Satire in Skynns', Prince Arthur and his knight, St George and the Dragon, and Diana and Acteon, were against the king's recent proclamation against playing. The defendants contended that Hole was misinterpreting the king's proclamation, which applied, they argued, only to playing during the time of divine service and not to the special circumstances of the May Day celebrations. (The mayor, Alexander Towse, who concurred with this interpretation of the proclamation, was named as a defendant.) Insisting that his interpretation was the right one, and arresting several of their number, Hole placed himself in solid opposition to the carnivalesque spirit of the games. The defendants proceeded to make him the subject of their play in the street 'shewes' they mounted on subsequent Sundays. They did so most aggressively in the show called the 'Holing Game'.

In the 'Holing Game', several actors carried a wooden construction upon which there were three painted figures. These were taken to be Hole, a friend, Hugh Mead, and the wife of another friend, Anna Yard. From the figures jutted forth three tracks along which bowls could be 'trundled' towards holes that had been cut out beneath the figures. By 'holing' and encouraging others to do so, the actors enacted a lewd form of symbolic revenge, displacing the violence that they would have liked to do to Hole on to the balls that entered the holes. The game also performed a symbolic arrest: in it, Hole was a trapped figure – a hart like the Acteon to which 'My Loving Friends That Love to Play' refers ('Acteon from man converted was into an hart . . . & all him chast to see him fall' [268]). Symbolically castrating or cutting Hole by turning him into a hole – a space of lack, a cut man? – the show made Hole the site for a violent enforced filling. He could be struck, and figuratively filled and killed, over and over by anyone who chose to trundle a ball along the track leading to his painted figure. If Hole had attempted to prevent the symbolic inversions that destabilized authority and the usual social hierarchy, the defendants performed, as a substitute for the disrupted May Games, another kind of inversion, one in which Hole had to endure the full force of the carnivalesque energy that the May Games traditionally embodied. May Day and everything it represented prevailed, at his expense.

The 'Holing Game' also called Hole's authority into question. In an exchange between two of the actors, one of whom impersonated a constable of the peace, and the other of whom impersonated a notary or scrivener, the defendants insinuated that it was Hole's activities, rather than their own, which ought to be forbidden:

> . . . some other of the said confederacy did then & there in like sort with a loud voyce often say vnto the said Gamage [the actor playing the constable of the peace] theis wordes (videlicet) Holinge is against the kinges procla- macion & not sufferable in the streates & therfore yf you will needes hole it goe Hole it in the Mead, whervpon the said Gamage speaking to the said pretended scribe or Notary said with a loud voyce, Sett it downe Notary Holinge is against the kinges proclamacion. . . .
>
> (266)

This is the defendants' slanderous activity at its cleverest, for through it they mocked the processes through which Hole attempted to prohibit their activi- ties. At the same time, they symbolically appropriated the very forms of writing that he was attempting to use against them. If Hole had prohibited their activ- ities, they here prohibited his; ostensibly mocking their own 'holing' as against the king's proclamation, the defendants insinuated that it was Hole, not they, who had a tendentious relationship with authority. They insinuated, in short, that he was using others as the instruments through which he wrote (author- ity) rather than read (it), and they represented the mechanisms through which he would usually exercise his authority in order to demonstrate that they too were capable of appropriating media to similar ends.

The 'confederates' took care, however, not to name Hole directly in either the 'shewes' or the two libellous 'rymes' written in connection with them. The chorus of 'My Loving Friends That Love to Play', the first line of which I quoted above, claims that the 'Holing Game' was best of all the May Day 'sports' and 'shewes'; but since it does not specify what the 'Holing Game' entailed, or whom it was about, a reader or listener would have needed other knowledge of the allegedly slanderous activities for the reference to have had any defam- atory resonance. The second libellous rhyme, 'Tell Me of Flesh', likewise berates a figure of authority as a 'Puritane' and a 'Rascall', but explicitly refuses to 'pre- cisely tell' of whom it speaks (271). It gloats that the 'Rascall' has been put into a 'mad condicion' by his attempt, 'in informacion trottinge to and fro', to secure legal action against the 'confederates' but conspicuously avoids accus- ing him of anything specific (272). In the words of *Twelfth Night*'s Fabian, these are 'good notes', strategies that would have helped keep the writer from 'the blow of the law'.[2] As the seventeenth-century legal writer John March notes in

Actions for Slander, you were free to call someone a variety of names as long as you did not, in the course of your name-calling, refer to, or cite, a specific act for which your victim might be indicted. You were entirely free, for example, to call someone a 'seditious knave' because the words 'import an inclination' to sedition but do not specify, or claim knowledge of, any actual act of sedition; and '[t]o say of a man that he deserve[d] to be hanged' would not have made you vulnerable to an action for slander, for the words fail to prove that your victim has done anything to deserve hanging.[3] In general, the more foolish your slander, and the less reasonable, the better off you were from a legal standpoint. To have claimed, for example, that your horse could 'piss as good Beer as Dickes doth brew' would not have constituted actionable slander against Dickes the brewer because it would have been impossible for your horse to piss beer of any quality whatsoever (35). In the first decade of the seventeenth century, talk nonsense, and you may say what you will.

If 'Tell Me of Flesh' is filled with matter that would have been, from the law's perspective, either nonsense or 'winde' (its coded references to the people involved in the allegedly slanderous 'shewes' are largely gibberish), the 'Holing Game' yielded, according to Hole, a readily discernible text. Although the precise meaning of the street shows remains unclear, Hole contended that the 'Holing Game' insinuated his adultery with Anna Yard, by 'cast[ing] an ymputacion & scandall of incontinency vpon them' (266). Perhaps in anticipation of the objection that this interpretation of the action involved a 'strained construction' (3 March), the lawyer or lawyers assisting Hole presented his claim about the defamatory character of the 'Holing Game' in more general terms, contending that they were 'vnlawfully representinge' (263) Hole and his friends, no matter what the meaning, intended or perceived, of the 'leud representacions' (264). They took this tack in part because there was as yet no formal legal mechanism for holding 'ignominious signs' actionable; it was this facet of the trial that made *Hole v. White* a leading case. To further strengthen Hole's case, the 'Bill of Complaint' also argued that he was not the only person whose authority was being 'traduced' in the shows. Situating the street theatre in Wells in the larger political context of concurrent uprisings against the king in Northamptonshire, the 'Bill' suggests that the defendants' actions constituted an offence against the king. Through their 'common playes' (261), the defendants 'derided' the king's proclamation, and struck at authority writ large. If the king did not take action against the defendants, the 'Bill' argues by way of closing, he would provide others with a 'perilous example' of how they could use 'shewes' to 'manifest [their] contempt of the good lawes and statutes of this your highnes Realme' (274).

The defendants attempted to keep, in the words of *Twelfth Night*, 'o'th' windy side of the law' by portraying themselves as inadvertently drawn into the 'sport' at the last minute without having any conception of the purpose of the 'shewes'. Their narratives make it appear as if they simply stepped on to a (figurative) stage where all of the props lay waiting and ready for their use without themselves having been in any way rehearsed for their parts. Even Walter Smith, the man who cut, framed and painted the 'Holing Game' board and trundles, claimed not to know how his work would be deployed. Not only did Smith not know, he claimed, 'who was meant or intended to be represented or signified by the Pictures which this defendant painted vppon one of the saied bordes' (289), he was not certain who commissioned the construction.

The defendants claimed, in short, that they were all part of a spontaneous, authorless form of play that was wrongly construed by a certain figure of authority as a libellous attack upon him. The defendants' contention that they had all acted without any set script and with props that were provided by an unknown agent had clear legal ramifications: if the defendants could successfully claim that they had simply performed 'for mirth's sake' (312), 'sporte' (299), or their own delight actions that had no author (and thus no particular end or intention) and no real object (that is, no particular person whom the representations were intended to signify), they might have been able to elude, or at the very least, attenuate their judicial punishment. They thus responded evasively to the Star Chamber interrogatories that sought to discover who was the 'occasioner', 'urger', or 'first mover' of the speeches that they uttered in the course of the various spectacles. The prosecution sought out the 'occasioner' or 'urger' of the speeches because it wished to trace the physical manifestation of the slander back to its first cause, or its original source or 'author', a person who was thoroughly screened (as Maria, the occasioner of the plot against Malvolio is screened in *Twelfth Night*) behind the representations themselves. Since the prosecution did not possess any material evidence of authorship in the form of written parts for the actors, it had to conceive of authorship in broad terms, and posited the author as an adviser who may not have put pen to paper but nevertheless performed the function of a dramatist by putting words into actors' mouths. The interrogatories thus demanded of the defendants 'whoe contrived the said spich or gaue the plot or directions for it' (303) and, alternatively, 'who urged you by anie speeches to vse the sayde words of holinge or not holinge for a crowne, what weare the speeches and trewe manner of the occasion that vrged you thearevnto, and what weare the name or names of the person or persons that weare or was the occasioner or vrger of anie sutche speeches' (315). These questions, which clearly use the word 'person' to account for an 'author' of either gender, were consistently met with the response that no man had urged them to utter any set speeches or provided them with the instructions on how to play their parts.

The defendants' claim that they had no written text for their representations and did not act according to the instructions provided by any 'author', instantiates the idea of an authorless theatricality behind which the actual author or authors might be screened. Even if the prosecution could successfully prove that the representations had an intended meaning, a meaning that the 'voice of the people' could confirm (278), there would be no certain person from whom this intended meaning arose, and no certain original speaker of the slander – nobody, in theory, to prosecute as the author – although the prosecution could still have found guilty anyone who 'published' or passed on the slander by reciting or singing either of the two libellous rhymes. But the real import of this authorless theatricality may lie not in the defendants' attempt to evade any legal culpability for their actions, but rather in the opposite, the choice to take collective responsibility for a corporate act of authorship for which no one person should be responsible. The author of the 'Holing Game' acted, after all, as the first libellous rhyme suggests, on behalf of a collective – a collective of those who loved to play. In this model of authorship, if there was anyone at all who engaged in the material act of writing that involves paper and a pen, the person who took up the pen to inscribe the 'instructions' according to which they all operated was himself or herself the mere agent, actor, or instrument of the communal will to turn against Hole. In other words, while the fiction that the spectacles had no 'author' may have been legally expedient, it was also of the essence: there was no single author because the slanderous spectacle was a joint venture in which all the defendants merely took a part.

It is nevertheless of some importance that the surviving documents suggest that the defendants were equivocating when they claimed that they were 'not procured to doe this by any man' (308). It may have been a woman, Thomasine White, who orchestrated the slanderous 'shewes'. It is not clear just how great a role Thomasine played in the various activities for which the defendants stood indicted, but it is certain that at the very least she took the part of the Lady of the May in the May Day festivities that first sparked Hole's ire; attired children for their participation in the same; along with her husband, provided free room and board to an itinerant drummer, whose drumming, Hole contended, was responsible for drawing up to 3000 people to watch the 'Holing Game'; permitted one of her servants to read the verses celebrating the 'Holing Game' aloud in her shop; had at least one direct verbal encounter with Hole in the streets during the shows; was involved in a physical confrontation with him at the time of his reading aloud of the king's proclamation against playing; and had been heard to call for a maid to bring a broom to sweep down the 'filthy Hole' outside when John Hole had passed by her house. It was presumably on the basis of this heavy-handed pun on his name and her display of animus against him that Hole assumed that Thomasine was the animating spirit behind the 'Holing Game' and the libellous verses that celebrated it.

Thomasine herself was careful to contend that she played only one role in relation to the spectacles – that of an inadvertent and uncomprehending spectator. To the twentieth interrogatory for her examination, she claimed that, when she found herself a spectator to the street shows on 18 June, she watched them without perceiving or comprehending the slanderous meaning that Hole attributed to them: 'this def did not then know nor perceive by any circumstance or otherwise that the now complainant or Yarde, Meade, or Palmer mentioned in this interrogatory were there represented, or abused thereby' (6^v). The answer does double duty, since it simultaneously undermines Hole's contention that the show had a readily discernible 'common intendment'. To the twenty-fifth interrogatory, she denied that she 'procured' the boards upon which the complainant and his friends were represented in the 'Holing Game', and that the boards were currently in her possession (7^r). In fact, her responses all tend the same way: Thomasine sought to disprove that she had done anything of which the defendants were accused, other than costume little girls for their participation in the May Day festivities.

More importantly, Thomasine White attempted to defeat the prosecution's attempts to identify her as the author of the 'Holing Game' by contending that she could neither read nor write. Perhaps in anticipation of this claim of illiteracy, the prosecution framed all of the related interrogatories in terms that set up a division of labour between the person who 'contrived' or 'invented' the speeches and the verses, and the person who 'penned' them – the very division of labour, we might note, that the defendants themselves represented in the 'Holing Game', where one actor presided as 'author' and another as the 'scrivener' or scribe who set down his proscriptions. The 'Holing Game's' representation of authorship as an act to which individuals make various, disparate contributions clearly mocks, as I suggested earlier, the ways in which Hole writes his authority through others by parodying Hole's own emulation of the means by which the king asserted his power through proclamations and subaltern figures. But the representation may also constitute a theatrical in-joke, for this is also the model of authorship upon which the confederates might have had to rely if Thomasine White were indeed illiterate. Even though two of the actors in the street spectacles, William Gamage and William Morgan, claimed responsibility respectively for the two libellous rhymes, the prosecution pursued the possibility that the purportedly illiterate Thomasine was the first 'occasioner' of all of the slanderous activity, including the writing of the rhymes. It found some support for the suspicion that Gamage had acted as a scribe, setting down words that had originated with someone else, in his curious ignorance about the text. When pressed to explain what particular lines from 'My Loving Friends That Love to Play' meant, Gamage claimed that he 'kn[e]weth not' (146^r). This claim of ignorance extended to the wording of the chorus, 'yett I doe lyve in quiett rest and thinke my holinge game the best'. The line merited an interrogatory of its own because it so flagrantly held up somebody's proprietary relationship with the 'Holing Game' as author even as it withheld that author's name. On the one hand, Gamage's contention that 'he [could] not express any special meaning or yield any reason why the closing of every staff or verse of the rhume or libel mentioned' should use those words (145^v) may have constituted a simple refusal to supply representatives of the law with the meanings that would permit them to define the verses as libellous within the law's terms. But Gamage's evasiveness on this point supported the prosecution's general notion that he was doing with the verses precisely what he had done in the shows themselves, pass on the words of another. Fixing on his answer as evidence that he had acted as another's scribe, the prosecution demanded, in a subsequent interrogatory, 'who [had] advised [him] so to make the end of every or any verse or verses of the said rhyme in that manner' (153^r).

The prosecution's use of a broad conception of authorship in its attempt to establish Thomasine's authoritative relationship with the 'histrionicall shewes' and libellous 'rymes' has a certain allure for the materialist scholar who would like to be able to find evidence of women playing an authoritative role of any kind in theatrical production in the period. It would allow me, for example, to posit the idea of Thomasine White as an 'author' who was able, despite her purported illiteracy, to make use of theatrical media to her own ends even though I lack, along with the prosecution in *Hole v. White*, any conclusive material evidence to support this claim. Amongst her various other denials, Thomasine claims that she did not 'invent, contrive, or make, nor cause any other person to invent, contrive or make the first Libel, rhyme or verses', and there is no evidence anywhere in the records that directly confutes this. The trial records do, however, reveal that Thomasine White was lying on at least one other front.

Amongst her many denials, Thomasine claimed that not only had she not read, never mind written 'My Loving Friends', she had never so much as seen a copy of the verses. Her testimony on this point was directly contradicted by three other deponents. These deponents claimed that they were present at the Dean of Wells' house one evening when Thomasine arrived with a copy of the libellous verses in hand. The Dean's clerk, Henry Downton, claimed he found Thomasine, the Dean's wife, and several other women in the sitting room reading the verses aloud. It is not clear from his deposition which of the women was doing the reading, or if they were taking turns, but his deposition makes it clear that Thomasine not only had knowledge of the verses, but she was taking some pleasure in disseminating or 'publishing' them to others. This evidence would have been sufficient, from the prosecution's perspective, to establish her as a participant in the slanderous campaign, since the clerk witnesses her voluntarily passing on defamatory words. But other depictions of this scene of reading suggest that it furnished evidence to those present that Thomasine played a more assertive and more substantial role in the slanderous campaign.

Another deponent, Richard Bourne, suggested that all was being done at Thomasine's direction. He claimed that when the Dean's clerk entered the room, Thomasine commanded that he continue the reading for them: 'the said White's wife willed him to proceed' (50ᵛ). He also deposed that she 'willed him to tell Hole' that 'My Loving Friends That Love to Play' represented 'not a quarter of that that was intended' (50ᵛ). That statement suggests that Thomasine occupied a privileged position within the slandering circle. Even if she herself did not instigate all of the activities, she knew everything that would be done. Given that only one thing remained to be done by the date this statement was uttered – the defendants had not yet made their attempt to have 'My Loving Friends That Love to Play' published in London – it suggests that Thomasine imputed a great deal of value to that act of publication.

Other evidence in the records suggests that both Hole and the prosecution were right to home in on a woman as the 'first mover' of the slanderous activity in Wells. I have already suggested that both the 'Holing Game' and 'My Loving Friends That Love to Play' speak, each in its own way, to the identity of the author, the 'Holing Game' by representing the act of writing as a task shared between scrivener and constable, or between someone who conceives the text and someone who actually writes it down, 'My Loving Friends' by presenting its poetic voice as the 'Holing Game's' author. The second libellous rhyme furnishes us with another of the hints to the author's identity that the 'confederates', motivated by a sense of play, may have scattered throughout their texts – much as, we might note, Shakespeare builds cryptic references to Maria's writing of the riddling letter for Malvolio into that text. The second 'ryme' goes beyond the claim made in 'My Loving Friends That Love to Play' that several women of 'every sort' with their 'wealth maynteine[d] the sport', by suggesting that a single woman engineered or spearheaded the campaign that exposed Hole's 'secreat vices' to the world: 'Capten Fa: ra: ra: Cameleon like is tourned Apostata by sweete St Johane hee's like a felters hatte turnd wronge side outward' (272). The line speaks of the dynamic of slander in much the same terms as *Twelfth Night* speaks of the performative power of language, and curiously uses, as *Twelfth Night* does, a sumptuary figure: *Twelfth Night's* Feste likens the performative power of language to the turning wrong side out of a chevril glove ('A sentence is but a chev'ril glove to a good wit. How quickly the wrong side may be turn'd outward' [3.1.11–13]) while 'Tell Me of Flesh' likens the exposure of Hole's vices to the turning wrong-side-out of another garment, a felter's hat. These correspondences suggest that one group of provincial players may have been defining their activities and perhaps their aesthetic in relation to the work of a well-known playwright; and at least one other deponent, William Tyderleigh, confirms his sense of a connection between the activities in Wells and professional drama by claiming that when he heard William Morgan reading 'Tell Me of Flesh' aloud, Morgan's delivery, complemented by his moving hand and foot, convinced Tyderleigh that 'the said verses had been a parte of some play' (354). These connections are not, however, what is most important here. What should give us pause is the reference to 'sweet St. Johane'. Captain Fa: ra: ra, a bombastic, pretentious figure, has not simply been turned wrong-side-out, and had things that he would have preferred to keep hidden, like his adulterous affair with a friend's wife, made public to all, he has been cast out of the community, thrust into the role of apostate by a woman – a woman, we are to understand, who has taken, as the Joan of legend did, a leadership role in a domain or a realm of activities conventionally dominated by men. Joan led a cohort of men into battle; Wells' 'sweet St. Johane' leads a cohort of men, the men whose hands and feet she may be animating, into serial slanderous play. Hole's challenge was to find a way of convincing the prosecution that the woman whose identity was shielded by the appellation 'sweet St. Johane' was Thomasine White; and it is amusing that, in his attempts to accomplish this, he sought a slanderous text in Thomasine's speech about an everyday domestic activity, finding, in her command to her maid to 'sweep down that filthy hole outside' an otherwise irrecoverable link between 'sweet St. Johane' and her handiwork.

But if the documents suggest in myriad ways that Thomasine White was the 'first maker' of the slanderous activity in Wells in 1607, one thing is clear: if Thomasine White did indeed operate in any sense like an author in relation to the slanderous spectacles in *Hole v. White*, her participation in an aesthetic of slander in which the author disappears thwarts the attempt to find any material traces of her 'hand' or concrete evidence of her contributions. If she wrote anything, that act of writing was as ephemeral as the scene of reading at the Dean of Wells' house; and if she were indeed illiterate and incapable of writing anything other than the scrawl with which she signed her deposition, her text disappeared when the actors in whom it was made manifest walked away from the streets that were their stage. I contend, however, that the trial records provide us with more than just the tantalizing possibility that Thomasine White orchestrated and in one sense or another wrote the series of street 'shewes' that took place in Wells in 1607, and that the most decisive evidence that she was held by the prosecution to be the 'first mover' or 'first cause' of the slanderous street spectacles in Wells lies before us in the summary of punishments for the trial. *Twelfth Night*, that play concerned with the 'blank' that certain cultural dynamics make of women's histories, draws our attention both to the legal fiction crucial to our reading of the summary of punishments and the dangers for women of their participation in an aesthetic in which they disappear.

The law requires persons upon which to act – persons to whom it can distribute punishments and from whom it can extract economic penalties. In the early modern period, the law generally sought to distribute punishments to and extract penalties from one kind of person, men. Under the fiction of coverture, women's legal identities were subsumed under that of their husbands or fathers, who were held responsible for their deeds. *Twelfth Night* draws our attention to the dynamics of coverture and the 'blank' it makes of women's histories as writers, in its final scene, where Fabian, who is not so much as present when the plot against Malvolio is concocted, claims co-authorship, along with Toby, of the riddling letter that induces Malvolio to turn himself into a spectacle for ridicule. With this move, Shakespeare both exposes and denaturalizes the fiction of coverture: by supplying Olivia with culpable persons in the form of Toby and himself, Fabian plays into the law's ordering principles and its gender regime, effectively 'covering' Maria, as if she were, at the time of the letter-writing, already Toby's wife and thus not herself an autonomous person responsible for her own acts. He thus performs a symbolic cutting by which Maria is deprived of both the responsibilities and the benefits of authorship. By threatening to 'cover' Maria's role, but not conclusively doing so, the play exposes the kind of erasures that occur as a result of the law's fiction, under which it does not hold early seventeenth-century women accountable for their own acts.

Shakespeare's text underscores the idea that the term 'woman writer' constitutes, within the fiction of coverture, an oxymoron, by fancifully imagining what a woman might *gain* if the law permitted her to take responsibility for her own acts of writing. If an authorial signature is, in legal terms, the mark through which a writer asserts his or her right to be identified as the author or originator of a text, and thus the mark through which he or she takes legal responsibility for it, it is also the mark through which he or she asserts the right to benefit materially from the text's publication and circulation, if there is any material gain to be had. If Maria were married, she would not technically be able to claim either the liabilities or the benefits of authorship. But she is not married when she writes the letter. She is therefore in a position to benefit from being identified as the 'author' of a work, especially if she could produce a theatrical spectacle for a paying audience considerably larger than that of three men in a box-tree. *Twelfth Night* highlights the difficulties of Maria's position by having Sir Toby imagine what would result if the law identified libelling authors not to punish them, but to reward them. In his fantastical formulation, Maria's 'device' will be brought to the bar so that her authorship of it can be established and she in turn rewarded: 'we will bring the device to the bar and crown thee for a finder of madmen' (3.4.134–5). Imagining the obverse of the legal culpability that comes with being identified as the 'author' of a slanderous text or representation, the text underscores the difficulties of coverture for women: they cannot reap the rewards of authorship until they are also liable for the penalties. Or, to put this another way, Thomasine White may have been a writer, but in the eyes of the law, she could never have been an 'author.'

This is precisely what the summary of punishments for *Hole v. White* makes clear. The summary shows that everyone who took a role in the 'Holing Game', or any of the other slanderous shows in Wells in 1607, was fined a sum ranging from £20 to £30. William Gamage and William Morgan, the two men who claimed responsibility for the libellous rhymes that celebrated the slanderous campaign, received harsher punishments: they were fined £40 each, and were required to do public penance in the pillory for their 'infamous libelling' (310). Their harsher punishments make it clear that, within the terms of the seventeenth-century's evolving conception of libel, authorship constituted a greater offence than the acting of a part in a slanderous show, even if one's authorship had not been conclusively proven. But here is what is both commonplace and extraordinary about the summary of punishments for *Hole v. White*: although Thomasine White's name appears on the list of defendants to be examined for their role in events, in a group including William Gamage's name and her husband's, alongside an annotation that reads 'publishers of the first Libell and the Common Intent' (361), it is not amongst those who were in any way punished or fined; and despite the fact that Edmund White was not associated with any of the street shows, and was not associated with any piece of writing connected to the slanderous campaign, activities for which his legal tab should have totted up to about £70 if he had been guilty of them, his name appears, with the single descriptor, 'imprisoned' and a note indicating that he received the whopping fine of £200 – a fine five times greater than that received by the writers of the libellous rhymes, and ten times greater than that received by any of the actors in the shows. The entry for Edmund White shows us the legal fiction of coverture in action: he received a fine of such magnitude because the prosecution believed, despite its lack of success in acquiring material evidence against her, that *Thomasine* White was the first source, or the principal 'urger', or the 'author', according to one definition or another, of all the slanderous activity in Wells in 1607. Our knowledge of the legal fiction of coverture allows us to fill in the blank in women's history to which White herself contributed by participating in an aesthetic that required her disappearance, for through it we recover, under the name 'Edmund White' what the defendants themselves had already obscured under the moniker 'sweet St. Johane', the woman's name that has been overwritten by another, that of a man.

But to write Thomasine White's story, and possibly the history of other women's hands in theatrical practices in the period, we have to go beyond the data that the *REED* volumes are presenting to us in the form of county-by-county transcriptions of references to theatrical activities in surviving documents in the Public Record Office and county record offices throughout England. The medieval scholar Teresa Coletti has already drawn our attention to the ways in which the *REED* project's claims of editorial objectivity and neutrality should be treated with some scepticism. As Coletti has noted, the *REED* editors claim that they are acting according to a 'non-interventionist' policy and that 'their aim . . . is to collect written evidence of drama . . . *not* to interpret it'.[4] That claim, Coletti contends, is belied by the volumes' 'selective quoting of brief references to dramatic activity from documents whose unquoted portions might provide a much fuller picture of the social framework of such activity' (269). The selections from *Hole v. White* that the editors at *REED* have chosen to publish prove her right, for the Somerset volume, by reproducing only certain portions of the case records, occludes much of the evidence that I have drawn upon here. Perhaps taking White's denials at face value or perhaps seeing little value in them, the editors at *REED* have chosen to reproduce very little of her deposition. They do not reproduce her denial that she asked her maid to say the words 'filthy hole' as John Hole passed by her house; her denial that she arranged for the production of the 'Holing Game' props; her denial that she was the 'first maker' of the slanderous shows; her denial that she wrote or had another write, at her direction, the first libellous rhyme 'My Loving Friends That Love to Play'; her denial that she not only circulated copies of these verses but had them read aloud at the Dean of Wells' house at her 'direction'; or her denial that she attempted to have 'My Loving Friends That Love to Play' published in London. An earlier school of feminist criticism would have regretted the attendant loss of White's 'voice'. But that is not the problem, for Thomasine's voice does receive one instance of striking representation in the Somerset volume. Although the *REED* editors do not reproduce Thomasine's responses to the accusations she denies, they do reproduce her response to one of the most important things she grants, that she did have an encounter with Hole in the streets. This response shows Thomasine asserting herself in no uncertain terms. In her account of that episode, Thomasine provides us with a striking image and a striking statement: she claims that while she

> and others of the then company were then standing still hand in hand at the door of this defendant's house, the now complainant came amongst them and would have thrust this def from her door without any occasion given him by this def whereupon this def used these words to the said complainant, viz., Mr. Constable, I am at my own door and here I will stand.

This speech is unique within the trial documents: it is the only instance in which a defendant concedes that he or she has indeed contested Hole's authority in any shape or form. It is also the only statement in which a defendant asserts the integrity of his or her own identity in the face of Hole's attempts to regulate the behaviour of others. With this statement Thomasine asserted her right to act in public space as she chose, the relatively mild claim 'Here I will stand' standing in for more controversial claims like 'Here I will play on May

Sundays'. The utterance thus constituted the essence of all of the other slanderous activities directed against Hole: the rejection of his authority to determine who might occupy public space and what the members of the neighbourhood might perform or 'play' within it. It also shows Thomasine functioning as a representative of the community – a representative of those with whom she stood 'hand in hand' when Hole 'came amongst them'. The statement is thus singular (there are no others like it), and about Thomasine's individual rights ('Here I will stand'), but through it she spoke for the others from whom Hole had, for whatever reason, singled her out. Through its very singularity, then, the statement comes to express, for those who stood 'hand in hand' with Thomasine, the essence of the communal opposition to him – the assertion of a self-defining 'I' in the face of his contested authority. But the absence, in the *REED* volume, of Thomasine's reponses to any of the interrogatories that link this 'I' with the other theatrical and literary activities that comprised the slanderous campaign makes it impossible for us, within the scope of the volume, to link that voice to any acts of writing, figurative or otherwise, in which Thomasine engaged. It is back to the archives, then, that we must go, prompted to do so by this single striking instance of her voice. When we return to the trial records themselves, we recover persuasive evidence that in Wells, in the early seventeenth century, at least one woman was working in the way that any other dramatist would, taking a variety of objects including painted figures, bowls, horses, wigs, and a variety of other props as well as actors' bodies as the media through which her voice issued and through which she shaped a text. A dramatist, this trial reminds us, animates others from a distance; and can write, it suggests, without necessarily lifting a pen.

Notes

1. The trial documents for *Hole v. White* are located in PRO STAC 8/161/1, and have been partly published in the Somerset volume for the *REED* (Records of Early English Drama) series, *Somerset Including Bath*, ed. James Stokes (Toronto: University of Toronto Press, 1996), Vol. I, 261–367. I have supplemented the transcriptions available in the Somerset volume with transcriptions of my own. This particular citation is to the Somerset volume, p. 267. Further references to *Hole v. White* will be cited directly in the text, and, unless otherwise noted, are to the Somerset volume. Where I cite PRO STAC 8/161/1 directly, the text is provided in modernized spelling along with the sheet number.
2. William Shakespeare, *Twelfth Night* in *The Riverside Shakespeare*, ed. G. Blakemore Evans (Boston: Houghton Mifflin, 1974), 3.4.148–9.
3. John March, *March's Actions for Slander, and Arbitrements* (London, 1648; rev. 1674), 30–1.
4. Theresa Coletti, 'Reading REED: History and the Records of Early English Drama', 248–84, in *Literary Practice and Social Change 1380–1530*, ed. Lee Patterson (Berkeley: University of California Press, 1990), 249.

11

The Sharer and His Boy: Rehearsing Shakespeare's Women

Scott McMillin

This chapter takes its lead from the two editors of this volume, Peter Holland and Stephen Orgel, although they did not know this when they brought me on to the line-up. The initial impetus comes from something Peter Holland wrote about boy-actors in 1988:

> So far, there has been remarkably little sustained and thoughtful consideration of the effects of boy actresses on the creation of female roles in English Renaissance drama; too little for us to be able to assess yet what effects they may have had on the development and formation of gender roles within the drama.[1]

Given the attention that has been paid to boy-actors, cross-dressing, and gender-construction since 1988, that remark might now be seen as a successfully provocative remark, but Peter Holland was pointing to a broader gap in Shakespeare studies which has not yet been filled, and the point about a shortage of work on boy-actors belongs to that more general argument. The general argument is that Shakespearians do not think often enough about the material conditions of theatre performance, about the bodies and persons of the actors, their other roles in the company, the popular reputations they have gained with their audiences, their costumes, their rehearsals, and in that context the comment that we have been overlooking the boy-actors still seems provocative and true. The boy-actors are hard to think about as real persons, with real bodies and minds: we do not even know their names in most cases, or how long they stayed with the company, or which roles they played. One of the excitements of theatre history just now, incidentally, is that the names of some of the boy-actors in Shakespeare's company have come to light and more are to follow. I shall say something about that in a moment, but we still do not know very much about where the boy-actors came from, how they were

found, where they trained before gaining major female roles, and what combination of roles each boy played across the repertory.

The boys were taken up as apprentices, of course. We have known that for a
long time, but not many people have thought about the apprentice system and
how it figured in the affairs of the acting companies. Stephen Orgel is an exception to that generalization, and the other impetus for this chapter comes from
his book on *Impersonations*, where Orgel takes Old Historicists to task for not
asking enough questions about their own material and proceeds to ask the
missing questions himself. One condition he interrogates is the apprentice
system, and how it was applied to the acting companies and their boy-actors.[2]
Master actors could take up apprentices only by being members of the existing trade guilds – there was no guild for the theatre. Many of the actors were
members of existing trade guilds, and they followed the usual procedures of
binding apprentices within the existing guilds even though the boys were really
going to be trained in the acting profession.

Why should the actors have gone this round-about route, Orgel asks, and his
answer is that the apprentice system was an established way of controlling child
labour under the economics of the patriarchal guild system. The apprentices
were housed and fed and clothed in the master's home and they were paid no
regular wage: 'apprentices were good investments' (p. 68). Thus a master actor
who was also free of the Grocers' guild, as John Heminges was, would bind
apprentices under the regulations in effect for the Grocers and would then raise
and educate the boy to play women's roles, without incurring the expenses of
wage payments. That is the economic answer: boys were a source of profit. But
there is another question in Stephen Orgel's book: why were the boys used to
play *women's* roles. Here again the answer has to do with the patriarchal society:
there are analogies between boys and women in the structure of early London
society, and the one analogy that seems most telling is that boys and women
are 'objects of sexual attraction for men' (p. 70).

So sex and money are the patriarchal interests that led the theatres to train
boys on the apprentice system. I would like to dwell for a moment on the Old
Historicist answer, the one that is passed over in favour of sex and money, for
the Old Historicist answer is not a wrong answer, in Stephen Orgel's view, it is
just not far-reaching enough. The Old Historicist answer is that boys were hired
as apprentices in order to receive training in their craft under the guidance of
a master. The boys were learning a skill, and although they were doing so under
the regulations of the Grocers' guild or the Weavers' guild, what they were
really learning was how to act under the tutelage of a master actor like John
Heminges, who was free of the Grocers but was acting with the Chamberlain's
Men, or John Dutton, who was free of the Weavers but was acting with the
Queen's Men. Why were the boys training to act women's roles? I like the
answer that they were training to act women's roles because Heminges and

Dutton found boys sexy as well as profitable, but the humdrum answer is that boys could speak in the alto register, which gave a touch of verisimilitude to their impersonations of women. So, adding the humdrum answers to the more searching answers, we find that the sexy boys and profitable boys were apprenticed before their voices changed in order to receive training in how to act female.

We are educators ourselves. We know that sex and money enter into education. We understand that students are a source of profit for the teachers, and my colleagues tell me that the students are sexy too. These truths should not obscure the third reason for the student–teacher relationship, though, that the teachers often have something to teach that the students will sometimes benefit from learning.

I wish to bring the interests of these two essays together in order to think about what Stephen Orgel asks us to, boys serving as apprentices to master actors, at the same time as we think about what Peter Holland asks us to, boys learning how to represent women on the stage.

I will begin with the boy playing Desdemona in 1610, when the King's Men gave performances in Oxford which moved one spectator to make notes on what he saw. The spectator was an Oxford scholar named Henry Jackson, a learned and religious man of twenty-four who wrote his account in Latin. This is a translation of what he said about the performance of *Othello*, in its entirety.

> They also had tragedies, which they acted with propriety and fitness. In which [tragedies], not only through speaking but also through acting certain things, they moved [the audience] to tears. But truly the celebrated Desdemona, slain in our presence by her husband, although she pleaded her case very effectively throughout, yet moved [us] more after she was dead, when, lying on her bed, she entreated the pity of the spectators by her very countenance.[3]

This is a remarkable account for a number of reasons, many of them already discussed by Anthony Dawson and Paul Yachnin in *The Culture of Playgoing in Shakespeare's England*. I will just mention of few of these briefly. First, for Henry Jackson this was Desdemona, not a boy playing Desdemona. He writes of the woman, not the boy actor. Moreover, he focuses almost entirely on Desdemona, relegating Othello to 'her husband' who slays his wife in our presence. Third, Henry Jackson separates theatrical performance into two elements, speaking and acting, as though elocution was noticeable as one thing, and bodily presence – or what we might call 'body language' – was another. Finally, although Desdemona was effective at elocution – 'she pleaded her case very effectively throughout' – she could especially grip the audience by keeping still and saying nothing, by playing dead.

This production of 1610 did not protect the boy-actor by letting him face upstage or by covering him with bed-clothing. His countenance was visible through the final lines of the play, eloquent in its stillness, entreating the pity of the spectators by his very countenance. One has to learn how to play dead. Breath control is hard to master, especially after what Desdemona has just been through – and Desdemona has 250 lines during which she must hold still.

Perhaps the Desdemona of 1610 was the boy who had played the role originally, in 1604. The span of a boy-actor's career would have been six or seven years in the female roles. If the Desdemona of 1610 was the same boy who had played the part for some six years, we can imagine how he learned to be eloquent of speech, for he would have been acting the female roles of Shakespeare's later tragedies and romances when they came into the company's repertory. Did he play Hermione in *The Winter's Tale*? That would be a good role for developing eloquence of speech, and an exceedingly good role for learning how to hold still and practise breath control. Cleopatra is a good role for holding still too, in a death scene where she is said to look 'like sleep,/As she would catch another Antony/In her strong toil of grace'.[4] A Desdemona of 1610 tinged with the experience of playing Hermione and Cleopatra might very well command Henry Jackson's attention with his silent eloquence. But this points to what we do not know. We do not know who the boy was, what roles he had played, how long he had been with the company.

Surprisingly, there is something we do know about the boy, whoever he was. We know something about how he rehearsed his part. He rehearsed his part in response to cue lines from other actors in the King's Men. I dedicate the rest of this chapter to Tiffany Stern, who has opened the way to reading drama according to its cue lines and who has argued that the actors would have done much of their rehearsal alone, with nothing but the cue lines to trigger their speeches, or in partial rehearsals, in the presence of the other actors who deliver those cue lines.[5] Learning Elizabethan roles alone in one's room would have suffered from one prominent disadvantage: the actor would not have known from whom his cue lines were coming. As far as we can tell, each cue line was nothing more than the last few words of the preceding speech, with no indication of what that speech was about, or by whom it was spoken. Much of the memorization must have been done by a sort of trigger-system: whatever the source of the cue line, those words set off *this* speech. There must have come a moment when the actors did partial rehearsals in order to familiarize themselves with the source of the cue lines, and, given the system of apprenticeship that obtained for the boy-actors, some of the boy-actor's rehearsal and memorization would have been done in the presence of his master.

I have made a list of Desdemona's speeches and the sources of her cue lines (using the Folio text), and I think it shows us something about how the partial rehearsals were done. More than half of Desdemona's cue lines are given her by one character, Othello. More than half of the cue lines she gives are answered by one character, Othello. More than half of her speeches can be rehearsed with one actor, the actor playing Othello, and probably that is how they were rehearsed. The master actor probably rehearsed the boy-actor one-on-one, teaching the boy how to respond, teaching him enunciation, gesture, and movement.

Moreover, Desdemona's role changes as the play proceeds. She begins with three of her longer speeches, in the Senate scene. To Brabantio's line 'Where most you owe obedience?' she has nine lines about her divided duty. She speaks six lines asking the Duke to listen to her 'unfolding', then she 'unfolds' for twelve lines on her love for Othello. This is Desdemona at her most voluble. She responds to three characters in this scene, they respond to her, and she speaks at some length. Her next scene, where she jokes with Iago on the quay in Cyprus then welcomes Othello upon his arrival, connects her with four characters: Iago, Cassio, Emilia, then Othello. These are her widest-ranging scenes, involving exchanges with six different characters.

Her role becomes much more restricted after that. Peter Stallybrass has noted that there are two Desdemonas in the play, two 'constructions' of Desdemona, the active Desdemona of the first half and the subservient Desdemona of the second half.[6] I am describing this difference in terms of her cue lines. After welcoming Othello in Cyprus, she comes increasingly under the control of Othello, as though being under his suspicions, or under his jealousy, or under his murderous misconception of her character, is allied with being under his instruction. The boy playing Desdemona is taking lessons from the actor of Othello in the second half of his role, and they are lessons in the one-liner. Most of Desdemona's speeches in her scenes with Othello are one or two lines long. There is a pace to this exercise in the one-liner, a pace which culminates in her final speeches with Othello:

> What, my lord?
> How? unlawfully?
> He will not say so.
> O, my fear interprets. What, is he dead?
> Alas, he is betray'd and I undone!
> O, banish me, my lord, but kill me not!
> Kill me tomorrow, let me live tonight!
> But half an hour!
> But while I saw one prayer!
> O, Lord, Lord, Lord.

This is the pace leading to strangulation. Henry Jackson's impression was of a wife being strangled in our presence by her husband. Other viewers have seen this as a white woman being strangled in our presence by a black man. I am adding the perspective that comes from the rehearsal process: the apprentice learning to die at the hands of his master, and advancing in talent as he does so. The stark representation of the scene probably comes from all of these perspectives.

Could Desdemona rehearse her entire role with only Othello as partner? To some extent she could, but the other leading boy-actor would be important to these rehearsals too. Desdemona needs Emilia along with Othello to rehearse the last half of her role, but she needs very little else. In Acts 4 and 5, nearly 90 per cent of her cue lines come from those two, Othello and Emilia. Her final forty-seven cue lines come entirely from Othello and Emilia. If Burbage played Othello (and he did), Burbage can rehearse Desdemona in the last half of her part without the rest of the company being present. He can train Emilia in much of her role at the same time. Over 70 per cent of Emilia's cue lines in the last two acts are cued by Othello and Desdemona. This group of three, Burbage and the two boys, can rehearse most of the boys' roles in Acts 4 and 5 by themselves. If Iago is counted into the rehearsal group, virtually all of the cue lines for the two boy-actors throughout the entire play are provided.

We know one other play the King's Men were performing at Oxford in 1610. Henry Jackson mentions *The Alchemist,* which bothered him for its anti-Puritan satire. What sort of rehearsal pattern were the boys of the King's Men following with this play? The longest boy's role in *The Alchemist* is Dol Common, who like Desdemona and Emilia is cued mainly by one or two sharers. Her role in Acts 1, 2, and 3 has forty speeches, all of which are cued by Subtle and Face. In Acts 4 and 5, she has 66 speeches, 97 per cent of which are cued by Subtle, Face and Sir Epicure Mammon. Thus Dol can rehearse all of her first forty speeches with just two actors, and virtually all of her remaining sixty-six speeches with those two plus Sir Epicure Mammon. The other boy's role, Dame Pliant, only appears in Acts 4 and 5. All but four of Dame Pliant's cues are given by Subtle and Face. It appears that both boys' roles in *The Alchemist* are conveniently rehearsable with two master actors or three, counting Sir Epicure.

One wonders which role in *The Alchemist* was assigned to the Desdemona boy. Did the Venetian wife who cannot bring herself to say 'whore' spend the previous evening playing Dol Common? Or was she Dame Pliant? In either case, a certain aura from *The Alchemist* attends Desdemona, and vice-versa, but we cannot tell which aura it is.

At any rate, the leading boys' roles in both plays are, in the parlance I am now adopting for the sake of shorthand, 'restricted' roles, largely rehearsable with one or two master actors, perhaps with a second boy. It seems clear that the boys could have rehearsed both of the Oxford plays with the same master actors in each play. That is, if Burbage played Othello in one play and either Subtle, or Face, or Mammon in the other, and if it is reasonable to imagine the

actor of Iago playing one of those three roles in *The Alchemist*, then one is imagining that the boy-actors in the two plays were rehearsing with the same combination of master actors for both plays. Possibly these boys were apprenticed
to these master actors, were living with them, being fed and clothed by them,
but we do not know these things. The facts of the matter are that *Othello* and
The Alchemist were performed together at Oxford in 1610 and both have boys'
roles which are closely tied to a small group of master actors.

Is that always the case in the plays of the King's Men? Would we find
'restricted' patterns of cue lines in all of the boys' roles written for the
company? That would itself be worth knowing if it were true, for the company
would then appear to have had a permanent system of relating their apprentice roles to a few male actors, even training the boys through roles written to
be rehearsed with the masters. But in fact it is not true of all the boys' roles
written for the company. Casting about in the other plays Shakespeare is
thought to have written in the first decade of the seventeenth century, we come
upon the role of Cleopatra. It is impossible to think of Cleopatra as a 'restricted'
role. Cleopatra talks to just about everyone. She has 200 speeches, which are
cued by eighteen characters. Her three leading suppliers of cues are Antony,
Charmian and the woebegone Messenger of 2.5 and 3.3. Altogether, these three
supply 116 of her cue lines, but that leaves over eighty cue lines to be rehearsed
with other characters. Cleopatra has important exchanges with Enobarbus,
Alexis, Thidias, Proculeius, Dolabella, Iras, Caesar, and the Clown who brings
the asp. She begins new scenes eight times – that is, she speaks the opening
lines without a cue when she enters after the stage has been cleared of its previous grouping. That takes a certain command of the stage, entering and
opening the dialogue simultaneously. Desdemona does it twice, Doll Common
does it once. Cleopatra does it eight times. Cleopatra has to be set apart
from the 'restricted' roles of Desdemona and Doll Common. I shall call it a
'wide-ranging' role.

There is no reason to assume that 'restricted' roles were played by neophyte
actors who had not yet learned to work their way up to the 'wide-ranging' roles.
The boy-actor capable of Cleopatra could have gone on to play 'restricted' roles
like Desdemona and Doll Common at Oxford in 1610. But it is worth remembering that the career span of a boy in female roles would have been about six
or seven years, and that the first Desdemona when *Othello* was new in 1604
would have been replaceable by another Desdemona some time before about
1611. Shakespeare's company would have needed a second Desdemona by
about 1611, in other words, then another some time before 1618 – in all at
least six Desdemonas by the closing of the theatres in 1642. The probable need
for a new Desdemona around 1611 or before is particularly close to our Oxford
performances. It happens that a new boy was taken up as an apprentice to the
company in 1610. David Kathman has found that an apprentice named George

Burge was bound to John Heminges of the King's Men on 4 July 1610, just two months before the Oxford performances. Just after that, on 12 July 1610, playing in London was ended by an upsurge of the plague. (That is, of course, what *The Alchemist* is about: an upsurge of the plague in London in 1610.) George Burge was hardly into his term of service before the King's Men were prevented from playing in London.

That is not to suggest that George Burge was playing the boy's roles in question that soon. Dol Common is not a role for a neophyte. It is a 'restricted' role in its contact with the adult actors, but within those restrictions it requires brilliant impersonations, as Dol goes into her fit over the works of Broughton or tantalizes Dapper as the Queen of Faerie. It is not a role for a new boy, in my little book of guesswork over casting for the King's Men, nor is Emilia a role for a new boy either. Dame Pliant seems a good role for a new boy, and I leave the question of Desdemona open. If there were boys who needed to be trained up to play the leading roles in 1610, they would probably have been apprentices who had acted smaller roles in the past and were now advancing. But we do not know this. We know that a new apprentice was taken up by the company in July 1610, and we also know that the apprentices' roles played by the company in Oxford two months later were 'restricted' roles in that they are rehearsable with two or three sharers in the company. There is no way to hammer these two facts into a cause and effect relationship. Let us just keep them in mind.

I would now like to look back six years in the career of the King's Men, to a time when *Othello* was a new play, and particularly to the court season of 1604–5, where we have an unusually full record of the plays performed by the company. In the kind of windfall that only occasionally comes to theatre historians, the titles of the plays performed at court in 1604–5 actually appear in the Revels Account. The table below lists the plays from this winter season, derived from Leeds Barroll's book on *Politics, Plague, and Shakespeare's Theater*.

The first play of the court season was *Othello*, the performance falling on 1 November 1604. Then comes a revival of *The Merry Wives of Windsor* three days later, then the first known performance of *Measure for Measure*, about a month later. It seems likely that *Othello* and *Measure for Measure* were new plays. Barroll has shown that the London playhouses had been closed most of the time from the death of Elizabeth in March 1603 on into the plague-ridden summer of 1604. Barroll estimates that the playhouses had not been open for a sustained repertory run at any time for the previous eighteen months. So *Othello* and *Measure for Measure* may have been given their first performances during the court season of 1604–5. Perhaps one or both had originated in an abrupt run at the Globe the summer before. In either case, they are the newest two plays in the court season and their first performances either occurred then, at court,

King's Men Court Performances, 1604–5. Lead Boy Roles[7]

Date	Play	Lead Boy Lines	Speeches 10+ Lines
1 Nov. 1604	*Othello* (new)	391	7
4 Nov.	*Merry Wives*	347	4
26 Dec.	*Measure* (new)	424	7
28 Dec.	*Errors*	262	6
1–6 Jan. 1605	*LLL*	290	5
7 Jan.	*Henry V*	63	0
8 Jan.	*EMO*	172	
2 Feb.	*EMI*	65	1
3 Feb.	play not given		
10 Feb.	*Merchant*	578	17
11 Feb.	*Spanish Maze*		
12 Feb.	*Merchant*	578	17

or a little earlier at the Globe, during a long period of disruption in the London commercial theatre.

That *Othello* turns up here as it does later in Oxford, being staged after a plague-disrupted period in the commercial theatre, catches the eye. Remembering that both plays staged at Oxford had restricted roles for the leading boys, I think it worth a glance at the other new play for the King's Men in the court season of 1604–5, *Measure for Measure*. The cue lines for Isabella seem at first to differ from the pattern of Desdemona's cue lines. No one master actor speaks over half of her cues, as Othello does for Desdemona. (Angelo gives 43 of her 127 cues, the Duke gives 37, and the two account for 63 per cent of the total.) But there is a restricted quality to Isabella's role, in that nearly all of her cues come from four male actors: Angelo, the Duke, Lucio and Claudio. And if one divides Isabella's role into halves, one sees the pattern. In Acts 1 and 2 Angelo and Lucio give 94 per cent of Isabella's cues. In Acts 3, 4 and 5, the Duke and Claudio give over 95 per cent of her cues. Isabella hardly speaks to anyone but these four, two of them for the first half of her role and two others for the second half. The boy-actor rehearses the first half with two adult actors, the second half with two other adult actors.

The second-longest boy's role in *Measure for Measure*, Mariana, is confined to the second half of the play and is largely cued by the Duke (fifteen of twenty-four cues). Isabella is always present in Mariana's scenes. Isabella and the Duke give 80 per cent of Mariana's cues. So *Measure for Measure*, the other new play at court in 1604, has restricted roles for boys too, although the pattern is different in that Isabella rehearses the first half of the play with two master actors and the second half with two others, in a group which also rehearses Mariana.

What of the revival that was positioned between these two new plays? *The Merry Wives of Windsor*, given just three days after *Othello*, has three important roles for boys: Mistress Page and Mistress Ford have the largest numbers of speeches, and they give each other over 50 per cent of their cues.[8] If Falstaff is added to the group, 72 per cent of the cues for Mistress Page and Mistress Ford can be rehearsed. If we broaden the group by including Ford, so that we have two master actors and the two boy actors, 82 per cent of the boy-actor cues are provided. This seems to me 'restricted' in the sense of being closely rehearsable with a small group of adult actors, and it gives us three such plays at the beginning of the court season.

Again, we need to wonder if the restricted quality of the female roles is unusual at this stage in the career of the King's Men. Perhaps their boy's roles over the previous six or seven years had all been restricted in somewhat the same way. But looking back, one finds some wide-ranging roles for boys, in the romantic comedies the company was performing in the later 1590s. There are two clear examples of the wide-ranging role: Rosalind in *As You Like It* and Portia in *The Merchant of Venice*. They are two of the longest female roles among the extant plays of the company. Rosalind has 721 lines, Portia has 578, Desdemona 391. The more telling difference is in the lengths of the speeches, for no one has much luck reducing Rosalind and Portia to one-liners, as Othello does to Desdemona. Portia has seventeen speeches running ten lines or more. Rosalind has fourteen or fifteen, if we allow a little leeway on prose speeches.[9] Isabella has seven. Desdemona has seven. Rosalind and Portia dominate their plays. Theirs are wide-ranging roles.

And cue lines for Portia and Rosalind come from a fuller range of the play. Bassanio has 22 per cent of Portia's cues. He and Shylock counted together have under 40 per cent of her cues. Altogether Portia's cues come from fourteen characters. Rosalind's cues come from thirteen characters. These two female roles range through their plays, whereas Desdemona's cues come from eight characters, mainly from Othello and Emilia. Isabella's cues come mainly from two characters in the first half of the play, two others in the second half. There is a difference between the restricted boy roles of 1604 and the wide-ranging boy roles of the 1590s, and this reminds me of the difference between the restricted boy roles of 1610 and the wide-ranging boy role of a few years before, Cleopatra.

There is now a hypothesis lurking in these figures: that these restricted roles for boys were restricted for a reason, the same reason in 1604 as in 1610, namely that a new generation of leading boy actors was being trained and rehearsed by their master actors in each case. The boys who originally played Rosalind and Portia in the later 1590s would have reached the end of their indentures in the early 1600s. By the court season of 1604–5, it is virtually certain that the original Rosalind and the original Portia had come to the end of their apprenticeships. David Kathman's research into the Guildhall documents has found that a boy was apprenticed to John Heminges, Grocer, on 12 November 1595 for nine years. He would have ended his period of indenture in November 1604, just the month *Othello* and *Merry Wives* were performed at court.[10] Another boy was apprenticed to John Heminges, Grocer, on 26 January 1597 for eight years. He would have ended his period of indenture in January 1605. This was Alexander Cooke, whose voice must have changed before his indenture ended, for he was playing adult roles for the King's Men in 1603. He appears to have been married in 1603, he was a father in 1605. That is not to say these particular apprentices were the original Rosalind or the original Portia (although they are the only known candidates from our present evidence). We do not know who originally played Rosalind or Portia. But we do know that the component of apprentices in the King's Men was undergoing a change in about 1604–5, when new boys would have graduated to the leading roles, and that is exactly when we see restricted leading female roles being rehearsed and performed at court.

At the end of the 1604–5 season comes one of the wide-ranging boy's roles from the 1590s, Portia in *The Merchant of Venice*, twice. The hypothesis being considered here holds that the training and rehearsal of the recently graduated boys had advanced to the point where one of them was ready to play Portia by February 1605, some three months after the court season began the previous November. Looking at the other revivals staged before *The Merchant of Venice* in the court season, we find some noticeably light boys' roles. Jonson did not write many good parts for boys, and the two Jonson plays in this season have slight women's parts (although Fallace in *Every Man Out of His Humour* is distinctly longer than Bianca in *Every Man In*). Shakespeare's *Henry V* has two good scenes for a leading boy-actor as Katherine, but the role is short and restricted. These three roles are among the shortest ever written as leading boy's roles for the King's Men. Perhaps they were clustered here to make rehearsal space for a boy to learn Portia. The rehearsal patterns for the three short boys' parts are restricted: the leading boy in those three plays is cued by two characters in *Henry V*, then by four characters in *Every Man Out of His Humour*, then by seven characters in *Every Man In*. These three short and restricted roles all go back to the final years of the 1590s – 1599 to 1600. I think they were chosen deliberately for the court performances between early January and 10 February, in order to give a leading boy a relatively free stretch of rehearsal time for Portia on 10 February and for whatever role he played in *The Spanish Maze* the following night.

What of the court roles which fall just before this cluster of three short ones? The Princess in *Love's Labour's Lost* (early January) has 290 lines; Adriana in *The Comedy of Errors* (28 December) has 262. Each is about half the length of Portia's role, each has less than half the number of speeches of ten lines or more. But they are not easy parts. They are certainly more substantial than the three short roles which follow in the *Henry V/Every Man In/Every Man Out* group of early January and early February, and they are cued from rather large numbers of roles. Adriana is cued by fourteen characters, the Princess by twelve. These would smack of the wide-ranging type, were it not for one thing. Both parts become wide-ranging only in the final scenes. Both begin restricted and open out into wide-ranging at the end. The Princess has over 60 per cent of her cues in the final scene, those cues coming from ten characters. This scene has to be rehearsed by the entire company. By contrast, the Princess in the first two acts has only twenty-one speeches, cued mainly (81 per cent) by two characters, the King and Boyet. The role begins as rehearsable with two master actors and becomes wide-ranging in the finale. The same thing happens with Adriana, whose role all the way to 4.4 is cued mainly by Luciana and Dromio of Syracuse (72 per cent). Then, in the two busy scenes which end the play, Adriana has half of her speeches and is cued widely, by eleven characters. The leading boy in each case could rehearse much of his part with one or two master actors and one other boy, down to the busy final scenes, where the entire company would be needed and where about half his part in each play would be spoken. This strikes me as a miniature of what was happening in the court season at large, where relatively short roles for boys were scheduled before one wide-ranging boy's role, Portia, came before the king on 10 February and again on the 12th.

Rehearsal time is needed for working up to the big effects. This is true for all actors, but especially for boys expected to be Portia eventually. If a boy in December 1604 was preparing to play Portia in February 1605, he might have been scheduled to act smaller roles in the meantime, although they might be smaller leading roles. If one of those roles has challenges of its own, such as the Princess has in 5.2 of *Love's Labour's Lost*, this boy is going to be able to rehearse the earlier scenes of that play largely with the King and Boyet, in what I am imagining as training sessions with master actors. A boy might have to work up to being the Princess in 5.2, or Adriana in 4.4 and 5.1 of *The Comedy of Errors*. These things take time and practice – and that is what the schedule of leading boys' roles suggests were being provided at court in 1604–5, both within the season and within individual plays.

I am running ahead of the evidence, to be sure. Who knows if one boy played the lead role each time in these plays? Who knows if the boy-actors in 1604 were relatively inexperienced? Who knows if the texts on which I am basing these observations correspond to the versions performed at court before the king? No one knows these things. The tale I am telling pretends to a narrative completeness that cannot be true to history. No complete narrative can be true to history. We make narratives in order to organize and remember the evidence. I do not intend to believe what I am saying so much as I intend to remember it. For new evidence does come before us – David Kathman's discoveries are one case in point. New ways of thinking about play texts do arise – Tiffany Stern's study of rehearsals is another.

I am remembering the evidence at hand by turning it towards a narrative about leading boy-actors being trained by master actors during time provided by a careful scheduling of parts. The narrative originates in the historical situation of the actors – boys were apprenticed to masters for their training in the theatre. The scheduling of the parts is where the narrative takes over. Did such a scheduling take place? The three leading boys' roles performed at court during the month before Portia was played there were among the smallest ever written for Shakespeare's company. Together those three roles amount to a little over half of Portia's. For more than a month of the court season, in other words, the Portia boy was given no role more important than these small ones. I think he was actually doing something more important, rehearsing Portia. But he may have been playing the small roles too – or the small roles may have been played by the lesser boys while Portia was memorizing his lines and rehearsing with the entire company. For two weeks before that, when *The Comedy of Errors* and *Love's Labour's Lost* were staged, the leading boy's role was the kind that holds to restricted groupings down to the final scenes and then blossoms a little into wider participation with virtually the entire company.[11] That is one way to learn how to play roles like Portia – by advancing from restricted to wide-ranging within the earlier plays. For two months before that, two new parts were played, Desdemona followed by Isabella a month later, challenging and distinct roles arranged so as to be largely rehearsable with another boy and small groups of master actors. The one revival in those two months, *The Merry Wives of Windsor*, has a similar arrangement. I doubt if these are the appearances of chance. The company had just been through a year and a half of interrupted playing, at a point when some of the leading boys of the 1590s must have been moving on to other things. There must have been fine talent among the remaining boys, perhaps among newly apprenticed boys – Desdemona, Mistress Page and Isabella are hardly a tame beginning for the court season – but there does appear to be a schedule to the 1604–5 female roles, and I think its purpose was to combine training with performance in the main parts. If something like the same situation occurred about six years later, around the time of the Oxford performances of *Othello* and *The Alchemist* witnessed by Henry Jackson, we would not be very surprised. Six years is approximately the range of a boy-actor's career.

A great deal of unexamined evidence about theatre history lurks in the texts that remain to us from the Elizabethan playhouses. The size of the roles, their distribution across the play so as to allow for doubling, their patterns of cue lines – these are indicators of the theatrical intentions of the texts. The opportunity before us is to study that evidence with an eye to what the real actors

Peter Holland asks us to think about had to do in order to rehearse and stage their plays. Andrew Gurr's contribution to this volume points to the gap between the play texts and what transpired in the playhouses. Scepticism about the texts as theatre evidence has to be maintained, and I am a close follower of a distinction Gurr made in an earlier paper between 'maximal' and 'minimal' texts.[12] 'Minimal' texts will often be found, I think, to be revealing of particular stage occasions (the so-called 'bad' quartos will be among these examples), and 'maximal' texts will in many cases have to be seen as including more than was normally staged. Yet 'maximal' texts can be read for their bearing on the theatre. They were written with performance in mind. These texts do not come out of the blue. They come out of the theatre. A second phase of the present argument would have to test the Folio texts against the quartos of *Henry V* and *Merry Wives* to see if the relative proportions of the boys' roles are the same in the shorter and the longer texts, for there is a possibility that the court season in question consisted of the shorter kind of script represented by the quartos.[13]

I am proposing that the printed plays are 'readable' for their theatrical intentions in ways that have not yet been fully explored. This is meant to be a note of optimism. Reading the texts with a theatrical eye seems appropriate and urgent – appropriate because the texts were written in close adjustment to real actors and real stages, urgent because the evidence the texts contain about real actors and real stages can tell us some of the things we most want to know.

Notes

1. Peter Holland, 'The Resources of Characterization in *Othello*', *Shakespeare Survey*, 41 (1988), 119–32. The quoted passage is on p. 128.
2. Stephen Orgel, *Impersonations: the Performance of Gender in Shakespeare's England* (Cambridge: Cambridge University Press, 1996), 64–74.
3. Quoted from the *Riverside Shakespeare*, ed. G. B. Evans et al., 2nd edn (Boston: Houghton Mifflin, 1997), 1978. It is discussed in Paul Yachnin, *Stage-Wrights: Shakespeare, Jonson, Middleton, and the Making of Theatrical Value* (Philadelphia: University of Pennsylvania Press, 1997), 27 and in Anthony B. Dawson and Paul Yachnin, *The Culture of Playgoing in Shakespeare's England* (Cambridge: Cambridge University Press, 2001), 19–20, 127–8.
4. The *Riverside* text is used for all Shakespeare quotations.
5. Tiffany Stern, *Rehearsal from Shakespeare to Sheridan* (Oxford: Clarendon Press, 2000). David Grote, *The Best Actors in the World: Shakespeare and His Acting Company* (Westport, Conn.: Greenwood Press, 2002) occasionally speculates about the relationship of actor and apprentice in Shakespeare's company, but seems unaware of Stern's book or of David Kathman's discoveries of apprentice records.
6. 'Patriarchal Territories: the Body Enclosed', in *Rewriting the Renaissance*, ed. Margaret Ferguson, Maureen Quilligan and Nancy J. Vickers (Chicago: University of Chicago Press, 1986), 141.

7. Dates are from Leeds Barroll, *Politics, Plague, and Shakespeare's Theater* (Ithaca, NY: Cornell University Press, 1991), 125. Numbers of speeches and lines are from Marvin Spevack, *Complete and Systematic Concordance to Shakespeare*, 9 vols (Hildesheim: Georg Olms, 1968–80). For the authenticity of the list, see E. K. Chambers, *William Shakespeare: a Study of Facts and Problems* (Oxford: Clarendon Press, 1930), 2: 330–1.
8. Mistress Quickly has more lines than Mistress Ford (278 to 197), but fewer speeches (74 to 85).
9. I count eleven speeches of over ten lines in the *Riverside* setting, plus four more prose speeches of nine lines each.
10. David Kathman has kindly allowed me to see his work in advance of publication.
11. *Love's Labour's Lost* was pressed into service when the company had no new play the queen had not seen. See Barroll, *Politics, Plague, and Shakespeare's Theater* 126–7.
12. 'Maximal and Minimal Texts: Shakespeare v. the Globe', *Shakespeare Survey*, 52 (1999), 68–87.
13. The quarto of *Merry Wives* has 67 per cent of Mistress Page's cues from Falstaff and Mistress Ford, the same percentage as the Folio. Where Mistress Page is cued by eleven characters in the Folio, she is cued by eight in the quarto. So, as a preliminary note, the roles for the boys seem to be more restricted in the quarto.

Index

CPSIA information can be obtained at www.ICGtesting.com
Printed in the USA
LVOW130752101112

306745LV00004B/43/P

9 781403 933430